MAX WEBER'S THEORY OF CONCEPT
`ORMATION

TO MY MOTHER AND FATHER

MAX WEBER'S THEORY OF
CONCEPT FORMATION · ·
HISTORY, LAWS, AND IDEAL TYPES

Thomas Burger

1976
DUKE UNIVERSITY PRESS
Durham, North Carolina

Burgess
H
61
.W42
B87

Material herein from Max Weber, *The Methodology of the Social
Sciences*, Copyright 1949 by The
Free Press, a Division of Macmillan Publishing Co. Inc., has been
reprinted by permission of the Macmillan Publishing Co. Inc.

L.C.C. card number 74–31592

I.S.B.N. 0–8223–0332–9

Printed in the United States of
America by Heritage Printers, Inc.

We wish also to make acknowledgment to J.C.B. Mohr
(Paul Siebeck), Tuebingen, for permission to quote extensively from *Gesammelte Aufsaetze zur Wissenschaftslehre* by M. Weber, and from *Die Grenzen der naturwissenschaftlichen Begriffsbildung* by H. Rickert; The
University of Illinois Press, Urbana, for permission to
quote from C. Menger's *Problems of Economics and Sociology*; and Arno Press, Inc., New York, for permission to
quote from O. Spann's *The History of Economics* (reprinted by Arno Press, Inc., 1972). We regret that this
acknowledgment was inadvertently omitted from this
page as originally printed.

ACKNOWLEDGMENT

John C. McKinney and John Wilson, through their criticisms and suggestions, forced and helped me to clarify my thoughts and their expression. I gratefully acknowledge their efforts.

Thomas Burger

TABLE OF CONTENTS

INTRODUCTION

The present essay is an attempt to interpret the central segment of Max Weber's writings on the methodology of the empirical sciences. Although not everybody may share the opinion expressed by one writer, that these methodological writings are probably Weber's "greatest achievement,"[1] it is a fact that historically they have been of great significance and that they continue to exert influence. The postulate of ethical neutrality, *Verstehen*, and the conception of the ideal type come immediately to mind. Especially with regard to the latter, however, it is also true that at present a curious situation prevails. On the one hand, those constructs which Weber called "ideal types" still occur rather frequently in sociological writings. It seems, therefore, that Weber's reasoning about them can still command some interest, although, of course, the possibility cannot be excluded that it may no longer have a direct bearing on the current state of affairs. On the other hand, numerous people have tried to make some sense out of Weber's statements without entirely succeeding in their attempts. As a result, a feeling of resignation seems to have spread, if the number of irritated and polemical remarks by commentators can be taken as an indicator. Often the impression is fostered that the ideal type is the confused result that sprang from a confused philosophy. This is frequently accompanied by the attitude that, although admittedly Weber has laid his finger on something worth mentioning, it is best not to waste time trying to clear up old confusions, but to go ahead and analyze the problem with which Weber was dealing with the help of the more advanced means now available. This looks like a rather straight-forward suggestion—although it also amounts to an admission of defeat as far as the understanding of Weber is concerned—but it begs the question, of course, of *what* exactly Weber's *problem* was and *how* he *formulated* it, that is, *in what frame of reference*.

In the secondary literature on the topic, this question has never been answered in a satisfactory fashion. In a way, Alexander von Schelting's contributions are an exception to this. However, von Schelting took Weber's approach too much for granted to be of much analytical help. Therefore, it is fair to say that the shortcomings of existing interpretations have been the result of a failure to carefully and step by step think through Weber's methodological arguments with a clear understanding of the premises from which he started, while maintaining a guarded attitude toward these basic assumptions. Consequently, the core of Weber's difficulties as well as the crucial features of his proposed solution have never been properly recognized.

One cause of the poor state of the secondary literature may be found in the fact that sociologists and historians, who have produced the bulk of interpretations, often are not very competent philosophers of science. Another cause of the shortcomings may be found in historical circumstances. Weber's methodological essays are essays mainly in the logic of the historical sciences. Since Weber's time, the logic of science has undergone fundamental change, which has made much of the literature on the ideal type obsolete. The change is reflected in the diverse interpretations, in the approaches taken by different authors, according to the extent to which the new developments have penetrated the ideas of the authors. This has been the case to very varying degrees. At the same time, the increased influence of modern philosophy of science has been accompanied by a decreased interest in, and understanding of, the intricacies of old-style methodology. In the present context, this must be regarded as a very unfortunate circumstance, for there is little hope for a proper understanding of Weber without an adequate conception of the problem situation as he perceived it. Thus it seems to be a fair characterization of the current situation to say that, on the one hand, there are those writers who have not been influenced by modern philosophy of science and who, with regard to methodology, employ a predominantly traditional frame of reference. Most of them have been so little aware of the problematic character of their own presuppositions that they have not even realized that the ideal type is a conception designed by Weber to overcome certain—and basically insurmountable—difficulties deriving from these very presuppositions. Thus they were in no position to properly understand Weber who, although no specialist, apparently had a superior grasp of the methodological problems which he had to face, and to elucidate his difficulties and their causes. In general their analyses are based on so many doubtful assumptions that they are practically worthless, and in any case unilluminating (e.g., Oppenheimer, Weippert). On the other hand, those writers who have a background of modern philosophy of science have rarely made efforts to become sufficiently acquainted with the details of the intellectual heritage of Weber's methodological arguments—probably finding this unrewarding—to be able to realize precisely what troubled Weber. Accordingly their analyses, although in general valuable in themselves, have neither clarified Weber's reasoning in a satisfactory manner, nor provided entirely convincing reformulations of his conception in an up-dated frame of reference. None of these authors made a systematic effort to penetrate to the true *sources* of Weber's problems (e.g., Hempel, Watkins). They approached him from points of view and with regard to problems which were not his, and which he did not try to answer. There is, of course, nothing illegitimate in this procedure, especially when the viewpoints and questions issuing from the modern problem situation seem more promising than those over which Weber was concerned. However, it does not easily lead to a better understanding of what Weber's labors were all about. Because of these shortcomings in the existing literature a renewed attempt is being made in the present essay to come to grips with the riddle of Weber's methodology, and especially the ideal type. Admittedly such an undertaking must look somewhat foolhardy, considering the impressive amount of literature on the subject. However, the latter may also be taken as indicative of the formidable difficulties involved which so far have precluded a solution. In any event, it is a somewhat disturbing fact that more than sixty years after Weber's publication of his essays the puzzle is still unsolved. This in itself is sufficient reason to justify a renewed attempt.

The interpretation presented in this essay was guided by the principle that any scientist's theoretical work must be seen as a more or less reasoned argument in support of certain solutions to certain problems. In the present case this meant that the fundamental question to be asked was: "To what problem, as conceived by Weber, does his methodology (and especially the conception of the ideal type) constitute the solution?" Only by answering this question was it possible to establish the proper frame of reference within which Weber's statements make full sense.

The substantive body of the present essay consists of four chapters. The first deals exclusively with Heinrich Rickert's theory of concept formation which—it is claimed here—heavily influenced Weber. This rather narrow focus, as far as Weber's intellectual ancestors are concerned, must not be misunderstood. It is not intended to imply that the influences on Weber's methodological considerations by thinkers other than Rickert are completely negligible. Any reading of, for instance, Menger's, Simmel's or Gottl's relevant works shows that such a claim could not seriously be maintained. The decision to limit the exposition to Rickert's thought was made (a) because the main aim of this essay is to show that the many arguments and considerations occurring in a hodge-podge fashion in Weber's methodological essays are components of a very systematic and comprehensive epistemological and methodological theory, and (b) because it can be shown that this theory is practically identical with that of Rickert. Thus Rickert's theory is singled out for treatment because those elements of Weber's methodological thought which stem from people other than Rickert seem to have been selected according to whether they fit into Rickert's theory or not. Rickert's relevant systematic arguments, however, Weber accepted in toto, as this essay will show.

The exposition of Rickert's theory has been entirely undertaken in view of the ultimate purpose, namely the clarification of Weber's thought. Thus mainly those arguments are presented whose knowledge is necessary for a proper understanding of Weber. Of course, this amounts to a neglect or underemphasis of several aspects to which Rickert himself attached great importance, e.g., his philosophy of value and his treatment of understanding. The presentation includes a few analytic comments in the form of explications of certain assumptions and tenets familiar to Rickert and his contemporaries, which nowadays do not seem to be as self-evident. Some of these assumptions are quite crucial to Rickert's argument (e.g., the immanent character of all empirical phenomena, i.e., the assumption that reality as such is inaccessible to human knowledge, that all humans can know is *phenomena* as they are perceived; the idea that knowledge is a picture of phenomena in the human mind; the conviction that abstraction is the process underlying all acquisition of scientific knowledge). Without carefully taking them into account, Rickert's (and Weber's) whole reasoning must appear incomprehensible, if not nonsensical. The requirement of placing one's thinking into an unfamiliar frame of reference in order to understand what is being said makes the reading of the first chapter a little difficult. This is aggravated by the fact that the terminology employed by Rickert is no longer in common use, and that some of the terms have meanings attached to them now which differ from those which Rickert attached to them (e.g., "law"). These inconveniences are unavoidable. However, they may be easier to cope with if they can be approached with a general idea of the sense of the whole argument presented in chapter one. The remainder of this introduction, therefore, is devoted to a short outline of the reasoning pursued in this chapter, and its significance for the essay as a whole.

As already stated, the main purpose of this essay is the interpretation of Weber's statements about the ideal type. It is presented in chapter three. A proper understanding of Weber's reasoning on this subject, however, requires a rather thorough knowledge of his entire theory of concept formation. This theory is outlined in chapter two. Its component parts are dispersed throughout Weber's methodological articles. Sometimes they occur in coherent clusters, often completely out of the systematic context in which they belong. In the majority of cases they are explicitly stated, but a few times they have to be inferred. Weber himself never gave a systematic exposition of his methodological theory. As a matter of fact, it would be extremely difficult to find systematic consistency in Weber's statements without the insight that they must be arranged in accordance with Rickert's theory of concept formation. For this reason Rickert's thought is presented in chapter one. This argument is less sketchy than the one in chapter two. It provides the detailed blueprint for the organization of Weber's statements. Indeed, it will be argued that Rickert's reasoning as presented in chapter one largely corresponds to what Weber would have said had he had any systematic inclinations.

The starting point of Rickert's argument is the presentation of the problem which is to be confronted: the declaration that only nomological knowledge is scientific knowledge. Rickert rejects this claim and then proposes a theory of his own as to what constitutes scientific knowledge. First he formulates the frame of reference which is peculiar to his approach. In it the establishment of knowledge is analyzed as a human activity which takes place only because the humans carrying it out connect a certain meaningful intention with it. This intention is the compliance with the value of truth. Thus, puzzling as it may seem, in Rickert's philosophy "truth" is interpreted as a value whose acceptance by scientists as binding induces them to establish knowledge. The question then becomes: In what does the establishment of knowledge consist? Rickert bases his answer on a version of the Idealist tenet that humans cannot know anything about reality as such but merely about their perception of it. Furthermore, it is important to realize, "knowing" for him is "having a reproduction of the object in the mind," as far as the content of knowledge is concerned. Knowledge, however, does not merely have a content, is not merely reproduction and copy of reality in the human mind; it also has certain forms. Knowledge occurs in statements; everything in a statement which is not reproduction of perceptions is interpreted as the form in which the knowledge occurs. Since perceptions in the human mind are not automatically reproduced and given a certain form, Rickert concludes that establishing knowledge consists in willfully combining a form with a content (the reproduction of a perception). It is a conscious act, an effort which takes place because it is demanded by all those who accept the value of truth.

After having established his conception of knowledge, Rickert next draws a distinction between mere knowledge of facts and science. This is necessary since for Rickert the human mind is too small to contain all facts which can possibly be stated. Scientific knowledge, therefore, cannot consist in stating all facts, for this would be a senseless undertaking under these circumstances. If there is to be any sense in human scientific efforts, these efforts must contain a manageable task. The amount of facts to be known must be limited. It must be limited in such a way that at the same time it both can be handled by the capacity of the human mind and also approximate as closely as possible the ideal of total factual knowledge. This elimination of certain facts from science as not worth knowing for Rickert constitutes a formative process.

According to Rickert there are two ways of forming the immense totality of facts in a scientific way. Each method reduces the infinity of facts to manageable proportions, and each comes as close as humanly possible to one of the two essential features of absolute, ideal knowledge. The establishment of complete knowledge in accordance with each one of the two procedures, therefore, must be the goal of everybody who wants knowledge, i.e., accepts the value of truth. In its entirety, this knowledge comprises everything which humanly can be known in a scientific fashion.

The two features of absolute knowledge which must be approximated by scientific knowledge are the following: (1) absolute knowledge encompasses all facts; (2) absolute knowledge is knowledge of each fact in its total concreteness. Absolute knowledge must have these two features due to the nature of empirical reality as Rickert postulates it: empirical reality, i.e., the totality of facts, for him is an infinity of individual concrete events. The task of scientific knowledge thus is to approximate complete knowledge of the infinity of things in their concreteness. According to Rickert, both tasks cannot be performed at the same time, given the nature of the human mind. He, therefore, proposes to divide the sciences into those in which the main endeavor is to come to grips with the infinity of reality, and those which above all deal with reality's concreteness. The former he calls "natural sciences," the latter "cultural," "historical," or "social sciences." In accordance with the different cognitive aim pursued in each kind of science, reality is formed according to a different principle in each. In the natural sciences only that is described which all phenomena have in common, i.e., only general concepts are formed. This is identical with the establishment of laws of nature. In history, only that is described which constitutes the uniqueness of, in each case, one particular phenomenon; in other words, individual concepts are formed. Thus the challenge is met by Rickert. The establishment of laws is shown not to be the only scientific undertaking which is legitimate.

Chapter two is practically another statement of the argument presented in chapter one, but this time in Weber's words. Since almost all existing interpretations of Weber's methodological writings have failed to see (or to take seriously the thought) that the latters' unity and inner coherence can be found in Rickert's philosophy of science, they have frequently not been able to reconcile all of Weber's statements with each other. The interpretation offered here, in contrast, can accommodate every one of Weber's pronouncements. One of the crucial insights in this respect is that Weber's methodology, if it is to make any sense as a whole, must not be understood as a treatise on the logic of explanation and testing. Rather, it must be realized that its central concern is to provide an answer to the question: What is it that makes the writing of history a justifiable undertaking? Or, put more generally: Of all the possible things that one could want to know, which ones are a legitimate object of investigation? Thus, the problem for Weber is that of determining what is worth knowing, not that of establishing how we can check and improve and expand the knowledge which we have. It is this starting point which gives Weber's reasoning its direction, and failure to realize this is to miss from the very beginning what preoccupies him.

Two other premises of Weber's arguments, whose significance is crucial for the solution of the puzzle of the ideal type, are (1) the equation of nomological statements and class concepts, i.e., the latters' treatment as identical with the statements defining them, and in turn their interpretation as empirical statements ("real definitions"); (2) the interpretation of nomological statements as the equivalent of conjunctions of singular statements, all stating the occurrence of events which are identical except for their spatio-temporal location. Neither one of these premises has been given any attention in the existing secondary literature. Consequently, it was never realized that the conception of ideal type was Weber's solution to the problem posed by certain class concepts with which historians necessarily have to work, yet which cannot be interpreted as conjunctions of singular statements (each of which reports an event which is identical with all the others, except for its location in time and space). Only with the help of this insight is it possible to make sense, complete sense, out of Weber's discussion of ideal-typical concepts (ideal-typical statements). The interpretation of these statements is presented in chapter three, together with Weber's application of Rickert's methodological theory to the problem of *Verstehen*.

In chapter four, finally, an attempt is made, using the notion of *model*, to reformulate, in a more appropriate frame of reference, the problem which Weber tried to solve through the conception of the ideal type. Whereas the objective in the first three chapters was merely the explication of Weber's and Rickert's arguments on their own grounds, chapter four goes somewhat beyond this. It is intended to indicate the way in which ideal-typical constructs must be interpreted so that their function in sociological theories is clarified. The considerations presented in this chapter are rather tentative and in no way exhaust or settle the issues raised. Hopefully they show, however, that Weber's considerations, when formulated in a more up-to-date language, are not entirely irrelevant to current concerns.

TECHNICAL REMARKS

(1) An attempt was made to consult all the existing secondary literature on Weber as far as it has a bearing on the topic treated in this essay, i.e., the understanding of Weber's theory of concept formation and ideal type construction. A few titles, almost all German dissertations, were not available to the author. Not all of the works are listed in the bibliography attached to this essay.

(2) It seemed useful to present and discuss the most important interpretations advocated in the existing literature, although in a rather brief fashion. In order not to disrupt and complicate the already difficult argument by frequent discussions of opinions expressed in the secondary literature, they have been partly relegated to the footnotes.

(3) Since the main objective of this essay is the correct interpretation of Weber's statements, and since so many divergent interpretations have been suggested, it was felt necessary to be pedantic and to include a considerable number of quotations as support and documentation. For the same reasons it also seemed advisable to give as many references to the original text as possible. Special care was taken to quote those passages which are hard to interpret, and to accompany them with a suggested interpretation.

(4) All quotations were translated by the author. They are accompanied by references to existing translations, where there are any. The attempt was made to retain already existing English translations with as little modification as possible. Still, considerable alterations were sometimes unavoidable. Occasionally, the altered portion is given within brackets together with the page reference. Stylistic considerations were completely subordinated to the attempt to give an exact rendition of the meaning of the German text.

(5) This author could not find any merit whatsoever in the common procedure of making Weber's writings "easier" to understand by eliminating the great number of italicized spellings and quotation marks around terms. Weber had good reasons for the frequent use of these devices. In the translated quotations, therefore, they occur as in the German original. Unless indicated otherwise, all the italics occurring in any quotation are as in the original.

(6) Page references to the German edition of Weber's essays are to the first edition. The same holds for Rickert's *Grenzen der naturwissenschaftlichen Begriffsbildung*.

MAX WEBER'S THEORY OF CONCEPT FORMATION

CHAPTER I. THE FOUNDATION OF MAX WEBER'S METHODOLOGY: HEINRICH RICKERT'S THEORY OF CONCEPT FORMATION IN THE EMPIRICAL SCIENCES

1. THE CONVERGENCE OF MAX WEBER AND HEINRICH RICKERT

Max Weber's views on methodological problems are contained in a number of essays which were written between 1903 and 1919, and in the opening pages of *Economy and Society*.[1] Posthumously, the essays[2] were collected and, together with several other articles which have little to do with methodology,[3] edited by Weber's wife Marianne in a book under the title *Gesammelte Aufsaetze zur Wissenschaftslehre*[4] (Collected Essays in the Logic of Science). Max Weber's theory of concept formation, which is the subject of this essay, is stated above all in the articles "Roscher & Knies,"[5] "Objectivity,"[6] and "Critical Studies."[7] *Economy and Society* also contains some relevant remarks, although nothing which cannot be found in the essays. All the other methodological writings are peripheral to the topic under consideration.

Weber completed only two of his methodological essays proper. Perhaps significantly, in both cases external circumstances required completion. The essay on "Objectivity" was written as a programmatic statement by Weber in his capacity as the new editor of the *Archiv fuer Sozialwissenschaft und Sozialpolitik*,[8] and the article on "Ethical Neutrality" was prepared as a position paper for a meeting of the Verein fuer Sozialpolitik.[9] The remaining three are critical discussions of methodological positions not in agreement with Weber's. Most of the articles are rather unsystematic, and there is no serious attempt to present the author's views, and the foundation on which they rest, in an integrated and coherent fashion backed up by reasoned argument. Rather, Weber's procedure consists mainly in confronting the opposed opinion on a particular question with his own tenets whose justification he apparently takes for granted. One of the problems of interpreting Weber's essays on methodology is finding the underlying systematic considerations—assuming that these exist—which give coherence to the expressed views. The assumption that they exist has indeed been made almost everywhere in the secondary literature, but it has not remained uncontested.

Friedrich H. Tenbruck in an article argues[10] that usually Weber's interpreters have operated under the influence of three suppositions which have vitiated their analyses. First, there has been the assumption that Weber's essays were written with the intent to present a coherent methodology for the cultural sciences.[11] Second, there has been a tendency to see this theory as the result of a creative outburst of a genius from whose mind it sprang practically full-fledged. Third, there has been the concomitant belief that for a proper understanding of the essays it is not really necessary to consider the specific historical situation in which they were written, or to investigate whether perhaps a development and change of ideas took place. A typical representative of this attitude, according to Tenbruck, is Dieter Henrich, who writes that the essays "are not only contributions to a possible future methodology, but already completely contain it."[12] He also declares: "A real change in core positions could nowhere be found. *The development of Max Weber's methodology is the unfolding of a conception which Weber possessed in all completeness.*"[13] Tenbruck thinks that such assumptions have to be dropped if Weber's essays are to make any sense. In his opinion, Weber never had any ambitions as a methodologist. He argues that for the supposed great methodological interest there exists "no convincing evidence,"[14] and that the methodological writings themselves "do not exactly testify vocation and passion. A certain carelessness, even indifference, is unmistakeable."[15] An interpretation, therefore, must not start with an image of Weber as the born methodologist but must view him instead as the specialized scientist who has been temporarily pushed into methodology.[16] "The concern of the essays is not the formulation of a methodology, but it is the methodological justification of a very particular substantive shift of the cultural sciences. The puzzle of content and function of Weber's methodological work cannot be solved, therefore, by even the most intensive study of the text when this study proceeds in an unhistorically systematizing fashion."[17] Tenbruck thinks that commentators trying to find a coherent doctrine, or at least a detailed sketch, have tended to twist Weber's arguments in ways which made them compatible with their own presuppositions. As a result, statements which Weber made in specific historical situations and with reference to particular historical constellations have been taken in an absolute fashion and interpreted as basic tenets of a coherent methodology. Against this tendency Tenbruck emphasizes that Weber's essays are "not a logic of science developed from an originally methodological viewpoint. They are the auxiliary methodological considerations of the specialized scientist which grew from a certain crisis in the field. Plan and frame of reference are not methodological but derive from the concrete problem situation in the writer's own field. The methodological reflection is not the end, but a means."[18]

To a certain extent, Tenbruck's criticism seems to be well taken. For in spite of the claims of some interpreters,[19] that the development of a methodology was one of Weber's great concerns, it is hard not to gain the impression that he was not too deeply interested in methodological problems.[20] It rather appears that as a result of external circumstances he felt compelled to deal with them and left off as soon as he could. The shape of the articles speaks in favor of this assumption. Furthermore, Marianne Weber's report documents the absence of any active desire on Max Weber's part to pursue methodological questions.[21] Finally, Weber's own statements support this interpretation:

> The following proposition recommends itself as essentially true: methodology can only bring us reflective understanding of the means which have *demonstrated* their value in practice, and raising them to the level of explicit consciousness is no more the precondition of fruitful work than the knowledge of anatomy is the precondition for "correct" walking. . . . Only by laying bare and solving *substantive* problems were sciences established, and are their methods developed. On the other hand, purely epistemological and methodological reflections have never played the crucial role in such developments. Such discussions can become important for the enterprise of science only when, as a result of considerable shifts of the "viewpoints" from which the material becomes the object of description, the idea emerges that the new "viewpoints" also require a revision of the logical forms in which the traditional "enterprise" has heretofore operated, and when therefore uncertainty about the "nature" of one's own work arises. As to history, this situation undoubtedly is given at present. . . .[22]

This is a social scientist and historian speaking, not a methodologist.[23] It does not sound like the opinion of someone who is overly committed to methodological considerations, and it may be conjectured that Weber, as far as his own substantive work was concerned, had no cause for such a commitment. His writings in this area, in any case, give no indications that he was ever plagued by methodological doubts. Alexander von Schelting's reasoning in this respect, which seems to stand at the beginning of the tradition criticized by Tenbruck, therefore has to be taken cautiously. He talks of the "passionate thrust" and "pathos" with which Weber "over and over again"[24] addressed himself to methodological problems and attributes it to the fact that for Weber the universality of methodological truths constituted a "compensation"[25] for the fragmented and particularized character of all empirical knowledge. Consequently he objects to Marianne Weber's characterization of the methodological work of her husband as a "byproduct."[26] However, this seems hardly justified. First of all it is not true, in the sense which von Schelting has in mind, that Weber over and over again was attracted by methodological problems. The important essays were all written in the three-year period between 1904 and 1906.[27] The later ones were repeat performances of an occasional nature. Secondly, there is simply no sign indicating that the transitoriness of all empirical knowledge constituted an emotional problem for Weber. Thirdly, there is no reason not to take at face value Weber's declaration that he wanted to try out Rickert's theory in the field of economics. Finally, as to the passionate nature of Weber's efforts, it has to be emphasized that passion is entirely lacking except when Weber is talking about ethical neutrality. Here, however, it is easily explained by Weber's involvement in the many fights over this issue in the Verein fuer Sozialpolitik, and elsewhere.

But there is yet another question raised by von Schelting in this context. He argues that in addition to the accidental stimuli of external circumstances Weber must have had some reasons of his own in dealing with methodology, an "inner necessity."[28] His suggestion is that the motive of Weber's search for the logical foundation of scientific knowledge was his commitment to an ethics of responsibility in political affairs. For without valid empirical knowledge such an ethics is not practicable.[29] Von Schelting's suggestion is rather interesting, and indeed there seems to be a meaningful relationship between Weber's position on ethical neutrality and his preference for an ethics of responsibility.[30] The question is, however, whether the existence of this relationship is sufficient to account for Weber's methodological concerns on the motivational level. To the present author, at least, it seems most plausible to assume that, surrounded by the *Methodenstreit*, Weber believed to have found, in Rickert, an already formulated theory capable of solving the most pressing problems, and, given an external stimulus, applied it.

If this consideration is valid, one should expect Weber to deal with methodological questions just enough to be able to refute particular concrete views whose acceptance would, in his opinion, entail calamitous results with respect to the substantive problems of history, and not more. This indeed seems to be the case, and to this extent Tenbruck's claims are correct. Tenbruck is wrong, however, in declaring that Weber, when he wrote his essays, was not in possession of a coherent and systematic methodological theory. He was, but this theory was not his own; it was taken over from Heinrich Rickert. The indebtedness of Weber to Rickert's thought has never been a secret, and interpretations have taken notice of it, for in a footnote to "Roscher & Knies" Weber says that one of the purposes of the article is ". . . to try out the usefulness of the thoughts of this author for the methodology of our discipline [i.e., economics]. For this reason I do not quote him in each single instance in which this properly would have to be done."[31] He also calls Rickert's *Die Grenzen der naturwissenschaftlichen Begriffsbildung*[32] (The Limits to the Concept Formation of Natural Science) "the fundamental work" in which "the exact logical formulation" of the difference between the "nomological sciences" and the "sciences of concrete reality" (*Wirklichkeitswissenschaften*) has been "comprehensively developed."[33]

These statements unhesitatingly can be applied to the "Critical Studies" which were written at the same time as "Roscher & Knies," containing several references to it[34] as well as to Rickert's work.[35] The question must be, of course, how far this agreement between Weber and Rickert really goes. The present essay will document that this agreement is almost total within the area under consideration, i.e., the theory of concept formation and its epistemological foundation.[36] It will show that Weber's and Rickert's positions in these respects are near-identical—with one or two exceptions whose significance will be discussed in the proper context—that all the gaps in Weber's arguments can easily and consistently be filled through recourse to Rickert's more systematic presentation, and that Weber's more cryptic statements make perfect sense when placed in the context of Rickert's theory. An implication of this is that Tenbruck is wrong in his conviction that only a developmental perspective can do justice to Weber's reasoning.[37] To the contrary, it is maintained here that Weber never changed his views in any relevant way.

In this author's opinion many of the problems encountered in previous interpretations of Weber's methodology were directly the result of an a priori underestimation of Rickert's influence and the consequent failure to analyze it in detail. This may have been due to the tendency described by Tenbruck to see in Weber the "Founding

Father" of methodology in the social sciences.[38] However this may be, in any case it prevented any systematic attempt to complete what was taken to be the torso of a more or less original methodology with the help of Rickert's detailed exposition, and to answer on the basis of this reconstruction the questions that had arisen. This had particularly lamentable consequences for the interpretation of Weber's statements concerning the ideal type. For one author, the history of the successive interpretive attempts qualifies as "a major mystery story."[39] However, there is nothing mysterious about the ideal type. As will be demonstrated later in this essay, Weber's conception represents an absolutely consistent and unambiguous attempt to solve *within the systematic framework of Rickert's theory of concept formation* a specific *logical* problem (in the sense in which Weber understands this term) arising in it. This problem concerns the *logical* status of certain concepts which could not be described adequately in terms of the available theories of knowledge, and it was encountered within Rickert's theory as well as within any other theory existing at the time. However, Rickert did not address himself to the question, whereas Weber was forced to face it.

The emphasis which is placed in the present essay upon the influence of Rickert's thought on Weber's theory of concept formation must not be misunderstood. It does not imply a claim that this was the only influence, nor does it imply that Rickert's ideas were always particularly original. Both Rickert and Weber stood in a tradition which had led to the formulation of certain problems and to particular attempts of solving them.[40] Weber undoubtedly was familiar with the ideas of the major thinkers in that tradition, like Sigwart,[41] Windelband,[42] or Simmel,[43] and with those of their opponents, like Menger[44] or John Stuart Mill.[45] Certain ideas were very common—they were "in the air," so-to-speak—and thus it would hardly be justifiable to give Rickert the sole credit for the fact that Weber adhered to them. The contention here is, however, that the particular fashion in which Weber approached the solution of the commonly recognized problems of concept formation, the way in which he used or modified rather familiar ideas, is—with one or two qualifications—exactly the same as Rickert's. In other words, whoever else's views may have influenced him, figuratively speaking Weber read those theories through Rickert's glasses. He used the same analytical perspective and the same terminology. He accepted only what could be fitted into Rickert's methodological framework and thus often became undistinguishable from this philosopher's views.[46]

From everything that has been said so far, Weber the methodologist does not emerge as a very independent thinker. In two respects this impression has to be corrected: the ideal type represents a rather original synthesis, although altogether within the framework of Rickert's theory, and some of the arguments advanced by Weber in connection with the issue of ethical neutrality seem to be his own. However, with these two exceptions, Weber is content to apply ideas already formulated by other thinkers,[47] not only as far as the theory of concept formation is concerned, but with respect to the whole of his methodology.[48] This attitude appears perfectly understandable when the idea is accepted that Weber's main concern was not the formulation of a methodology of his own but the refutation of certain methodological positions adopted by some historians and social theorists. There were above all three methodological tenets which Weber felt compelled to combat: The inclusion of value judgments in accounts claiming to be of an empirical, scientific[49] nature, the contention that it is the aim of the science of history to establish laws, and the negation of the conceptual character of historical knowledge. A theory existed that could provide the basis for a rebuttal, i.e., Rickert's, and Weber made extensive use of it. He added to it in the two just-mentioned instances: the argument in favor of ethical neutrality, and the ideal type. The addition of the latter—which alone is of concern in this essay—was necessary because the methodological status of certain general concepts occurring in economics and the historical sciences required clarification. Here Rickert's theory was not sufficiently specific, and Weber was forced to do it on his own. Significantly—in relation to the here adopted view that Weber was not very eagerly pursuing problems of methodological character—he chose *not* to do so in another instance for which neither Rickert[50] nor anybody else had provided in a satisfactory way:[51] the theory of understanding (*Verstehen*). This was an open field which Weber did not really enter, presumably because he did not perceive any practical necessity to do so.[52] The theoretical problems involved apparently did not stimulate him. He was satisfied to show that for understanding to be empirical knowledge it has to be in the form of concepts. Otherwise, he took it for granted that understanding was possible and left the whole set of problems related to the "How?" and "What?" of understanding unanalyzed. This would hardly seem to be the proper behavior for somebody who called his sociology "interpretive" (*verstehend*) and supposedly tried to lay the methodological foundations of social science. It rather insinuates a general lack of commitment to such matters. The implication of the foregoing paragraphs is that Weber on the whole was rather willfully unoriginal in his methodological writings. Only in two or three instances was he forced out of his reserve. Since Weber relied heavily on Rickert's writings it may, therefore, be said that in Weber's view the foundation for a logic of the social sciences had been laid by Rickert. Thus, any assessment of Weber as a methodologist has to consider that in this area he largely was the advocate of another person's ideas. It is a rather tenuous interpretation to argue as Henrich does that Weber found in Rickert's works only a confirmation of his own previously and independently developed views.[53] Henrich bases his opinion on the following statements of Weber's: "I have finished reading Rickert. He is very good. To a very large extent I find in his book what I have thought myself, although in logically untreated form."[54] This quote proves only that Weber agreed with Rickert, and that before he had read him he had not been in possession of a coherent logical argument. It also provides a rather good explanation for the congruence of Weber's argument with Rickert's, even in details, which otherwise would be truly astonishing.

Once Weber's dependence on Rickert is fully taken into account, it is very easy to arrange his dispersed statements in the proper way. Correctly interpreted, his writings on methodology reveal an internally consistent theory of concept formation which is practically identical with the one proposed by Rickert.[55] With respect to this internal consistency it is entirely justified to proclaim "the unity of Max Weber's methodology."[56] There is no evidence that Weber's methodological convictions changed through the years:[57] the earliest and the latest essays contain entirely identical or compatible arguments. This is not at odds with Tenbruck's opinion that Weber's methodological essays originated as occasional articles in response to external stimuli. However, it is in clear disagreement with his contention that Weber's methodology is an "extremely contradictory structure in which the most diverse impulses, concepts, and problems are solved in a thoroughly superficial and very general fashion."[58] This is not to say that as a whole his methodology stands valid even today. The only contention is that Weber went as far as the logic of science of his days permitted him to go, and that within those limits he arrived at a reasonable, defendable, and consistent position. The body of this essay will have to provide the justification for this contention.

2. SOME FUNDAMENTAL TENETS OF HEINRICH RICKERT'S EPISTEMOLOGY

Heinrich Rickert's major work on methodology, or logic of science, bears the title *Die Grenzen der naturwissenschaftlichen Begriffsbildung* (The Limits to the Concept Formation of Natural Science) [1] and represents a systematic attempt to provide a foundation for the historians' claims that theirs is a science. The issues which it tried to settle had existed for a long time, yet had remained somewhat latent, at least in Germany. However, under the impact of the rapid advances made by the natural sciences, the philosophical and methodological traditions which had carried their successful development gained in significance. On their basis some people felt justified to deny the status of science to history. To Rickert, this was a challenge which had to be met.

The fundamental objection of the critics of history was that the writing of history merely amounts to a description of constellations of singular facts and provides no insight into the laws of nature. These critics declared that compared with the natural sciences, history as traditionally written, therefore, yields an inferior kind of knowledge. The suggested remedy was to adopt the methods which elsewhere had proved to be so successful. Thus, Henry Thomas Buckle stated:

The unfortunate peculiarity of the history of man is, that although its separate parts have been examined with considerable ability, hardly anyone has attempted to combine them into a whole, and ascertain the way they are connected with each other. In all the other great fields of enquiry, the necessity of generalization is universally admitted, and noble efforts are being made to rise from particular facts in order to discover the laws by which those facts are governed. So far, however, is this from being the usual course of historians, that among them a strange idea prevails, that their business is merely to relate events. . . .[2]

The conclusions which he draws from this were not flattering to historians: "At present it is enough to say, that for all the higher purposes of human thought history is still miserably deficient, and presents that confused and anarchical appearance natural to a subject of which the laws are unknown, and even the foundation unsettled."[3]

The main thrust of this and similar arguments must be correctly understood. They were not put forward as considerations concerning the logic of explanation, based on the insight that without nomological hypotheses the occurrence of specific singular events cannot be explained. Although this problem played a role, the main consideration was metaphysical and in some form involved the belief that in the universal features of things lies their essence. On the basis of such an assumption, the discovery of these features would seem to be the obvious goal of all scientific investigation. In any case, Rickert fully acknowledges the function of nomological statements in scientific explanations[4] and takes issue only with the latter idea. In his view it is erroneous to believe that the essence, or nature, of things can be discovered;[5] all that can ever be known is phenomena, that is, objects as they appear to the human mind. Thus, as long as it is based on this kind of reasoning alone, the argument that the search for laws of nature is the only justifiable scientific undertaking is unfounded for Rickert.[6]

From the point of view of a philosophical position for which it is the task of science to discover the essential nature of things, believing it to lie in their general features, it is reasonable to doubt the scientific status of history. In rejecting this whole position and by confronting it with his own Idealist epistemology, it seems that Rickert has eliminated the issue together with the framework within which it arose, and, therefore, has no reason to pursue the matter further. However, this is not the case. In spite of the rejection of the philosophical approach from which the problem sprang, Rickert continues to treat it as a valid problem. Obviously, then, this question has some significance within his own theory. But within what kind of frame of reference would it make sense to treat the question whether or not history is a science, as a sensible and legitimate question? The answer, implied in Rickert's epistemology, basically is provided by the following considerations, as presented in Rickert's book *Der Gegenstand der Erkenntnis* (The Object of Knowledge).[7]

Science is the attempt to establish "knowledge" (*Erkenntnis*) of a certain kind, namely "objective" knowledge of the world, of empirical reality. This knowledge "abstracts" from the concreteness of empirical reality. It is possible to abstract from concrete empirical reality in many different ways, but not all lead to objective knowledge. Objective knowledge is knowledge which everybody wants to have, in which everybody is interested. Thus, historical accounts can be

considered to be scientific only if they contain what everybody wants
to know.

As this sketchy argument shows, Rickert proposes certain conceptions of "science" and "objective knowledge" which, of course, differ from those held by his opponents. On their basis, he sets out to
establish whether or not history qualifies as a science in his sense of
the term. Since he thinks that historical investigations are a worthwhile
activity, it is reasonable to conjecture that the results of his efforts
will be positive. Whatever the outcome, however, it can only be a
definitional truth. For whether or not history can be called a science
depends on the decision to use the term "science" in a particular fashion.
This does not mean that Rickert's whole effort is trivial, though. First
of all, given his definition, it is not immediately obvious that history
can indeed be properly called a science. It requires careful analysis
to find out whether it has the necessary empirical attributes which,
according to Rickert, characterize science. And second, Rickert deals
with the problem within the wider framework of a whole epistemology. This places considerable restrictions on his definitional decisions.
Thus, he is not simply free to choose whatever conceptions of "science"
and "objective knowledge" he pleases in order to make sure that history can be called a science.

To Rickert, the establishment of objective knowledge of empirical
reality is one of the goals pursued by humans. The efforts which are
necessary to reach it occur in the form of specialized activities, namely
scientific investigations. If one looks at objective empirical knowledge
as a goal to be reached, every investigation whose aim it is to yield
such knowledge, and which uses the proper procedures to that end,
seems to be a justifiable undertaking. It appears, then, that every effort in that direction, every methodical activity having that goal, qualifies as scientific. The problem, whether the search for laws of nature
is the only genuinely scientific endeavor, is resolved by showing
whether or not this is the only activity which can lead to the establishment of objective knowledge of empirical reality. Obviously, the
solution depends on what is understood by "objective knowledge,"
and, therefore, a clear idea of Rickert's conception is crucial to the
understanding of his whole argument.

Rickert, in accordance with the opinion prevalent at the time,[8] conceived of knowledge as a mental state: when humans have knowledge
of empirical reality, they have something in their minds. But he rejects the idea that this may simply be described as a copy in the mind

of a world existing outside it. For humans can only be aware of that which they have in their minds, and they have no way of finding out whether this faithfully reproduces a reality existing outside it and independently from it. Things as they are unmediated by the mind, independent from how humans perceive them and are aware of them, are not accessible to human reason. Man can never know things *as they are as such*, but only *as they appear to him*, as they appear in the mind as so-called phenomena. Thus, what humans have in their minds when they have knowledge of empirical reality, is not copies of things as such; it is phenomena.

Now, how may phenomena be described? What do they consist of? Rickert's answer is complicated. He starts by saying that the analysis of the cognitive content of the human mind, i.e., disregarding subjective states like feelings, emotions, etc., reveals the presence of a mass of most basic, least differentiated, and unorganized elements given in the consciousness. These "sensations," or "impressions," constitute the lowest possible level of awareness. They may be called "immediate (or directly given) experiences," but this expression must not be misunderstood. It is not to imply that such sensations are unmediated, faithful copies of a reality existing beyond, or transcending, the awareness of them. It is merely to state that for the cognitive endeavors of man, these are to be treated as the ultimate givens, and not some reality "behind" them. They are the basis of everything else, and it is not possible to go beyond them by reducing them to more original or immediate components.

Sensations occur as an undifferentiated flow of diverse and unclear states of consciousness. Having such sensations, according to Rickert, does not constitute knowledge. Rather, he argues that they are the *object* of knowledge. Knowledge must be knowledge of something; sensations are its raw material. For nothing more immediate is accessible to the human mind.[9] Now it may seem, says Rickert, that knowledge can be adequately described as a copy or a reproduction, on another mental level, of the immediate sensations or directly given experiences,[10] and that knowledge thus consists in having "notions" or "ideas" of these basic states of consciousness. But he thinks that this conception is unsatisfactory; for the analysis of what is usually called "knowledge" reveals that there is more to it than just having ideas of something. For example, if someone asks: "Is the sun shining?" he has the ideas "sun" and "shine," but he certainly has no knowledge. For the conception of knowledge implies that it can be either true or false,[11] yet a question cannot be true or false, although it can contain ideas. Only *assertions* can be true or false, and ideas alone do not assert anything. Rickert, therefore, concludes that knowledge consists in asserting something of an idea. "Since having notions [i.e., ideas] is not the same as having knowledge, the contents of consciousness [i.e., immediate experiences] become objects of knowledge only through 'thinking,' i.e., judging [i.e., asserting something of the ideas of these experiences]."[12] Thus, according to Rickert, when someone says: "This is a cat," he asserts something of the notion "cat," namely that it exists. The notion, or idea, of one or more immediate sensations —in this case, "cat"—is called the *"content"* of knowledge. "Existence," which is asserted of it, is the *"form"* in which in this case knowledge is had.[13] The combined form-content is what is usually called a *"concrete fact."* It is the idea of a segment singled out from the undifferentiated mass of dimly experienced states of consciousness on the level of immediate sensations, which is given the form of "existence," i.e., which is thought to be "real."[14] Thus, when something is stated to exist, to be real, it is not asserted to exist outside the mind. It is only stated that, as a mental content, it is thought of in a certain form, that of existence, rather than in another, for instance, that of "possibility."

A concrete fact, the combination of an idea and the form of existence is not something which simply occurs in the human mind on its own force, so-to-speak. Only sensations occur in an individual's mind without his being able to, or having to, do anything about it. Facts, however have to be constituted. A form and a content have to be combined, and this is a volitional act. Its performance is intentional activity. But why should anyone make this effort? Rickert argues that men constitute facts in their minds because they want to create something which can be said to be true. This, in turn, they want because they recognize truth as a *value*. Otherwise, there would be no reason for them to assert anything at all. They could be content in remaining on the level of just "experiencing" (*erleben*) their immediate sensations, which they cannot help having. "*Having knowledge* (*erkennen*), *as far as its immanent logical meaning is concerned, is an acceptance of values, or a rejection of un-values*, whereas *error* accordingly has to be understood as the *rejection of values and the acceptance of un-values*."[15] It is the recognition of a particular value as being valid which compels humans to combine a form with a content, i.e., to make a *judgment*. Thus, a judgment always involves a claim to truth, truth being a value. For, given the starting point of Rickert's whole argument,[16] what forces men to accept something as a fact (forces them to think of certain sensations as "real") cannot be the need to correctly reproduce in their minds a world existing outside it (for they cannot know anything of it). It has to be something else, and this can only be a value. Since they accept it as valid for themselves, the combination of a particular content and a particular form looks necessary to them. "Indeed, it is exactly our point to emphasize that simply *stating a fact of consciousness* always implies the recognition of the *necessity* to judge such and not otherwise . . . ."[17] Thus, Rickert can say: "Fact is what I ought to think."[18]

There are several forms in which contents are judged to occur, and their totality comprises any form in which man can have knowledge. The form-element is called the "category."[19] "Existence" is one of them. For instance, in the statement, "This is a man," the notion "man" is a content which is given the form of existence. Every concrete "fact," therefore, is categorically formed. People refer to such facts when, in the empirical sciences, they speak of "objective reality" or "empirical reality." Concrete reality consists of contents of consciousness which are judged by everybody to be "real."[20]

Objective reality in its totality is the subject-matter of *science*; it is the concrete material which constitutes the object of scientific investigations. In science, the "real" existence of the content of consciousness is not seen as being problematic; it is taken for granted.[21] Instead, the establishment of the substantive diversity of the content is focused upon. It may now seem that it must be the task of science simply to state what the facts are—that is, *all* facts, everything which is thought as real.[22] However, and this leads back to the very starting point of Rickert's considerations, exactly this problem is the substance of the question whether or not a particular group of facts—namely those referred to as "laws of nature"[23]—alone are a legitimate object of scientific investigation. Rickert has reason to think that it is not the task of science to state all facts; a selection is necessary.[24] Thus the principle of selection comes into question. As the epistemological considerations outlined above make obvious, from a logical point of view Rickert cannot acknowledge any differences in the essence of facts. They are all equal, so-to-speak, none are intrinsically more essential than others. There are no inherent qualities which make some facts worthy of scientific investigation and others not.[25]

Before proceeding to discuss the principles of selection, however, it is necessary to ascertain Rickert's reasoning in declaring that it cannot be the task of science to state all facts. His argument is that there are infinitely many facts, and that, therefore, it is impossible to state them all. This argument does not sound very convincing as it stands. Why should scientists not try at least to establish as many facts as they can? From the impossibility of stating them all it does not follow that it is not the task of science to try. Their complete establishment may be set up as an ideal. Why then does Rickert say that the establishment of *some* facts only is a justifiable scientific objective?

For the purpose of answering this question it is helpful to give the problem a different formulation. It was said that knowledge consists in asserting the combination of a content with a form. Thus, when Rickert declares that it is impossible to state all facts, this means that it is impossible for scientists to give all occurring contents a form. Why is this so? There is nothing intrinsic in either forms or available contents which would impose such a limit. Therefore, it seems that Rickert has to make some kind of assumption about the nature of the mind which necessarily implies a restriction. This assumption is that the human mind is *limited*. By this Rickert means that, on the level of ideas, humans are just not able to grasp all available contents; they cannot have them all in the mind.[26] Now, *as far as its content only is concerned*, disregarding the form in which it occurs, it is correct to describe knowledge as a number of ideas, or *images*, or *pictures*, which humans have of their sensations.[27] If, then, due to the limitations of the mind, humans can never have complete knowledge of empirical reality, it is obvious that their knowledge cannot be perfect in the sense that their minds can never contain an exact mirror-image of the sensation-contents of the consciousness in all their details. It cannot hold the totality of ideas which would exhaust the content of immediate experiences. The mind can embrace only a finite number of such ideas. This, of course, requires that a selection be made.

The fact that human knowledge of concrete reality in its entirety is impossible and, therefore, must be selective, must involve *abstraction*, poses for Rickert the problem of the "objectivity" of scientific knowledge. For this situation creates the possibility that each scientist's knowledge is different from everybody else's, that everybody abstracts in a different way and thus arrives at a merely subjective, private picture of the world. However, all science is based on the idea that it is possible to achieve objective knowledge of empirical reality, namely, to establish the *same* knowledge in every scientist's mind. In the context of Rickert's argument, thus, the problem of "objectivity" is *not* that of correctly establishing *what* the facts are (or *what* the relations among them are). The solution of this problem is taken for granted and not further discussed. Rather, the problem is that of the selection of the *same* facts by all scientists in their endeavor to present an account of empirical reality.[28] The precondition of the objectivity of science, therefore, is that all scientists abstract in identical fashion from the concrete reality constituted by the totality of ideas which are given the form of existence. Since the establishment of knowledge is due to an effort of the will, it is reasonable to assume that scientists would apply the same methods of abstraction only if they were all interested in identical knowledge. In Rickert's opinion, this commonality of interest is indeed the case; his reasons for holding this opinion will be presented later.[29]

It seems that with this the task of establishing Rickert's conception of "objective knowledge" is finished. For him, "objective knowledge" is knowledge of those selected facts which everybody wants to know. This knowledge is, therefore, intersubjective. "Science" is the systematic effort to establish this knowledge. Hence it can be said that, according to Rickert, every exposition of facts can legitimately claim scientific status, which is accepted by all those whose aim it is to establish knowledge, i.e., scientists, as (a step toward) a representation of an aspect of reality which is worth knowing. However, such an exposition can be presented only after a previous selection from among all available facts. Thus, its legitimacy has to stem from the circumstance that a standard of selection has been applied which is intersubjectively recognized as valid.[30] A standard is recognized as valid when it involves a method of abstraction leading to the establishment of those facts which every scientist wants to know. Conversely, when there is an agreed-upon standard of selection, it is used because it leads to generally desired knowledge. Therefore, if the knowledge of laws of nature is the only knowledge which everybody wants to have, then the method leading to their formulation is the only legitimate scientific method. In this case, it also would be the only one which is in use among scientists. If, however, knowledge of the laws of nature does not exhaust the facts which everybody wants to know, then one should expect to find additional methods of abstraction which are generally accepted by those scientists whose main interest it is—due to the scientific division of labor—to establish this additional knowledge.[31]

Based on these considerations Rickert, in his book on concept formation,[32] sets out to establish the valid standards of selection and to show how they fulfill their function: the reduction of the infinite number of concrete facts to proportions which can be handled by the human mind. He arrives at these standards by way of an analysis of the established sciences. He also tries to demonstrate that it is not accidental that these methods of abstraction underlie the formulations of the existing sciences. This analysis he calls an "inquiry in logic."[33] "Logic" to him is the inquiry concerned with those features of human knowledge which are functions of the human mind: the "form" of human knowledge, as opposed to the "content" of human knowledge—that which is processed by the mind. Thus, "... logic is the science of the *forms* of thought."[34] Since as scientists we can have knowledge only within these forms, it may also be said that logical inquiries have the goal of "finding out the conditions under which we can claim to have scientific knowledge."[35] It should be obvious here that Rickert does not refer to the formal requirements which an *inference* must fulfill in order to be valid in terms of the logic of syllogisms. Rather, he is concerned with the formal conditions which must be fulfilled if an account of facts is legitimately to be treated as a scientific representation of the world. "Before we make any statements about the facts we inquire in what sense science here has a right to state anything. Each *quaestio facti* for us becomes a *quaestio iuris* ...."[36]

Scientific knowledge, as far as its content is concerned, is a partial "image" on one level of the human mind of the sensations which occur on a different level. Such an image cannot be likened to a mirror-reflection.[37] It is a selective image which has to be constructed, or formed, with the intent of intersubjectivity. Its selectivity is *asserted* to be valid for everybody. Thus at this stage it is not the truth anymore which is asserted; it is assumed that what is said is true. Asserted now is the legitimacy of the selection of particular and true facts for an account of empirical reality, i.e., the conformity to a valid standard of selection. The process of selection involved in the establishment of scientific knowledge, in Rickert's view, is a *formative* process. Its end-product, a certain account of empirical reality, thus displays a certain *form* in which the substantive content appears. This form is called "concept" by Rickert. In this terminology, then, the formal aspect of scientific investigation is a process of concept formation. Its established outcome is a concept.[38] Strictly speaking, "concept" refers only to the formal aspect of scientific knowledge. However, the term is also used loosely by Rickert to denote the form-content combination as a whole. *The conceptual content consists of facts, the conceptual form is the kind of abstraction from concrete reality which they represent*, and due to which they are judged to constitute a valid account of this reality. This kind of abstraction is a function of the standard of selection applied in the process of concept formation. The application of such a standard represents for Rickert a method of overcoming the "irrational" infinity of reality.[39] It is a method of rationalizing it, i.e., treating it such that it can be grasped by human reason.[40] Therefore, Rickert calls concepts "methodological forms" as opposed to the categories, which are "constitutive forms," since through them objective reality is constituted. The analysis of the methodological forms is the object of "methodology."[41] It is the existence of these forms which makes science possible at all. Without them, humans could not have scientific knowledge but could only try to grasp the infinite whole of the concrete world through intuition or some other kind of all-embracing inner experience (*Erlebnis*).[42]

Before a more detailed outline of the methods of concept formation can be presented, one last remark is necessary. It was said earlier[43] that according to Rickert the facts constituting objective reality are categorically formed notions of sensations. The category, or "constitutive form," of existence was mentioned as the form which makes humans think of such notions as "real." Another such category is "possibility." Now still another one must be named which deserves special attention, namely "causality."[44] By giving a particular content the form of causality it is thought (judged) as having a cause and an effect. However, in contrast to the common opinion following Kant, Rickert insists that giving a content the categorical form "causality" is not identical to treating it as an instance of a general law. For when reality is constituted in the mind an individual content is combined with a categorical form—that of causality, in the present case. This means that every single fact of objective reality which is given this form is conceived as causing and being caused, not more and not less. This may be expressed by saying that the human conception of objective reality is governed by the *principle* of causality. This is not synonymous with any particular causal *law*. For in laws, general causal relationships are described which exist between all phenomena which are members of certain classes. Since objective reality confronts man as a totality of individual objects, causes, and effects, assertions about general relationships have to be the result of comparing and ordering many individual facts. Causal laws, then, cannot be forms through which objective reality is constituted in the human mind. Instead, they must be treated as forms in which humans have scientific knowledge of reality, that is, as forms of abstraction. As such they are methodological forms, concepts, or ways of overcoming the infinite multiplicity of empirical reality.[45] It is now necessary to turn to the description of these methodological forms.

3. GENERAL CONCEPTS

The systematic starting point of Rickert's methodological reflections proper is the fact that to the human observer, the empirical world represents itself as an infinite multiplicity of qualitatively and quantitatively different concrete phenomena.[1] Rickert calls it a "heterogeneous continuum."[2] Its infinity is encountered on two levels: first, any attempt to merely enumerate all concretely existing objects leads to the recognition of the "extensive" infinity of empirical reality; second, any attempt to describe the component parts of just one concrete object reveals the "intensive" infinity of elements of which any concrete phenomenon consists. The significance of this situation has already been indicated.

As a matter of principle, it is an insoluble task for the finite human mind to have knowledge (*erkennen*) of the world by individually representing in one's mind all the discrete phenomena as they concretely exist. . . . Whoever understands by "knowledge of the world" an actual copy of it, from the very outset has to renounce the idea of a science which would ever come near to representing knowledge of the world as a whole.[3]

If there is to be knowledge at all, the infinite multiplicity of things has to be somehow "eliminated or overcome."[4] This is accomplished by concepts. They reduce the mass of facts representing the empirical world to proportions which the mind is equipped to handle. "Thus, without concepts . . . any knowledge of the world, any grasp of physical reality in our minds, would be impossible. Concept formation, therefore, is necessarily connected with any judgment about reality which can be expressed in words."[5]

The scientific observer can overcome the infinity of reality only by limiting himself to the establishment of selected facts. The selection, in order to be valid, requires the application of a standard of selection which is recognized as valid by everybody who wants to have scientific knowledge. This standard states what parts of reality are to be considered as "essential" for its valid representation. Thus, being "essential" is not an inherent quality of certain facts, but a characteristic *ascribed* to facts by the scientist who is applying a particular selective criterion. Rickert refers to this situation when he says that it depends on the *point of view* adopted by a scientist, i.e., the standard of selection applied by him, whether a fact is essential or not.[6]

Empirically one finds, according to Rickert, two different formal principles of selection. Their application makes it possible to arrive at two different kinds of representations of reality. Each principle is recognized as valid by all those who are interested in the corresponding kind of knowledge. The pictures of reality resulting from the application of these standards are, therefore, generally recognized as valid by the respective groups of scientists. One of the standards prescribes the selection of those empirical elements which are *common to many* concrete phenomena. These elements are considered to be essential, whereas individual differences are neglected. The other standard requires the selection of those component elements of *one* individual phenomenon which in their combined occurrence constitute *the unique features* of this phenomenon and distinguish it from all others; everything else is neglected as irrelevant. The former method leads to "general" concepts. According to Rickert, it is characteristic of the natural sciences. The latter procedure results in "historical," or "individual" concepts. In their most elaborate form they describe complex historical developments, e.g., the decline of the Roman Empire. The use of the term "concept" for such descriptions is uncommon. However, in Rickert's terminology "concept" denotes any kind of thought-construct, any methodologically formed mental content which is intended as a valid representation of empirical reality, no matter how complex its verbal formulation.

Rickert's considerations are based on a specific conception of empirical reality. The main idea involved is that every concrete phenomenon—be it a "thing," be it a process—is composed of smaller concrete parts, that every concrete component part, in turn, is a structure consisting of even smaller concrete elements, and so on. Furthermore, every concrete phenomenon is viewed as being caused and as having an effect; the same is thought to hold true of all the concrete component parts of phenomena, of the parts of parts, etc. On any given level of complexity no concrete phenomenon is exactly like any other. None has exactly the same concrete cause, none the same concrete effect.

Every concrete phenomenon in its totality is a unique, individual structure of component parts, uniquely caused, and uniquely causing. However, the concrete composition of any phenomenon, as well as its cause and effect, may be partially the same as, or like, that of other concrete phenomena. In this case, some of their component parts, and the ways in which they are related to each other, are alike. The same also holds of their causes and their effects. When a scientist decides to acquire knowledge of only these common features of phenomena, their causes, and their effects, he decides to *generalize*. When he decides to ignore them and instead to focus on the particularities of just one concrete phenomenon, i.e., those component parts and their interrelationships which make this phenomenon unlike any other, he decides to *individualize*. In either case, the method of ignoring some facts in favor of others involves the selective procedure usually called "abstraction." All concept formation involves abstraction.[7] Therefore—as far as their content is concerned—scientific concepts are, in Rickert's view, abstracted accounts of reality. Considering that he calls his inquiry a study in "logic," it may thus be said that the logic of science, for him, deals with methods of abstraction, the derivation of concepts from reality. As should be clear from the whole argument presented in the foregoing section of this chapter, Rickert's opinion is a direct implication of any approach in which the problem of knowledge is treated as the problem of mentally grasping or conceiving of a multitude of concrete contents. Before the advent of modern logic of science, this was the dominant view on which methodological discussions were based. It was the rationale underlying distinctions such as those between ideal types and real types, exaggerated abstractions, isolating abstraction, average types, etc. All these distinctions referred to different ways of abstracting from concrete reality; they were treated as logical distinctions.[8]

In this section the concern is with Rickert's solution to the problem of overcoming the infinite multiplicity of empirical reality by representing in the mind "what several concrete individual phenomena have in common."[9] With this somewhat vague expression Rickert describes the kind of knowledge which typically is desired in the existing natural sciences. It is his conception of the structure of concrete reality which helps to clarify what he means. This conception is that all phenomena are composed of smaller elements, and that the properties which phenomena exhibit are nothing else but the distinctive modes in which they are built out of a distinctive diversity of these smaller components.

In Rickert's view, then, the natural scientist attempts to identify the regular and recurrent features of the so-conceived empirical reality. This procedure begins with the establishment of classes of phenomena on a relatively low level of abstraction (such as Linné's classification of plants). They are formed by grouping objects and processes together on the basis of similar properties exhibited by them. Increasingly, the relatively concrete level is left behind by the discovery that objects or processes which on the surface are distinct, on a more abstract level have things in common which justify grouping them together. For example, it may be found that planets and apples both can be treated as bodies having masses, and that as such they have many things in common in spite of their more concrete differences. Thus they can be classed together as instances of the class "physical body," a class which is rather more comprehensive (i.e., contains more instances) than that of either "apple" or "planet." In the same fashion, the formulation of ever more general causal laws is accomplished. Such laws are statements about the identical features of the many concrete cause-effect relationships of which phenomena are part. Causal regularities which can be established with regard to physical bodies are much more general than those which can be formulated about either apples or planets (since they refer to a greater number of phenomena). In the end, as a result of progressive abstraction, in the ultimate natural science, the world will be conceived of as composed of simple elements which occur in specific constellations and have like causes and like effects.[10] Knowledge of "what several (and ideally, all) concrete individual phenomena have in common," then, is a picture in the mind of these elements, the constellations in which they occur, and the "laws," which govern them. These "laws of nature" are nothing else than conceptions of the causes and effects which are common to many, and ultimately all, phenomena.

Rickert is, of course, aware of the fact that the actually existing natural sciences are not characterized by the exclusive use of this generalizing method. In order to avoid misunderstanding it has to be emphasized that when he speaks of "natural science," he does not talk about any actually existing natural science. Rather, "natural science" for him denotes any systematic activity whose ultimate aim is the formation of general concepts. "Natural science" is defined as the use of this method. The actually existing sciences come more or less close to this definition. Psychology and sociology, since they use the generalizing method, are to be classified as natural sciences. The ultimate natural science consists in concepts of elements which are common to all physical, psychic, social, etc., phenomena, and of the relationships of cause and effect in which these elements stand.

The procedure which scientists use to approach this final goal, according to Rickert, consists in comparing many, and ever more, phenomena in order to identify the component parts which they all have in common, the constellations in which they occur in all of them, as well as the causes and effects which are common to all. Eventually, a specific constellation of specific parts shared by many phenomena is established (e.g., an organism with four legs, which is furry and barks); this is what scientists are aware of, what they have in their minds, when they "have a concept" of something (of a dog, in this case). They are conscious of a combination of parts which they designate by a term, and every concrete phenomenon displaying this combination is "subsumed" under the concept. Such concepts may represent things or relations of cause and effect between things; they are "thing-concepts" (e.g., "tree," "stone") and "relational concepts" (e.g., "attraction," "motion"), respectively. "We reduce the extensive multiplicity of the world around us by designating a plurality of phenomena with one word. The intensive multiplicity of each single phenomenon is overcome because we are able to subsume it with certainty under the meaning of a word..."[11] Even in prescientific discourse, terms denoting general concepts are constantly used. Communication would be impossible without them. However, since they have not been formed with the intention to *completely* overcome the infinite multiplicity of reality *in its totality*, they merely simplify a limited universe of events for the practical purposes of everyday life. They do not have the special characteristics required by scientifically useful general concepts. The latter have to be designed to completely overcome the infinite multiplicity of an unlimited universe of concrete facts.

In natural science as defined by Rickert, the aim is the construction of a system of general concepts which leaves no phenomenon "unconceived." This is its specific way of attempting to overcome the infinity of reality. No matter what phenomenon may occur, natural scientists want to be able to subsume every event under a general concept. In setting this goal, however, the assumption is that in each case it can be unambiguously decided whether or not a phenomenon is subsumable under a concept. As long as natural scientists work only with prescientific general concepts, this assumption does not hold. For instance, it is often impossible to decide whether to treat something as a "tree" or a "bush," a "mammal" or a "fish" (in the prescientific meanings of the terms). For Rickert, the cause of this is manifest: he has described the content of concepts as "pictures" (or images, or reproductions) of sensations which are thought as real. This description presents no problem as long as one is dealing with individual mental contents. Thus, having a concept of a particular tree may be adequately described as having a picture of tree-sensations in the mind. A general concept, however, cannot be said to be the mental image of, in this case, a general tree. For there are no general trees.[12] Rather, what people have in mind when they think a general concept like "tree" is the *vague* image of some particular tree. What may seem to be a general picture merely is an undifferentiated and indistinct particular image. Thus, Rickert seems to be forced to conclude that concepts which are both general and unambiguous cannot be formed.

If this were the last word on the matter, scientists might as well give up all hope of ever overcoming the infinite multiplicity of the empirical world by forming general concepts. It is Rickert's argument, however, that fortunately there is a way out of the dilemma. For he argues that it is possible to give a sufficiently precise statement of what is subsumed under a specific general concept through the procedure known as "*definition*." When such a concept is defined (in contrast to the *term* designating the concept),[13] it is made explicit just what particular elements or parts have to be present in a specific combination in a concrete phenomenon for it to be subsumed under the concept.

> In order to construct a really useful concept . . . we have to go beyond having *mere* images, for any image involves a disturbing multiplicity. . . . To achieve this, we apply a very simple procedure. . . . We specify the constituent elements of a conceptual content one by one. . . . Making a concept precise this way can be effected only by replacing a single image by a multitude of intellectual acts, namely a number of subsequent *judgments*. . . . A logically perfect concept, accordingly, is never a single image but always a sequence of images. It consists . . . of a series of assertions.[14]

In other words, a general concept is the short, but vague, holistic version of what a person has in mind when he asserts, one after another, the occurrence of several things in a certain combination. These things are those component parts which are alike in all the concrete phenomena comprised by the general concept. The concept and its definition are completely equivalent as far as the content of knowledge is concerned.[15] However, in the definition it appears much less ambiguous,

3. GENERAL CONCEPTS 27

and therefore, it must be the endeavor of all natural science to convert all concepts into definitions, i.e., statements about things standing in certain relations to each other.

If we imagine a state of complete scientific systematization of the content of our thought, we see that our thinking would never be able to grasp it in its totality, but could only successively go through it in such a way that at times it forms concepts out of the elements (i.e., a set of judgments) which are related to each other, at times again dissolves these concepts into judgments; thus, it always proceeds "discursively."[16]

A general concept is equivalent to a set of statements.[17] Both are reproductions of the same sensations. It is not made clear in Rickert's account whether they are two different mental modes of being conscious of these sensations, and if so, in what relation they stand to each other. In any case, Rickert declares that only a set of statements is suited for scientific purposes; a general image is not unambiguous enough. Thus the dilemma of generalizing knowledge is solved: "Even though images which are both general and clear do not exist, we have a substitute in form of a complex of statements which is logically equivalent to an image which is both general and clear."[18]

It is obvious, however, that defining a concept not only provides a solution to a dilemma, but also creates a new problem. For in the definition of a general concept, new general concepts occur which represent the relevant component parts of the defined phenomenon. They in turn require definition if they are to be unambiguous. Clearly, then, this definitional process can be carried on ad infinitum. This means that no concept can ever be completely defined. There always remains a relative ambiguity. Theoretically, this seems unavoidable (within empirical science); in practice, fortunately, there soon comes a point where for all immediate purposes there is sufficient agreement on the content of a general concept.

From the need to define general concepts for the purpose of unambiguously overcoming the infinity of empirical reality, Rickert derives his conception of the ultimate natural science. For defining a concept consists of nothing else than the identification of those component parts of several phenomena which are found existing in all of them, and of the constellations in which they occur. The elements in turn are subdivided into their respective constituent parts, and so on.[19] In short, the ongoing process of defining concepts consists in finding the component parts of which empirical phenomena are built up, and the relations of cause and effect in which these parts stand, then in finding the subparts of which the parts consist, etc. A concept initially representing concrete things through the definition procedure is transformed into a combination of concepts representing certain relations between more elementary things.[20] A concept initially representing certain concrete *relations of cause and effect* between things becomes a set of concepts representing relations of cause and effect between the more elementary components of which the concrete things in question consist. In principle, this procedure can go on without end as long as one remains within the boundaries of empirical science. This is an implication of the premise that every empirical phenomenon—no matter how small—consists of an infinity of component elements.

It is possible, however, to envisage theoretically a state in which no further definitions could be performed. This would be a science in which all the thing-concepts still occurring in the specialized natural sciences have been transformed into concepts describing the relationships in which the ultimate component elements common to all empirical phenomena stand. It would be the "ultimate natural science."[21] It would still have to contain some thing-concepts; their contents would be "ultimate things." Without being able to assert anything concerning their empirical existence, one can nevertheless infer the characteristics which they theoretically have to have. Things, in order to be ultimate, must be unanalyzable. That is, they must not consist of parts, but be absolutely simple, indivisible, and unchangeable. Their identification is the logically ideal aim of generalizing concept formation. "It must be possible to dissolve all the manifold concrete things into absolutely simple things."[22] They must stand in no further analyzable relations of cause and effect. For the specialized field of physics a relative approximation to the ultimate state can be imagined in a conception of the whole world as a mechanism, made up of elementary parts and governed by the laws of mechanics. Reality is conceived of as consisting of absolutely simple things standing in spatial and temporal relations to each other. The multiplicity of phenomena is viewed as a multiplicity of different arrangements of the ultimate things. All change is change of these combinations; it is movement in time and space. The infinity of the world, of course, still exists. But its problematic aspect—the possible occurrence of a phenomenon not conceivable by the available concepts—has disappeared. "Thus . . . each phenomenon of the physical world can be subsumed under the concept of constellations of ultimate things which, as far as these things are concerned, differ from each other only in their number and are, therefore, mathematically conceivable."[23] The same can be said of phenomena of change. "The multitude of the different movements is . . . entirely conceivable in a system of *mathematically formulated laws of motion.*"[24] A similar conception may be put forward for the field of psychology: all psychic phenomena may be conceived of as being made up of absolutely simple sensations governed by the laws of association. But this must be understood merely as a speculation for the purpose of illustrating the principle. In any case, as yet nobody has any substantive conception whatsoever of a science with concepts basic to physics, sociology, psychology, etc.

At this point it is necessary to indicate an important implication of Rickert's characterization of general concepts. Obviously, in his view, such concepts are summary representations of common aspects of many phenomena. Their definitions, i.e., the sets of statements equivalent to the concepts, must therefore be interpreted as constituting *descriptions* of those features which many or all known phenomena have in common. The earlier statement that the conceptual content is facts[25] also supports this interpretation. Now, laws of nature, in Rickert's terminology, are general concepts. They represent the relationships of cause and effect in which phenomena stand. These laws must be interpreted as *descriptions* of certain aspects of many known concrete cause-effect relationships, as summaries of such facts past, present, and possibly future. Their cognitive role thus consists in functioning as handy abbreviations for great (and eventually unlimited) numbers of singular statements, each describing a specific spatio-temporal event.[26] This view of laws of nature is shared by Max Weber and must be taken into consideration in the interpretation of some of his pronouncements concerning the ideal type.

The process of forming general concepts, as it is described by Rickert, starts as a clarification of the meaning of the terms occurring in everyday discourse, i.e., as a precise specification of the mental image evoked by the use of such a term. Basically, this procedure consists in providing an *analysis* of an already existing concept. It is clear, however, that such an analysis can be performed only because the conceptual elements have been previously combined in the mind. It seems, therefore, that it is really this synthetic process which determines the content of a concept.

Namely, if someone wants to indicate the meaning of a term designating a concept, a thought-process within the realm of *logic* must have *previously* taken place in his mind; only then can it be verbally formulated. . . . This thought-process, however, even in today's use of language, is nothing else than the formation of the concept. The act of logical thinking—which really is the actual definition of a concept—therefore has to be already terminated before the definition can be verbally formulated. For only after I have a concept completely defined in that sense, can I state a sentence in which I declare that I am to use a certain name as the linguistic sign for the concept designed by me.[27]

The synthetic process of concept formation may be described as follows: an observer is aware of a number of phenomena as really existing (e.g., elephants). The content of these concrete facts is complex (i.e., elephants have many parts, come in diverse sizes and shapes, different shades, etc.). The observer forms a general concept by singling out from each particular content those partial contents—which still are complex—which it shares with all the others (e.g., tusks, trunk, hairless grey skin, herbivore, mammal). Of these he forms a mental picture which he treats as a unity ("elephant"). This is the general concept. "Seeing now that the analytic definition of a concept . . . consists in a series of judgments, we may infer from this that the synthetic definition, which we have described as the process of combining elements, also must consist of a series of judgments."[28] The "content" of the general concept is the totality of the selected ideas of immediate sensations; these ideas represent the common component elements of those concrete objects which are subsumed under the concept. The total number of these objects (e.g., all elephants) constitutes the "scope" of the concept. The greater the number of concrete objects subsumed under a concept, the wider its scope, its extension (i.e., the greater the reduction of the extensive infinity of reality); the fewer the elements, or parts, which an object has to share with others in a certain combination, the smaller its content, its intension (i.e., the greater the reduction of the intensive infinity of reality).[29] (E.g., Indian elephants as a class have more features in common than elephants in general.)

Before concluding this section, it must be indicated that Rickert's whole account of concept formation in the natural sciences, since it is focused especially on the justifiability of the ultimate aim (knowledge of what things have in common), rather simplifies the intricacies of the process as it actually occurs. Thus, very often it is not possible to define concepts by the constellation of elements which things have in common, since they do not simply share them equally—as is presupposed by Rickert's argument—but exhibit them in degrees. Rickert has no difficulties accounting for cases sharing certain aspects to an equal degree, e.g., "Man is a featherless biped." Something either has feathers and then is not a man, or it has not, and then is a man, provided that it has two feet. However, there are many instances when the shared components occur in degrees, e.g., "Man is a rational animal." Just how rational does an animal have to be to pass for a man? If "selection of the common elements" means, as it does in Rickert's theory, that the elements also have to be present to the same degree, then it would be necessary to form a tremendous number of different concepts grasping the differences of reason exhibited by the beings commonly covered by the term "man"; if that cannot be done, no one can know where to draw the line between "ape" and "man."

The reason for mentioning this particular case is the significance which this problem assumes in Max Weber's discussion of the ideal type.[30] Rickert did not pay any attention to it, perhaps because he perceived it as a mere temporary difficulty due to the backwardness of certain sciences.[31] For in the ultimate natural science this would not play any role at all. There, such "qualitative" differences would be reduced to mere quantitative differences in the constellations of the same elements.

For Rickert, there remains one final problem. He realizes that the elimination of all ambiguity of content is not the only characteristic required of scientific concepts if they are to fulfill their purpose. For obviously, one may well possess completely clear concepts without thereby eliminating the infinity of reality, i.e., without providing such class concepts that every empirically possible phenomenon can be unambiguously subsumed under one. This is simply a consequence of the fact that all general concepts can only be derived from the comparison of a limited number of phenomena. The only way to completely overcome the infinity of reality through general concepts, however, is to form them such that their scope is infinite. Infinity of scope means that there is an infinite number of phenomena sharing the same component parts in the same arrangements. The only constellations of elements, however, which are common to an infinite number of phenomena are those which they necessarily have to share since the world is made that way, whose occurrences thus are "laws of nature." "We may, therefore, also say that through a concept we can grasp an infinite multitude of individual phenomena in the infinite space and the infinite time only under the condition that its content consists of judgments expressing a law of nature."[32] In this sense, since the content of a general concept is made explicit in the definition, the definition of a general concept may be said to express a law of nature (i.e., the correct definitions of "dog" or "elephant" refer to combinations of properties which are not accidental but cannot be otherwise). They imply the assertion that this is the way a particular part of the empirical world exists.[33] Thus, the coexistences of the properties as asserted by the definitions of general concepts are laws of nature. Accordingly, Rickert can say: "The concept of gravity and the law of gravity are just completely identical . . . as far as the content of theoretical knowledge is concerned. . . ."[34] The problem is, of course, that general concepts are always formed on the basis of an analysis of only a limited amount of empirical cases. This means that scientists can never be certain that their definitions definitely assert laws of nature. Their generalizations hold for whatever empirical facts they know, i.e., they are *empirically general*. They cannot be sure, however, whether or not there are some as yet undiscovered instances (like the famous black swans) which cannot be subsumed under the concept without modifying it. That is, they cannot be sure that the existing generalizations are absolutely universal. Now it is obvious that on the basis of empirical knowledge, i.e., within empirical science, there is no way of making the distinction between the empirical and the absolute validity of a general concept, since the latter cannot be known. Empirically general concepts, therefore—whether they describe things or relations of cause and effect—are treated by scientists just as if they were absolutely valid laws of nature. Scientists simply assume that they have overcome the infinite multiplicity of nature in an absolute fashion. This fact is highly significant for Rickert. For it means that on the basis of limited factual information, natural scientists feel justified in asserting more than what they already know. They do so on the basis of a particular presupposition: "We, therefore, have to presuppose that just a part of the world informs us about all of it, i.e., enables us to derive concepts from it which help us to acquire knowledge (*Erkenntnis*) of the whole."[35] Anybody investigating in the field of natural science makes this assumption, for without it he would have no reason to believe that by forming general concepts humans have a way of completely overcoming the infinity of reality. Of course, this assumption cannot be justified on the basis of ex-

perience; it is metaempirical. So it is apparent that the actual procedure
of empirical natural science is founded on an assumption made by
every investigator which cannot be justified on the basis of experience.

4. INDIVIDUAL CONCEPTS

General concepts are formed, in Rickert's view, because humans want
to have objective knowledge, and this procedure is generally acknowledged to be a valid method of achieving it. It was already mentioned,
however, that focusing on the common features of empirical phenomena is not the only direction which human cognitive interests can
take.[1] General concepts do not exhaust everything humans want to
know. For these concepts tell only what exists always and everywhere,
since their definitional elements refer only to those parts of empirical
reality which are common to (infinitely) many phenomena.[2] Ultimately they give an account of the world as a system of simple, i.e.,
nonconcrete elements occurring in changing combinations. The closer
general concepts come to this ideal, the more abstract they are, the
better. "We may, therefore, straightforwardly say that the logical perfection of a concept in the natural sciences depends on the degree to
which empirical concreteness has disappeared from its content. The
simplification [of empirical reality] through concept formation necessarily goes hand in hand with an annihilation of experienced concreteness."[3] Thus, general concepts do not provide any knowledge
of the specific features of particular events.

An interest in such knowledge, however, does exist. It is the interest
underlying the writing of history. A look into any book in that field
shows that very special and unique configurations of phenomena are
reported such as the French Revolution, or the American Civil War.
The question is, of course, whether these accounts can claim scientific
status. It is not answered simply by summarily denying the legitimacy
of the interest responsible for the writing of such reports, but has to
be shown by reasoned argument. However, according to Rickert,
nothing acceptable has been put forward so far. The existence of such
an interest, therefore, must be recognized, and one can only ask
whether, or under what conditions, investigations instigated by it
can lead to objective results.[4]

The proper point of departure for such an inquiry is the fact that every concrete phenomenon is different from any other. It is an absolutely unique, individual constellation of component parts. The cognitive interest which is not satisfied by the formation of general concepts is the interest in having knowledge of this individuality of empirical phenomena.[5] Of course, they can never be known in their total concreteness; this follows from what was said about the intensive infinity of every concrete phenomenon. Abstraction is necessary, for the human mind can handle only a limited number of facts. But it is possible to abstract from reality in such a way that the individuality of phenomena is not lost in the process. This is done by combining those elements into a conceptual unity which describes phenomena as specific constellations of particular component parts, so that each description fits only one empirical phenomenon.[6] In spite of the abstraction involved, such an account is rather concrete as compared to the knowledge provided by general concepts. It can, therefore, be said that this kind of concept provides the knowledge to satisfy an interest in the concrete individuality of phenomena, at least in a relative way, and in any case in the only possible way.

Accounts of individual constellations of things and events are "individual concepts." Since they are typically used in history they are also called "historical concepts." The objects they describe are "historical individuals"; this term refers to any kind of individual phenomenon, e.g., the Peloponnesian War, or Napoleon's retreat from Moscow, not just persons. The label "concept" for such accounts is unfamiliar but, in Rickert's opinion, justifiable:

> Thus, history does not form general concepts, but just as the natural sciences it cannot give an account of its objects as they concretely exist, e.g., Caesar . . . or the origin of knightly estates. Since these thoughts can never perfectly cover all the infinitely manifold real processes they are, although their content is not general, concepts in the sense that those parts of reality which are essential to history are selected and combined in them. Of course, these historical concepts can be really thought only when they are dissolved into judgments of existence, telling of the things and processes which the concepts are representing; however, as we have shown, the transformation into judgments is equally necessary when we really think the concepts of the natural sciences.[7]

While it is thus possible to abstract from reality without destroying the individuality of concrete phenomena it has yet to be shown that this can be done in an objective way. That is, a principle must be found which helps the scientist to decide what phenomena are to be accounted for in this fashion. Certainly it is not possible to describe the individuality of all of them since there are infinitely many. According to Rickert, such a standard of selection does indeed exist. As in the case of the formation of general concepts, it is related to a principle already operative in everyday life. There, for practical actors, many things are relevant to conduct, not with respect to their general properties, but as unique concrete configurations of elements. This is indicated by the existence of proper names. As long as something is important only on the basis of the qualities which it shares with many other things, only a generic term is used for it, like "rain," "wood," etc. But a friend, for example, is recognized as a very particular person, not merely as an instance of the human species. Just this person is the friend, and he cannot be exchanged for just any other. The cause of this special treatment is to be found in the fact that his individuality is *valued*.[8] Discrimination among things on the basis of practical evaluations is the principle

> . . . by which every feeling, intending, and acting man, everybody who takes a position toward things and events—in short, every concrete person, —is guided in his conception of the world; for him, it separates everything that exists into essential and inessential parts. Whoever lives, i.e., whoever sets himself goals which he wants to achieve, cannot look at the world exclusively with respect to the general. Its unique features are also relevant. For this is the only way a person is able to orient himself and be active in the concrete and everywhere individual reality. Also, some objects are relevant for him only as far as they are instances of classes; others, however, become important just because they are unique and, therefore, are individuals. . . .[9]

Only when in practical life the unique and particular constellation of elements of which a phenomenon is composed is valued, is there any reason for people to be interested in its individuality. Otherwise it is merely treated as an interchangeable instance of a class.

The valuation of phenomena by practical actors has two features which are of interest to the methodologist. First, it is the source of persons' interest in the *individuality* of phenomena, and second, it is a way of overcoming the infinite multiplicity of the empirical world. The extensive infinity of reality is overcome since only a limited number of things, events, and processes is valued. Its intensive infinity is overcome due to the fact that not every concrete component element of a valued phenomenon is relevant to the value, but only the particular combination of a limited number of these elements;[10] thus, what makes a person someone's friend is not the fact that he wears glasses or has black hair. Now it is obvious that valuing a phenomenon is an entirely practical method of overcoming the infinity of reality and in this form not suited for scientific purposes. For in practical life people express different and idiosyncratic valuations and have divergent purposes. But in science the infinity of reality must be overcome in a generally acknowledged way. Furthermore, the task of science is to provide an account of the world, to establish knowledge, not to value it. Value judgments do not provide knowledge.[11] Therefore, even if everybody had the same values, by making value judgments one would not give a scientific account of individual constellations of empirical phenomena.

Fortunately however, according to Rickert, although scientists in their role as scientific observers cannot make practical value judgments, there is a way in which they can make use of the selective function of such judgments for the purposes of descriptive science. For instead of actually valuing a phenomenon, i.e., connecting a value with it themselves, they can limit themselves to stating that, for them as observers a phenomenon *"embodies"* a particular value. That is, the scientific observers only acknowledge that *somebody* values (or valued) this phenomenon, that it constitutes (or constituted) a valued object for some persons. Thus, without being committed to a value judgment, a scientist can say that some painting embodies, e.g., a Romantic conception of art. This means that its painter had a Romantic aesthetic value in mind by which he was guided when he produced the painting. Treating a phenomenon as the expression, or embodiment, of a value—a value which some human individual connects with the phenomenon in question—Rickert calls "relating a phenomenon to a value." Relating an object to a value fulfills the same function as direct valuation, as far as the problem of selection from reality is concerned. By describing a phenomenon so related to a value, the extensive and intensive infinity of reality are overcome since the value is embodied only in a limited number of objects and events, and expressed in only a limited number of their components. The combination in which these components occur constitutes the individuality of the phenomenon in question. For such a phenomenon, its creation or its maintenance, is the product of actions guided by individuals' practical valuation, and practical valuations always attach to the individuality of things. Thus, relating a phenomenon to a value is not only a way of overcoming the infinity of reality; in addition, reality is overcome in a way which emphasizes the individuality of the phenomena under consideration.

Not all phenomena incorporate values. Looking at empirical reality, therefore, two classes of objects can be distinguished. One may be called "nature" and comprises all those things which originate and persist without human interference or concern. The other, "culture," comprises whatever is either produced directly by men acting according to valued ends or, if they are already in existence, whatever is at least fostered intentionally for the sake of the values considered to be attaching to it.[12] Such values are "cultural values."

A cultural value is either actually accepted as valid by all men, or its validity—and thus the more than individual importance of the objects to which it attaches—is at least postulated by some civilized human being. Furthermore, civilization, or culture in the highest sense, must be concerned not with the values attaching to the objects of mere desire, but with excellences which ... we feel ourselves more or less "obligated" to esteem and cultivate for the sake of the society in which we live. However, we must not think of these exclusively in terms of "moral necessity." It suffices that, in general, the value be connected with the idea of a norm of some good that ought to be actualized. This is what distinguishes cultural objects from those that are, to be sure, valued and striven after by all men, but only instinctively, as well as from those that owe their valuation not, indeed, to mere instinct, but still only to flights of individual fancy or caprice.[13]

The examples which Rickert gives are the values of religion, church, law, state, customs, science, language, literature, art, economy, etc. What he has in mind is the idea that the development of social institutions and other cultural phenomena in which such cultural values are "embodied," is not a "natural" disposition of humans in the same way in which, for example, bees by instinct are organized in a beehive. Rather, men recognize values which they try to embody in objects. They create and cultivate certain objects because they attach values to them. Only for this reason do these objects (intentionally continue to) exist.

Rickert now declares that by describing—without valuing—those aspects of concrete phenomena which for human observers embody cultural values, scientists can give an account of reality which overcomes its intensive and extensive infinity. For, as already mentioned, these values are embodied only in a limited number of phenomena, and not in all component parts of those in which they are embodied. Furthermore, the parts in which they are embodied represent individual constellations of elements of empirical reality. However, at this point another consideration becomes important. It concerns the requirement that an account of empirical reality, in order to be scientific, must be of interest to everybody who wants knowledge of the *kind* in question, must be generally valid. So the question must be asked whether this condition is fulfilled when those phenomena are described in which specific cultural values are embodied. Such phenomena are, for instance, monasteries, national states, kinship systems, the harmonic structure of occidental music, etc. Rickert's answer is given in the form of an example: Let us imagine some persons holding very divergent political convictions:

> Certainly their value judgments about contemporaneous or past political events, whether they happened in their own country or abroad, will coincide in only a few cases. But does that mean that one of them follows only such individual political events with interest which are totally indifferent to the other? Certainly not. Even among politicians of the most divergent persuasions conceivable, always the same individual events are the object of conflict, i.e., the differences in valuation have to be related to a shared conception of reality. Otherwise those involved in the conflict would not talk about identical things at all, and a conflict over their value would not be possible at all. But if this is so, then it must be possible to separate the divergent value judgments from the shared conception of reality through which only certain objects become individuals. That is, the separation of essential and inessential elements occurs in a way which is completely independent from the diversity of the direct value judgments.[14]

Unfortunately, this answer by way of an example is less than precise. It seems, however, that Rickert's idea is this: men are social beings living in societies. They engage in activities which are the results partly of persons' instincts, drives, affects, etc., partly of the more or less conscious ideas of men concerning things and arrangements which it would be valuable, in their view, to have and maintain. For instance, a particular state, or a church, or a work of art exist only because at least some people wanted such things. This does not mean that everybody wanted them, or wanted them just as they are. Obviously there are great and often irreconcilable divergences of opinion with regard to the desirability of certain things and institutions. This is due to the fact that different people hold different values which they try to "embody" in products. However, the circumstance that different people hold such differing values does not mean that they are oblivious to each other's views. The opposite is the case. This is so because the values in question relate to *common concerns*. The fact that such values are held and embodied in phenomena has an impact on some aspect of the collective life of a society. Nobody, therefore, who himself holds (and tries to embody) particular values concerning this aspect, e.g., the form of government, is indifferent to the other persons' values concerning this same aspect, and the phenomena in which they are embodied. By the same token, only those persons who try to embody their own values in some area of collective concern are interested in the phenomena which embody the values of other people with regard to this same concern. For instance, products which are claimed to be beautiful, to embody a particular aesthetic value, are of interest to those, and only to those people who themselves hold values of an aesthetic nature, no matter whether or not they are identical with the ones embodied in the objects in question. Rickert is convinced that there are certain areas of collective concern with regard to which every member of a society holds some value, that is, is not totally indifferent and unconcerned.[15] This is due to the fact that everybody in society, due to his socialization into its culture, is existentially involved in these areas and, therefore, not indifferent to developments which have significance in these contexts. Values which refer to such areas of collective concern Rickert calls "general cultural values."

On the basis of these considerations, Rickert is in a position to formulate the principle according to which concept formation in history proceeds. It is called the "principle of value-relevance," and its application results in a selection of those parts of empirical reality which for human observers embody one or several of those general cultural values which are held by people in the society in which the scientific observers live. For the embodiment of these values in those cultural products around whose creation collective life centers—like law, religion, and kinship—has existential significance for everybody living in the society, including the scientific observer. Such phenomena are "value-relevant," or *culturally significant.* Everybody living in the society in question is interested in the unique configuration of their component elements because general cultural values are embodied in them. For the purpose of knowledge, these phenomena then become the content of historical concepts. According to Rickert, these historical concepts contain that whereby different individual phenomena are distinct from each other, whereas the parts common to them all are not included.[16] They stand in extreme contrast to the concepts of the natural sciences which contain only those elements which are common to several concrete phenomena, since their particularities were eliminated through generalizing abstraction. The value-relevance of an object, as was just demonstrated, does not imply according to Rickert that everybody has to positively value this object as an embodiment of what for him personally is good and desirable. It merely means that for human observers it is an embodiment of a particular cultural value appertaining to an area of collective life which is of common concern in the society, or societies, in which the observers are living. They all are interested in such an object because they are cultural beings. As such, due to their own valuations of the collective concerns of the groups in which they live, they are not indifferent to the structures originating and existing as the results of valuations other than their own of these concerns. Thus, it is the necessary basis for the validity of an historical account that each scientific observer *in practical life* in a valuing fashion is committed to the cultural concerns of his group.[17]

If some object through its individuality is to acquire political or aesthetic or religious significance, if it is to become the object of conflict and is to be singled out from the overwhelming multitude of objects as an individual, then political, artistic, or religious life must not be held to be something absolutely indifferent. Rather, some kinds of political, artistic, or religious values must be explicitly accepted as values. For people who do not do this would have no reason whatsoever to direct to the individual configuration of certain objects an interest different from the one they direct to any possible others. Thus, if we call that whereby a conception of reality common to the most divergent value judgments originates a mere "value-relevance," we can strictly separate this relevance from the direct positive or negative valuation. Through the mere value-relevance a world of individuals originates which is the same for everybody. The practical valuation of these individuals, however, will always be subject to very different estimates.[18]

In short, what Rickert argues here is that, for example, an American historian may or may not agree with the political and ethical ideas embodied in American political institutions. Regardless of his approval or disapproval, however, he will be interested in knowing about them since as a socialized human being he is caught up in them and is, to the extent that he has political and ethical ideals, existentially affected by what is going on and prevailing in these areas.

There are many different general cultural values. Depending on which one human observers choose to pay attention to, different phenomena acquire importance. When historians look at the world guided by a certain general cultural value or, as Rickert puts it, *from the point of view* of a particular value, this means that they select those phenomena in which the particular general cultural value (collective concern) is embodied. Thus, certain individual constellations of facts become important. When the observers adopt a different value viewpoint, another part of the world becomes essential, or culturally significant. Thus, a political historian would write a different history of the early New England settlers than a cultural historian. But it is the same for everybody who adopts the same point of view, i.e., all political historians will basically treat the same phenomena as important. A description of this significant part of the world overcomes the infinity of reality in a valid way, for only a limited number of phenomena becomes generally important. Due to their value-relevance, the unique combinations of elements of which they consist can be treated as conceptual unities (i.e., individuals, something which must not be divided, like the "Depression," the War in the Pacific, the American Revolution, etc.). Thus the writing of scientific history depends on the existence of such general values which can serve as viewpoints.[19]

It may seem, however, that the objectivity of such accounts is of a specifically limited kind. For a value-relevant historical description can be valid only for those humans who are members of the same cultural community. But the cultural values and concerns of different social communities are different, and also they change through time. The contemporary American historian can hardly be said to be existentially involved with the ancient Chinese kinship structure. Consequently it appears that in principle there may be as many kinds of historical knowledge as there are culture areas. Furthermore, a universal history, i.e., a history of the cultural development of all mankind which is valid for *every* human observer, does not seem possible on this basis. These implications can be avoided, though, when an assumption is made which is analogous to the one made in the natural sciences about the existence of laws of nature. This assumption is that there are universally valid values (or cultural concerns) whose embodiment is more or less approached in actually existing cultural phenomena.[20]

It is, therefore, not sufficient to exclude the purely individual values and to designate those values as the guiding principles of a historical description which are shared by all members of a particular community. Rather, if history is to compete with the kind of universal validity which natural science claims when it establishes laws of nature, we have to assume that certain values are not only factually valid for all members of certain communities, but that the recognition of values universally can be demanded as necessary and inevitable from every scientific investigator.[21]

This assumption, of course, cannot be empirically justified and belongs to the philosophy of history. All that can be asserted on an empirical basis is the existence of general cultural values in the past and in the present. But since the distinction between the empirically general and the absolutely universal cultural values cannot be made within empirical science, the empirically general values are simply treated as if they were universal.[22]

The description of the formation of individual concepts for Rickert is an account of the logical aspects of scientific history. It shows the formal structure which every historical report must have, which alone can ensure the objectivity of the description, its intersubjective validity. However, according to Rickert, whereas in the natural sciences ideally the scientist does not report more than logically necessary in order to avoid the disturbing multiplicity of the conceptual content, this is not so in history. What is logically necessary here only sets a minimum requirement.[23] For the historical scientist's goal in writing history is to describe the concrete individuality of phenomena. In this endeavor he is, of course, bound to the limits imposed on human knowledge. This means that he can never offer an exposition of a phenomenon's individuality in *all* its concreteness. However, he must try to get as close as possible. For this reason Rickert calls history a "science of concrete reality" (*Wirklichkeitswissenschaft*).[24] Through artful presentation historians have to attempt to evoke an impression of actual concreteness, to re-create the phenomena as they really existed. They must try to come as close to a mirror-image as possible.

What we try to discard from natural science because it does not belong there ..., namely the transgression of the limits of that which can be conceptually known and the description of a concrete multiplicity, for history as a science of concrete reality, therefore, becomes a necessary task. It must attempt to represent the individual concreteness of its objects such that the teleologically[25] essential elements are combined with components which serve only as a stimulation of the imagination in order to bring the account as close to reality as possible, so that in historical concepts the two ... are combined into a unified concrete whole. Thus, also history tries to provide an unambiguous account; not through definitions, though, but through images which are as precise and clear as possible.[26]

Rickert is perfectly aware of the fact that the addition of those conceptual elements which "serve only as a stimulation of the imagination" rests on extra-logical considerations. He declares that it is a "necessary task," necessary because it is "implied in the conception of history as a science of concrete reality."[27] But beyond this statement he does not provide an explicit justification. Furthermore, he does not seem to realize that such an extralogical element inevitably sabotages his logical attempt to delimit the infinity of phenomena.

Although it is essentially a matter of tactfulness and taste how far in the interest of concreteness one wants to go beyond the teleologically necessary components and give room to details which are not relevant to the guiding values, nevertheless the impossibility of limiting from logical viewpoints the individual inclinations of the historian exists only with respect to those *individual* features which history *adds* to the exposition in excess of the teleologically necessary. . . .[28]

It is not entirely clear how tactfulness and taste can overcome the infinity of reality in an objective manner, and why they should not be excluded, if they can only be subjective. But apparently this does not seem problematic to Rickert.

5. HISTORICAL CONTEXT, HISTORICAL DEVELOPMENT, HISTORICAL CAUSALITY

Through the formation of individual concepts it is possible to overcome the infinity of reality in a valid way. The criterion which is used to separate the essential elements from the inessential ones is that of their value-relevance, or cultural significance. What makes knowledge of such individual constellations more than just subjectively interesting is the general existential import of the cultural concerns embodied in them to the members of the cultural community (which includes the historians). According to Rickert, therefore, the application of the method of abstraction described by him permits the establishment of generally valid historical knowledge. Now, a question which arises at this point is how men's involvement in contemporary collective concerns can provide the basis of a valid interest in individual phenomena that occurred way back in the past, e.g., the barbarian invasion of Italy, or the collapse of Alexander the Great's empire. The answer to this seems to be that such past events acquire significance to the extent to which the ideas and ideals embodied in them in some sense linger on in present concerns, or at least had some positive or negative influence on their development and maintenance. This answer is indeed implied in much of what Rickert says, yet is not put forward as the main consideration. Instead, Rickert derives the legitimacy of knowledge of unique constellations which occurred far back in the past as an implication of the characterization of history as a science of concrete reality, and from his conception of the peculiar nature of historical reality. It seems that this involves a somewhat illegitimate replacement of cultural significance as a criterion of selection by something else.

Rickert starts his argument by saying that culturally significant knowledge is knowledge of individual significant events. He immediately adds that the term "individual" must not be misunderstood, for it is not meant to imply an isolation of these events from the context in which they occur. Every event which becomes significant is located in a larger historical context.

In empirical reality nothing exists in isolation, and history as the science of concrete phenomena must not be "individualistic" in the sense that it dissolves reality into isolated individual phenomena. On the contrary, in our conception such a dissolution would be an unhistorical abstraction.[1] ... Rather, the task of the science of concrete phenomena is accomplished only when every object with which it deals is also placed in the *context (Zusammenhang)* in which it occurs.[2]

The description of this larger context follows the principles of the formation of individual concepts. When an historical object is placed as a part within a general historical setting, one individual phenomenon is placed within another more comprehensive individual phenomenon.[3] This, in turn, is located in an even larger whole. Thus, an historically important person has to be seen in the context of his society; the society has to be seen in its relationship to other societies. The existence of all these societies is part of the general history of mankind, and mankind is only a part of the world of living organisms, etc. The ultimate, or most comprehensive, historical whole is reached when it is impossible to think of a larger one of which it would be a part, and whose individuality as a whole would be significant. In practice, this is the universal history of the development of civilized mankind.

To this, Rickert adds another reason to account for the wider context in which events occur:

Namely, the historical facts not only do not exist in a separate and isolated fashion because they are always parts of a larger whole, but also because they influence each other, or are *causally* related to other facts. There is no part of empirical reality in which each thing is not the effect of other things, and does not constitute a cause of other things. Therefore, if history is to be a science of concrete phenomena, it will have to deal with this situation. It even must be an essential task of the science of concrete reality to describe not only what was and is, but also to investigate the causes which generated that which is or was.[4]

A further characteristic of concrete reality which assumes importance is that everything concrete is in a constant process of change. "History never describes finished things, but always processes in motion."[5] Historians deal with this situation by subdividing the individual phenomena in question into several stages or steps each of which is an essential link in the whole individual process. Such historical processes are called "developments." Thus, every historical concept contains a description of the historical development of phenomena embodying specific general cultural values. Of course, the described sequence of stages must not be valued in the sense that, for instance, earlier stages are represented as less desirable situations than the later ones, or vice versa. Rather, each stage is only to be seen as a necessary component part of the whole individual process of implementing a general cultural value, without any valuation either of a part or of the whole. Process must not be confused with progress. The latter notion has no place in scientific history. Here only a series of changes is described which has acquired significance as an individual whole whose component parts occur in temporal succession. The principle guiding the formation of the concept of an historical development is, of course, that of value-relevance.

As a result, certain stages in the totality and multiplicity of occurring events become significant and are combined into the concept of a unique development. With regard to the guiding value its character is teleological, but thereby it is not valued either as a whole or in parts. Through its value-relevance it merely is given a definite beginning and a definite end in so far as the previous and succeeding events are not significant any more. At the same time it is subdivided into a definite sequence of stages which are located between beginning and end. This is so because the continuous flow of becoming has to be subdivided wherever the slowly occurring changes have become large enough to acquire a modified significance with regard to the guiding value-viewpoints.[6]

The notion of development, in a nutshell, expresses the logical nature of history as a science.[7] But as it is actually written, an historical description contains more than what seems necessary from the point

of view of a particular value. According to Rickert, this is a consequence of the fact that all things stand in causal relations to others;
for the conception of causal interrelatedness "time and again pushes
beyond the teleological unit."[8] Since the teleologically significant elements are caused by, and the cause of, other things and events, these
acquire a *derived significance*. Thus, the causes of every historical development are traced back into the past beyond its significant beginning; the transitions between its important stages are outlined, and the
consequences beyond its significant end are reported. These elements
of derived significance may be called "secondary historical individuals"
in contrast to those of "primary" significance. A clear distinction between the two is not always possible. The function of the secondary
elements is to produce an understanding and possible reexperiencing
of the continuous causal process of becoming. "However, it is not
possible to give particular logical rules for this aspect of historical description since here again history addresses itself to the reproductive
imagination."[9]

It seems rather questionable whether the introduction of secondary
historical individuals gives a satisfactory rationale for the presence of
many elements in actual historical writings. But such factual considerations aside, it once again must be asked whether Rickert's argument at this point does not jeopardize his whole theory of concept
formation. For when do historians have to stop creating the impression of concreteness? Isn't there an infinite number of causes? Rickert
admits that there is no logical solution to this problem—that is, within
his theory—but states that one must rely on the practical inclination
and arbitrariness of each historian.[10] He does not appear to be dis-
turbed by the implications this has for his logical theory.

 The fact that everything which concretely exists is causally determined, i.e., is caused by something and is the cause of something,
is the focus of some additional considerations of Rickert's. For this
fact was used by some scientists as a basis for the argument that it is
the task of history to establish causal laws. Rickert argues that underlying this belief is the erroneous assumption that, since everything is
causally determined, in the natural sciences scientists have to establish
the laws of nature, and in the historical sciences the laws of history.[11]
The result of this conviction has been such constructions as Auguste
Comte's Law of Three Stages. This fallacious kind of reasoning is due
to the confusion of the *principle* of causality with causal *laws*. The
former merely asserts that everything which exists must be thought

as having a cause and being a cause of something else, whereas the latter asserts that all empirically known events of a certain kind are causally related to events of a certain other kind. Confusion of the two leads to the statement that in order to have true knowledge of something existing, the scientist must think it as an instance of a class of events all the instances of which are causally related to instances of a specific other class of events. However, the individual phenomena which are described in history, for example "Caesar's death," or the "Boston Tea Party" cannot be subsumed in all their concrete uniqueness under any law. Hence it is either argued that history cannot be a science, or that there is no causality in history, supposedly because of human "freedom of will."

In Rickert's conception, causal laws are not forms which are required to conceive reality as existing; they are not constitutive forms. Rather, they are methodological forms, or concepts, and therefore involve an abstraction from reality. Concrete reality is the totality of individual contents which can be had in the mind and can be thought as real and as being causally determined.[12] Every individual content is different from every other, and so is every individual causal relationship. Causal laws, then, state what many individual causal relationships have in common. They are a result of concept formation as it is practiced in natural science. But it is also perfectly possible to state an individual causal relationship in all its uniqueness. The latter is the focus of history.

Thus, it certainly is a causally completely determined event that on November 1, 1755, Lisbon was completely destroyed by the well-known earthquake, or that Friedrich Wilhelm IV refused the crown of German Emperor, but there are no general causal laws in which these unique individual events are contained. Indeed, the notion of such a law contains a logical contradiction, for every law is general and, therefore, cannot contain anything of the special causes of the unique event in which the historian is interested.[13]

The impossibility of establishing laws of history is entirely a consequence of the principle of abstraction used. Individual concepts just cannot describe something general.

The only component which is common to causal relationships both in history and in the natural sciences is the "nexus" between cause and effect. Rickert refuses to define its nature, but argues instead:

What we mean by the word "causal nexus" we can always clarify by reference to an experience. For example, when we drop our hand on the table in front of us, we hear a sound. We then designate the motion of our hand as cause and the sound as effect, and assume that they are necessarily tied together.[14]

In such a concrete causal relationship, cause and effect are always different. In the natural sciences, however, there is abstraction from all individual differences between phenomena. Therefore, it is then possible to say: *"causa aequat effectum,"* i.e., the cause is equal to the effect. In history, to the contrary, *individual* causes and effects are described, and the relationships between them, therefore, are causal *inequalities.*[15] According to Rickert, here it may be said, then, that small causes often have big results.

The establishment of an individual causal relationship, however, touches upon a problem which has not been mentioned so far. It concerns the fact that all scientific knowledge, in order to be communicable, has to be formulated in terms of general concepts.[16] Nevertheless, in Rickert's opinion this does not mean that, therefore, all concepts are general concepts. For the general terms which are used in the description of historical developments refer only to the conceptual *elements* of complex historical concepts. Their combinations into unitary wholes, the individual concepts, still are descriptions of unique processes. Thus, general concepts are used as a *means* for the description of individual phenomena. This alone also enables the historian to give an account of individual causal relationships. Since an individual phenomenon as a whole cannot be subsumed under a causal law, it is broken down into its component general elements. Each of these elements then is subsumed under a law.

When in this fashion the causes of each component of the historical effect have been determined in a way which can be generally acknowledged, the combination of the diverse elements which have been found and which, when taken in isolation, can all be subsumed under general causal concepts, in its totality again constitutes an historical concept. This then is the concept of the historical cause as a whole. Of course, when we are searching for the cause of an historical object which we treat as one unitary phenomenon, the historical concept describing its cause does not necessarily refer to another thing which is equally treated as one unitary phenomenon. Rather, the concept of an historical cause may consist of elements of the most diverse historical things and processes.[17]

This may also be represented in a rather simplied formal scheme: the task is to determine the cause of the historical individual X which is described in the individual concept Y. The conceptual elements of

Y are a, b, c, d, e; they are *general* conceptual elements referring to concrete parts of the phenomenon X. The historian searches for events which can be subsumed under a set of general concepts A, B, C, D, E for which it holds that an instance of A always causes an instance of a, an instance of B an instance of b, etc. A, B, C, D, E then are the general conceptual elements which are combined to form the individual concept O describing the historical phenomenon P which is the individual cause of X.[18]

6. ABSOLUTE VALIDITY; METHOD AND REALITY

Rickert believes that on the basis of the considerations presented so far there is no reason to doubt that historical knowledge is as objective as the knowledge established by the natural sciences. For in either kind of science concept formation proceeds in accordance with a valid principle of selection. In natural science, it is the principle to form general concepts by abstracting from all features of concrete phenomena except those which they have in common with a plurality of other phenomena; this method results in the formulation of class concepts, or laws of nature. In the historical sciences, it is the principle to form individual concepts by abstracting from all features of a multitude of causally interrelated concrete phenomena but those which in the uniqueness of their combination represent a culturally significant unified structure; this method results in the presentation of individual historical developments. The appropriate principle of selection is accepted by each scientist in natural science and history for the purpose of separating those elements of empirical reality which for the respective cognitive purpose are essential, from the inessential ones. With its help, each scientist is able to completely overcome the infinity of reality in a valid fashion. However, it must be realized that the argument so far has merely established what Rickert calls the "empirical validity" of the standards of selection applied in science. Through an analysis of the existing sciences two, and only two, principles of concept formation have been derived of which everybody concerned (i.e., each scientist in his respective field) actually makes use. They are generally accepted standards. However, it seems that the possibility cannot be excluded that this is due merely to an empirical coincidence. Rickert, therefore, is not yet satisfied. For the task which he has set himself is more ambitious: He wants to demonstrate that the existing agreement with respect to scientific standards of abstraction is not merely a contingent consensus. He attempts a justification in terms of logic, i.e., he tries to show that because of the nature of the ultimate cognitive goals of humans and the structure of their minds these two ways of forming concepts are the only ones which lead to results for which the status of objective knowledge can be claimed. Thus, he has to show that the existing consensus is not a mere empirical coincidence, but that it is absolutely necessary because everybody who wants knowledge has to accept these standards of selection. Their "absolute validity," not just the "empirical" one, has to be demonstrated.

Rickert's deduction is based on his idea that the logical nature of the empirical sciences must be understood on the grounds of the purposes for which they are established.[1] The formulation of scientific knowledge is a volitional act. It occurs only because scientists accept truth as a normative value.[2] To everybody who is committed to the value of scientific truth—and it is an a priori assumption that every scientist is so committed[3]—the establishment of absolutely comprehensive and certain knowledge, if it were humanly possible, must be an ideal. However, as was shown,[4] Rickert argues that the acquisition of comprehensive knowledge of everything which occurs is not possible for the human mind. For comprehensive knowledge is asserting the form of existence of every possible fact, and there are infinitely many facts, whereas the mind is only finite. Thus, since ideal knowledge is not accessible to humans, they will have to settle for a more practicable goal. It is to function as a substitute for the unattainable ideal and, therefore, has to be as close to the ideal as the circumstances permit. This substitute goal is just the knowledge which scientists establish by applying the two methods of concept formation which have been described. It is clear, therefore, that everybody who desires knowledge must conceive of the application of both these standards of selection to empirical reality as a necessary task.[5]

The humanly unattainable ideal knowledge may be described as the knowledge of every component part of the extensive infinity of empirical reality in all its concreteness, i.e., in its intensive infinity of constituent elements. Now, according to Rickert, as far as the *extensive* infinity of the world is concerned, the closest approximation possible for humans to the absolute ideal is contained in the conception of the ultimate natural science. Whoever wants to have knowledge of empirical reality, therefore, must be interested in the establishment of this science. But since the only procedure empirically available to this purpose consists in comparing a limited number of phenomena, everybody accepting that goal has to make the assumption that by using this method it is possible sooner or later to arrive at laws of nature.

The limited [human] intellect, in order to at least be able to approximate the goal which on the basis of absolutely certain empirical judgments is accessible to the ideal intellect, needs a substitute. The most perfect substitute conceivable to this end[6] is natural science, as we have already shown. It, therefore, is an absolute goal of human knowledge, and the interest in natural science is thereby shown to be absolutely necessary. But since one also has to want the means if he wants the goal, every natural scientist has to make the assumption—although it is meta-empirical—that on the basis of a limited number of facts a statement can be found which is valid for an unlimited number of facts.[7]

As to the second aspect of absolutely ideal knowledge, it is obvious that the knowledge established by the natural sciences is rather one-sided. It cannot account for the individual particularity of empirical objects. Rickert argues, therefore, that the need to come closest to the absolute knowledge of an ideal intellect makes it necessary that natural science be supplemented by another kind of knowledge.[8] It is provided by the science of history whose pursuit must thus necessarily be in the interest of everybody who wants knowledge. This involves the postulate of an "ultimate history" just as that of an ultimate natural science. Its implication is that there are absolutely valid values from whose viewpoint the unique development of human culture becomes universally significant. It is not possible to know what these values are, and whether those which have been guiding the writing of history so far are among them or not. "Whoever thinks historically must only assume that the world in its temporal development stands in relation to some absolute values which may be completely unknown to him."[9] Since the writing of history requires a value point of view, the absolute necessity of the historical interest requires the metaempirical assumption that some values provide universal and absolutely valid points of view.

This derivation concludes Rickert's argument that history as a science is as justifiable as natural science. The methods of concept formation ensure objectivity in either science. "Objectivity" is the universal necessity of a judgment. It means that all persons in all times, when confronted by a given segment of the empirical world, will be forced (through the acknowledgement of the value of truth) to judge thus and not otherwise.[10] It must be clearly kept in mind, however—and this point needs reiteration—that what is at stake for Rickert is the problem, why certain statements of fact are made in history while other possible ones are not made. Thus, his methodology is not designed to answer the question: What do we have to do in order to find out how the world works, and what is in it? Instead, it centers around the question: Of everything that can be known, what part do we really want to know? It is not the correct establishment of facts and laws which is made problematic, but the selection from among them. Due to this peculiar focus, Rickert does not devote much attention to such a major problem as that of the role played by theories and conceptual frameworks in empirical investigations. Of course, his notion that they are descriptive summaries of a multitude of facts is an obstacle to the realization that they also function as guides to facts. Rickert thinks that the necessary guidance is provided by methodological principles (methods of abstraction). However, the idea that all that is required in science is, equipped with a principle of abstraction, to open one's eyes and ears seems somewhat too simple. Scientific investigations are poorly described as the performance of some abstractive procedure. In this respect, Rickert's theory is a good illustration of what J. W. N. Watkins referred to when he said: "The hope which originally inspired methodology was the hope of finding a method of inquiry which would be both necessary and sufficient to guide the scientists unerringly to truth. This hope has died a natural death." [11]

Rickert's argument involves a basic assumption about human nature: humans are cultural beings. They recognize the validity of values and make it their collective concern to implement them, to embody them in social products and institutions. Science, for instance, is one of these values, and the knowledge which humans possess exists only because of the validity of this value to some human individuals. The different methods of concept formation are the means which scientists have to use because of the limits of the human mind. The validity of their application is a necessary consequence of the validity of the goal: objective knowledge. It is not a consequence of some intrinsic characteristic of the subject matter under consideration. Any empirical subject matter can be treated in a generalizing or in an historical fashion. The same reality can be presented as either history or natural science, depending on the method used.

It becomes nature when we look at it with respect to the general, it becomes history when we look at it with respect to the particular. All empirical science starts with the directly experienced reality. The most general difference between the methods can only be found in the ways in which the diverse sciences process this reality; i.e., it depends on whether they look for the general and nonconcrete in the [general] concept or whether they look for the concrete in the particular and unique. Natural science assumes the former task, history the latter.[12]

According to Rickert's theory, the substantive differences which exist between history and natural science are not of an ontological nature. They are the result of, and not the cause of, the application of different methods of concept formation. The original material—directly experienced concrete reality—is the same. Differences exist only after conceptualization has taken place. To show this, a distinction may be introduced between events and processes which embody valuations from those which are completely indifferent with regard to values. The former may be called "psychic" or "mental" or "spiritual" (*geistig*), the latter "physical" or "natural." The only psychic phenomena whose empirical existence is known, however, are the thoughts and acts of human beings.

Now, if we assume that among some empirical phenomena which are to be described historically there are such beings who themselves take a position toward the values guiding their description, then the focus of the historical report has to be on these beings; that is, all remaining objects are then historically essential not only in so far as they become historical individuals with respect to the guiding values of the reporting *scientist*, but also insofar as through their individuality they are significant for the spiritual beings whose intentions and actions are the *object* of the account. History, therefore, will relate them not only to the guiding values of the report, but at the same time to the described spiritual beings who are taking positions.[13]

For instance, in a history of Italy written from the point of view of the value "art," it is the plans and actions of artists which mainly become essential, and everything else is related to these plans and actions. These spiritual beings, i.e., beings who have a mind, upon whom history is focused, are called by Rickert "historical centers."[14] Their thoughts and ideas play a major role in all historical descriptions, and this is a result of the fact that the principle of value-relevance is used as a guide for abstraction. It is due to this principle that historical accounts focus on cultural developments of groups of humans, whereas in natural science these spiritual phenomena usually do not play an important role.

Historical centers occur in every historical account. This is not a coincidence, but the result of the method of concept formation used in history. For the individuality of phenomena becomes value-relevant only due to the fact that these phenomena are the embodiments of general cultural values. They embody such values only because certain things were practically valued by empirically existing human individuals. Had there not been such humans, there would be no reason to treat these phenomena in an historical fashion. It is not possible to write a history from the point of view "art" of a period in which there were no artists, or people being something like artists. To write the history of a period makes sense only if the value guiding it was also recognized by the humans living in that period, or at least related to one recognized by them. "In an 'objective' scientific account, the values guiding concept formation always have to be taken from the historical material itself."[15] Thus, the central historical process always is either the development of a single person living in an individual social context, or that of a social whole whose members are treated as group members because each is historically significant through the same voluntaristic acts and behavior.[16] Examples are the development of things like a church, a nation, or a legal system. In the natural sciences, in contrast, it is always the general features of things which are treated without regard to any significance from the point of view of general cultural values. Nature is value-indifferent.[17]

"Natural science" and "history," as Rickert operates with these notions, have logical connotations and must be seen as conceptions of logical ideals. They in no way adequately describe the actual structure of any empirically existing account in either natural science or history in the common sense of the terms. However, Rickert says, such a description was not his task; he merely wanted to clarify the ideal forms of two kinds of concepts. It is possible, though, to interpret these two kinds of concepts as the opposite poles of a dimension, with many possible gradations between them.[18] Thus, every concept in natural science as it actually exists, which is valid for only a limited number of phenomena, i.e., which has not completely overcome the infinity of reality, is only relatively general with regard to the ideal. It still contains conceptual elements referring to concrete things and is not completely a relational concept. Obviously, every natural science except the ultimate one deals with such "relatively historical"[19] parts. Equally, in every historical account concepts occur whose content is general.[20] But this must not obscure the fact that in each kind of science these relatively historical concepts are the result of an entirely different method of concept formation. In natural science, they are constructed in an effort to establish what is shared by many phenomena. In history, they are found because what is significant from the point of view of a general cultural value occurs in many cases which are part of a larger individual phenomenon. So it seems that the existence of such concepts is not incompatible with the analysis of the differences between history and natural science, as it is presented by Rickert.

With this, the presentation of Heinrich Rickert's methodology can be concluded. His theory has been criticized on various grounds and from various philosophical positions[21] with which it is impossible to deal here, since this would involve going deeper into matters not of immediate importance for the present purpose. In general, the statement must suffice that in modern philosophy of science the problem of abstraction is seen as belonging to the context of discovery of a theory, not to the context of justification, and that the logical structure of a science cannot be described in terms of a method of abstraction. In any case, it does not require much sophistication to see from the outline given that Rickert has considerable difficulties accounting for all the elements present in actual historical writings in relation to the standard of value-relevance. This refers not only to those aspects which are included in order to enliven the report.[22] In addition, for instance, most historical accounts also contain causal relations holding among secondary and even tertiary historical individuals. Of course, by widening the reference of "historical context" or "derived significance" it may be possible to account for everything of which a historical description consists. But this procedure in itself would demonstrate the impossibility of using a clear-cut standard of selection. Also, as Bienfait has observed, the principle of value-revelance says nothing about the scale on which historical descriptions are to be presented, whether in one volume or in twenty.[23] In addition to these difficulties, the whole theory is built on a basic misconception. This concerns the identification of the difference between natural and cultural, or historical sciences with the distinction between theoretical and historical sciences.[24] In fact, theory and history are significant and distinct in both branches of knowledge although—it is true—the emphasis is somewhat different in each. Rickert's treatment of historical descriptions in natural science as mere preliminary data collections without intrinsic interest and justification is insufficient. Generally he suffers from an inadequate view of the interrelationship between theory and data.[25]

Rickert heavily influenced the methodological thinking of Max Weber, who accepted large parts of the theory. But his acceptance took the form of making use of it in special cases rather than presenting a general and systematic formulation. In his reasoning, he took much of Rickert's theory for granted, and, therefore, many of his statements and particular expressions must remain cryptic unless they are related to the framework of Rickert's thought. The present chapter is intended to provide the necessary background for an understanding of Weber's methodological essays. The extent of the congruence between Rickert and Weber will be documented in the next chapter.

CHAPTER II. MAX WEBER'S THEORY OF CONCEPT FORMATION

1. PRELIMINARY REMARKS

It is the purpose of this chapter to demonstrate the extent of the agreement existing between Rickert's and Weber's epistemological and methodological theories. To accomplish this, it seems best to present Weber's reasoning in the same order in which Rickert's argument was outlined in the previous chapter.

Concerning the extent of Weber's indebtedness to Rickert, there is a great divergence of opinion among interpreters. Eugène Fleischmann, for instance, agrees with Ernst Troeltsch's contention that Weber refers to Rickert only out of politeness,[1] and states: "Of all the Neo-Kantians of the time (and there was an abundance of them) it was probably him [Rickert] whom Weber considered the least...."[2] (No documentation to substantiate this claim is given.) Tenbruck takes a similar position: "Indeed, Weber's thought has, at best, a thin veneer of Rickert's philosophy."[3] In contrast, two authors who seem to have made extensive comparisons of Rickert's and Weber's writings —Alexander von Schelting and Dieter Henrich— note far-reaching agreement in spite of important differences.[4] Henrich's account unfortunately shares one weakness with almost all existing interpretations of Weber's methodology, namely the absence of *comprehensive* documentation for the claims made. At the present stage of the controversy surrounding the interpretation of Weber's methodology it is not possible any longer to accept anything bona fide, nor is it possible any longer to be satisfied with accounts of certain aspects of Weber's theory without regard for the systematic structure of the methodology as a whole. What is required is an exhaustively documented comprehensive interpretation of the whole theory which gives a plausible meaning to *every* ambiguous or contested statement of Weber's, which must then be compared with Rickert's argumentation. All too many interpretations have derived whatever plausibility they may possess from a selective emphasis conveniently neglecting some statements or aspects which are part of Weber's whole theory. Alexander von Schelting's attempts probably come closest to a comprehensive treatment. Like everybody else's, however, they deal only with the methodology of the cultural sciences, and fall short of providing an account of the systematic considerations underlying the whole of the methodology. The epistemological premises of the theory, as well as the analysis of concept formation in the natural sciences, have received scarce attention and have frequently been completely ignored by interpreters.

In this and the following chapter, an effort is made to provide a comprehensive interpretation of Weber's methodology and its epistemological premises. Given the age-old controversy, it seemed wise to document every step in the interpretation as amply as possible, either by supplementing it with quotations and numerous references or by giving the reasons on which the occurring inferences are based. An effort was made to include every possibly controversial statement of Weber's in the form of a quotation, accompanied by an interpretation. In general, the aim was to provide an explicit interpretation for every ambiguous, controversial, and obscure statement occurring in any of the writings here considered. This was felt to be necessary partly because it is the ideal goal of any interpretation. However, in the present case there is the additional reason that it is relatively easy—and, therefore, seductive—to arrive at rather sensible interpretations as long as one is not forced to take into account the totality of those statements of Weber's which are open to several interpretations, be it by oversight or by limiting oneself to only one or a few aspects of the whole theory. As soon as all such statements are included, the problem of internal consistency becomes crucial, assuming that Weber was consistent. From this point of view, practically all existing interpretations appear inadequate.

This chapter deals with those parts of Weber's theory which were taken over from Rickert. The next chapter is concerned with Weber's own developments. As to the extent of the agreement between Rickert and Weber, it will become apparent that it reaches very far. It is possible to find in Weber's essays a parallel statement to almost every important step in Rickert's argument. The only difficulty involved is that of finding them, since they are dispersed throughout the essays, taken out of their systematic context, and sometimes rather cryptic. Arranged in the proper order, however, they are consistent with each other, their meaning is no longer obscure, and they constitute a perfectly reasonable argument. Although a few problems remain which will be discussed in the proper places,[5] their importance should not be overestimated.

2. EPISTEMOLOGICAL PREMISES

Any reader of Max Weber's essays on methodology who is familiar with Rickert's work must be struck by the many similarities of opinion and even mode of expression of the two men. To begin with, it is apparent that Weber's overall concern is the same as Rickert's, namely, an answer to the charge that it is not justifiable to consider the historical disciplines as really coming under the heading of science.[1] In his writings on concept formation he argues against the belief that the ultimate aim of all science, and, therefore, of history, is the formulation of the *laws* governing the occurrence of events. On the basis of an analysis of the relationship between empirical reality and the forms in which humans can have knowledge of this reality, he declares that it is a "false contention" to maintain "that 'scientific knowledge' is identical with 'establishment of laws.' "[2] He is quick to assert, however, that the refutation of this opinion cannot be based on an ontological argument.[3] Thus, the fact that the data of history contain elements which can be *understood* does not affect the logical principles of concept formation.[4] Rather, the correct counterargument is that knowledge of laws is not the only possible form of scientific knowledge, and that the scientific investigator chooses the form of knowledge according to its appropriateness for what he wants to know, i.e., the *type* of his scientific interests.[5] It then becomes apparent that in the field of history scientists are not interested in the establishment of laws as the ultimate aim of knowledge. Instead, they want to give accounts of "historical individuals,"[6] i.e., the uniqueness of particular phenomena. The logical difference between these accounts of individual phenomena and laws is "fundamental."[7] "Neither of these two kinds of ordering reality in thought (*denkende Ordnung des Wirklichen*) has any necessary logical relationship with the other."[8]

Knowledge is always knowledge of humans, and it is not something with which humans are naturally equipped; it must be acquired. Its establishment requires an effort. Since it is thus the result of willful acts, it may be asked what the *intention* is which is behind the pursuit of scientific knowledge, and especially what meaning there is in the establishment of *historical* knowledge.[9] Weber's answer is that these acts are committed by humans as a result of their acceptance of "the value of 'correct' knowledge."[10] In this value "the meaning of all our scientific knowledge is anchored. . . ."[11] But in establishing scientific knowledge scientists are bound to the means provided by the human intellect. This imposes certain limits to what can be achieved.

By analyzing the formal structure of knowledge and the reasons underlying its existence Weber arrives at his position that nomological knowledge is not the only legitimate form of scientific knowledge. There is also knowledge in the form of individual (historical) concepts, and its scientific status is equally undisputable. In addition, one kind of knowledge can in no way functionally replace the other.[12] Therefore, Weber concludes that "an 'objective' treatment of cultural events which proceeds according to the thesis that the ideal goal of science is the reduction of empirical reality to 'laws' is senseless. This is so— *not* at all, as is often maintained, because the cultural or, for instance, the psychic events are 'objectively' less governed by laws"—but because this is not the only goal of science, and furthermore not the one which is pursued in history.[13] Julien Freund is mistaken when he states:

> While Weber accepted the distinction between generalizing and individualizing methods, he rejected Windelband's and Rickert's conclusions, notably their classification of the sciences on the basis of differences of method. . . . Consequently, while the distinction between the general and the particular and between the different procedures they call for is logically valid, it is wrong to say that in practice the natural sciences use exclusively the naturalistic or generalizing procedure, and the cultural sciences the historical or individualizing procedure.[14]

Windelband and Rickert never held the criticized opinion. Freund's claim, therefore, that the insight into the incorrectness of this belief gives "authenticity"[15] to Weber's theory of method, is without foundation.

All the statements of Weber's which have been referred to so far express ideas which had also been put forward by Rickert.[16] This in itself may not have too much significance, though, since such ideas were rather common currency at the time. In order to assess Rickert's influence on Weber it is above all necessary to compare the basic premises underlying each man's reasoning. As is the case with Rickert, the theory of concept formation embraced by Weber is based upon an epistemological theory without knowledge of which certain features of the methodological argument—the theory of concept formation—do not make much sense. In the present section, therefore, the task is to reconstruct Weber's epistemology as well as is possible from his fragmentary remarks. Since the objective of epistemology is to present an account of how humans acquire knowledge of empirical reality, it seems best to start with the analysis of what Weber understands by these two terms.

(1) Scientific knowledge, according to Weber, is an "ordering in thought of empirical reality" (*denkende Ordnung der empirischen Wirklichkeit*);[17] it is "the intellectual mastery of empirical data."[18] These expressions point to the fact that for Weber the human mind is not merely a passive receptacle but plays an active role in the acquisition of knowledge. This, however, is only one crucial component of Weber's view. The other is not explicitly stated and has to be inferred from what he does *not* say on certain occasions. It is the conception that knowledge is a kind of image, a representation of reality in the mind.[19] This has to be concluded from the fashion in which Weber argues against the idea that scientific knowledge is a faithful copy of empirical reality in the mind. For his objections are never directed against the conception of knowledge as a mental "picture" but only against the conception of scientific knowledge as a picture in the mind which shows *every detail* of concrete reality like a mirror image. He says that it is a "thoroughly erroneous" opinion to assume that knowledge is a "'reproduction of concrete empirical data' (empirische Anschauungen) or a copy of 'experiences'. . . . Even one's own experience, as soon as it is to be grasped *in thought*, cannot simply be 'copied' or 'reproduced'. . . ."[20] Knowledge is not a photograph of reality.[21] From such an argument it can be inferred, then, that for Weber knowledge is a selective mental image of reality, and that it is the process of selection in which the mind plays an active role.

(2) Concrete empirical reality, "the reality of the life around us,"[22] cannot be thought of as it exists independent from the human mind being aware of it. Weber says that the things and processes constituting empirical reality are "given in our consciousness" (*vorstellungsmaessig gegeben*).[23] Thus, concrete empirical reality consists of data in the human mind. It is a content of the mind; it is "immanent" to the human consciousness.[24] It may be concluded, then, that for Weber human knowledge of empirical reality consists in the selective mental image which a person has of the data given in his consciousness. But this must not be taken as more than a very general and preliminary statement. For Weber is much more specific than that, and the exact details of his conception are of importance. Their correct assessment, however, presents some difficulties in interpretation. At this point, therefore,

a return to Rickert's theory might be helpful. Rickert, to remember, argues that what is immediately given in the human consciousness is a flow of unformed sensations, of experience. They are vague and formless contents of human awareness. When humans have ideas of such sensations and assert that these ideas have certain categorical forms, such as existence, *knowledge of concrete facts* is constituted. Humans know a concrete fact when they judge that the idea of a particular sensation has the (categorical) form of, e.g., existence. Concrete facts which are thus known are the material of science. In science, the totality of known concrete facts is subjected to the process of concept formation. Concept formation is the scientific treatment of facts. Its outcome is a special kind of knowledge, namely *scientific* knowledge.

Weber's opinion on these matters is in complete agreement with Rickert's position.[25] This has not been seen by all interpreters. Their difficulties in this respect derived from the fact that unfortunately this agreement is obscured by many statements—especially in "Roscher & Knies"—whose formulation is so unprecise that a different impression can be gained. Thus, for example, Weber declares that a concept, i.e., in Rickert's terminology, a methodologically formed set of facts, "under any circumstance is something different from the 'experience' to which it refers; it is a thought-construct (*Gedankengebilde*), produced either through generalizing abstraction or through isolation and synthesis."[26] Here—as in several other places[27]—"experience" and "concept" are contrasted without any reference to an intermediary level of categorical formation as it is postulated in Rickert's theory. Consequently it may seem that in Weber's conception the immediately given sensations are directly formed through scientific concepts.[28] Such an opinion would be erroneous, though. For, on the one hand, there is clear and unambiguous evidence provided by explicit statements of Weber's that he subscribes to the tripartition of formless content (immediate sensations), categorically formed content (concrete facts), and methodologically formed presentation of facts (scientific concepts). On the other hand, none of the occurring ambiguous statements is incompatible with the assumption of such a tripartition. The following statements will document Weber's acceptance of this part of Rickert's theory:[29]

★ (a) Weber frequently talks of "experience," namely "the psychic[30] (*psychisch*) and *physical world* immediately given to us," whereby

... "experience" does not refer to the reality which is to be formed by the *scientific* way of looking at things, but to the totality of "sensations"

together with the "feelings" and "intentions" which entirely without differentiation are connected with them—those "attitudes," that is, which we
assume in each moment to a very different degree and in a very different
sense. In this sense, however, that which is "experienced" is something
which has not been made the object of judgments in the sense of an explanation of empirical facts; therefore, it remains in a state of indifference
as far as any empirical knowledge is concerned.[31]

In short, "it makes a logical difference" whether something "*is* 'experienced' or whether we have 'knowledge' of this experience."[32]

(b) The "brute and undifferentiated" (*ungeschiedene Dumpfheit*)[33]
immediate sensations cannot possibly be known as they are experienced.

Let us take a limiting case: the reflective analysis of one's own actions, of
which logically untrained opinion tends to believe that it certainly does
not present any "logical" problems whatsoever, since it is directly given
in experience and—assuming mental "health"—is "understandable" without
further ado and hence is naturally "reproducible" in memory directly.
Very simple reflections show indeed that this is not, however, so, and
that the "valid" answer to the question: "Why did I act in that way?"
constitutes a categorically formed construct....[34]

Thus it is obviously Weber's opinion "that all our 'knowledge' refers
to a categorically formed reality...."[35]

(c) The material of concept formation in science does not consist
of immediately experienced sensations but of *facts*,[36] "the empirically
given."[37] Facts, however—through a categorical judgment—are categorically formed sensations; "through the category of causality the
'world' as a 'perceived complex of facts' becomes an 'object.' "[38]
Science is "... the ordering in thought of facts."[39]

The transformation of sensations into facts, and the organization of
facts into a scientific account of the empirical world, i.e., scientific
knowledge, are seen by Weber as processes of giving forms to contents,
namely sensations and facts, respectively. For him, just as for Rickert,
giving a form to a content is the work of human effort. This effort is
made in response to the acceptance of truth as a value which is to be
pursued. Science is an undertaking "... in which truth is sought."[40]
Only for this reason are human raw experiences given the form of
"precise, articulate, and demonstrable *judgments*."[41] They now constitute valid knowledge, they are recognized as scientifically and (or)
categorically formed facts. "This 'recognition,' conceived as an element
of the taking of a position [toward the value "truth"] ... is attached
to the *validity* of one's own *judgments*, or those made by others."[42]
Only because humans accept "truth" as a value which has validity for

them can they and do they have knowledge at all. "For scientific truth is only what *claims* validity for all those who *want* the truth."[43] As soon as questions about sensations have to be answered in a valid way, therefore, "the category of validity assumes its formative function. . . ."[44]

In accordance with the tripartite hierarchy of sensations, facts, and science it can be expected that Weber makes a distinction between the category (or principle) of causality and the methodological forms of causality. This is indeed the case. Weber says that the "form" in which the "category of causality" is used in different disciplines (i.e., in either natural science or in history) is different.[45]

Its full, so-to-speak "primordial" meaning contains two things: on the one hand, the idea of *"effecting"* as a, so-to-speak, dynamic bond between phenomena which are qualitatively different from each other; on the other hand, the idea of something being subject to "regularities." The idea of "effecting" as substantive content of the category of causality, and, therefore, the idea of "cause," loses its sense and disappears whenever through quantifying abstraction the mathematical equation is arrived at as the expression of purely spatial causal relationships.[46]

What remains is the idea of a regularity "as an expression of the metamorphosis of something whose essence is eternally the same."[47] The idea of a regularity loses its meaning when one looks at reality as one single process which as a whole as well as in all its parts is qualitatively unique, and

. . . if the category of causality is to retain any meaning with regard to that infinity of concrete processes which cannot be embraced by any knowledge, *only* the idea of "causation" remains in the sense that everything which in each time differential is absolutely "new" "had to" originate from everything "past" just so and not otherwise. . . .[48]

Also, there are numerous statements in which the equation of "causal law" and "causality" is rejected.[49] Here too, Weber follows Rickert's lead.[50] Julien Freund's interpretation is not correct. He says that in its "full and original sense, causality comprises two basic ideas: the idea of rational action, a sort of dynamic between two qualitatively different phenomena, on the one hand, and the idea of subsumption under a general rule, on the other."[51] This is plainly not what Weber says.

The double step by which immediate sensations are finally transformed into scientific knowledge is required by the conditions under which the human effort to establish knowledge operates. As soon as humans *think* about their sensations and not just *experience* them, they cannot help doing so but in categorical forms. The human mind is just built this way. The categorical formation converts a subjective experience into what is called an "objective" fact, an "objectification."[52] A fact is "objective" because it is a content which has been given a categorical form as the result of the acceptance of the value of truth by all those who want knowledge. This is exactly what Rickert says.[53] A fact is "objective" because due to the acceptance of this value by all those who want knowledge there is intersubjective agreement that a certain content *ought* to be given a particular categorical form.

The objectivity of a *fact*, of course, must not be confused with the objectivity of a *scientific account* of empirical reality. Weber never states this, but it is an obvious implication of his reasoning. The objectivity of a scientific account of empirical reality depends on correct concept formation and presupposes the availability of objective facts, since the material of concept formation is facts. The objectivity of concept formation will be dealt with in the next section, in the proper context. At the moment, only one more thing must be mentioned: the ambiguity of Weber's statements with regard to the distinction between experience, fact, and science is particularly strong wherever he talks about the objectification of subjective inner experiences, like feelings, emotions, etc. Thus, e.g., Weber declares that no such experience "escapes" objectification "whenever we are dealing with a scientific account of facts, whose nature it is to claim supra-individual validity as 'objective truth.' "[54]

3. METHODOLOGICAL PREMISES

Knowledge of facts per se is not scientific knowledge (although all scientific knowledge is knowledge of facts). Weber calls the opposite assumption a "naive popular idea"[1] based on the fallacious belief that science is an attempt to faithfully copy reality.[2] For this idea implies that the ultimate goal of science is a complete reproduction of empirical reality. But this assumption is plainly nonsensical. Two considerations make this clear. On the one hand, there are infinitely many facts.[3] There is an infinite amount of potential mental contents which can be thought of as existing, that is, as facts. On the other hand, the human mind is limited, "finite";[4] no infinite amount of concrete facts can be contained in it.[5] A complete copy of reality, therefore, cannot be the goal of science, and to interpret the existing sciences as steps toward such a goal does not make sense. It cannot be denied that "the infinity and absolute irrationality of the multiplicity [of elements] of which everything concrete consists provides an epistemologically really cogent *demonstration* that it is an absolutely senseless thought to attempt a 'copy' of reality through any kind of science."[6]

On the basis of this insight one is forced to conclude that what scientists have to settle for is only a partial representation of concrete empirical reality. Since *as a matter of principle*[7] the human mind can hold only a limited number of facts, a selection from among their totality is necessary. There is nothing in the facts themselves determining which ones are included in or excluded from scientific accounts of reality. Instead, this depends on the aim of each particular scientific investigation, on what the scientists in question want to know, i.e., unique individual phenomena or the laws governing all of reality. Scientific knowledge, therefore, is not just any knowledge of facts, but knowledge only of those facts which are relevant to the aims of a scientific investigation of a particular kind.[8]

It is important to realize that by "aim of a scientific investigation" Weber does not refer to the substantive content of the interest responsible for the undertaking of a particular investigation, e.g., the interest in establishing the course of a planet, or the interest in describing the assassination of Lincoln rather than anything else. Rather, "aim" means "formal aim" and refers to the conception by which Weber replaces the refuted notion that the goal of science is a faithful copy of reality. According to Weber it seems that, rather than by this unattainable ideal, scientific investigations are instigated as attempts to approach either one of two ideals which *are* attainable by humans.[9] Either ideal formally limits in a different way the amount of facts to be known to such a degree that the human mind is theoretically capable of achieving complete knowledge of the remaining facts. One such ideal is the establishment of the laws of nature governing all empirical phenomena. The other is "knowledge of reality in the characteristic qualitative particularity and uniqueness in which it exists without exception and everywhere."[10]

The formulation of the goals guiding the human efforts to acquire knowledge provides the basis for the reflection on the means, or methods, to be applied in order to reach these goals. Their establishment is undertaken in methodology: "methodology can only bring us reflective understanding of the means which have *demonstrated* their value in practice by raising them to the level of explicit consciousness."[11] These means are two standards of selection whose application determines in each case which facts are *worth knowing* or, as Weber also says, "essential."[12] They are *interesting* facts, they are to be included in a scientific account of reality. A fact is worth knowing when its inclusion in an account of empirical reality is a step toward reaching one of the two formal goals of knowledge, depending on which one has been adopted in a particular instance. The standards of selection state under what conditions this is the case. If the goal is knowledge of the general laws governing all empirical phenomena, only those elements of reality are worth knowing which are *common to all phenomena*,[13] i.e., their *generic (gattungsmaessig)* features.[14] If the goal is knowledge of the uniqueness of concrete phenomena, then only those things are worth knowing in which the "individual particularity"[15] of the phenomena in question manifests itself, those parts which are "characteristic,"[16] or "historically essential,"[17] or "significant" for scientific researchers.[18]

Weber here is in agreement with Rickert.[19] The difficulties which Talcott Parsons believes to appear at this point do not exist.

The starting point [of Weber's methodology] is Weber's statement that these standards are to be found in the subjective "direction of interest" of the scientist. In interpreting what are in turn the determinants of this direction of interest in the two groups of sciences, Weber's position is not altogether clear, and hence it is here that the first serious methodological difficulty of his position arises.[20]

Parsons thinks that, for Weber, the natural sciences exist as a response to the human desire for practical control, the cultural sciences due to their relevance to the values of the scientist and the epoch in which he lives.[21] He denies that this is a well-founded distinction and wonders how Weber with his emphasis on the role of nomological knowledge for rational action could have maintained such an opinion,[22] especially in view of the existence of such social sciences as economics. The source of Parsons's puzzlement is a twofold confusion. The first of these concerns the distinction between the genetic aspect (psychological causes) and the logical aspect (reasons) of the application of the two methods of abstraction. It is obvious that Weber is concerned with the logical question. The justification for the two methods lies entirely in the fact that with their help it is possible to overcome infinite reality in a generally accepted fashion. The desire for practical control cannot establish their validity as abstractive procedures. The second confusion results from Parsons's apparent failure to realize that in Weber's terminology "cultural sciences," "history," and "social sciences" are interchangeable terms; they all denote historical sciences whose concept formation is individualizing. In this terminology, sociology and economic theory then are *not* "social sciences" ("cultural sciences," "historical sciences"), but natural sciences, since their concept formation is generalizing. Parsons, however, uses the term "social sciences" such that it includes reference to economics and sociology, apparently assuming that this conforms to Weber's usage. This, however, is not the case. "Social science," for Weber, is synonymous with "history."

The scientific process of selection from concrete reality, according to Weber, is a formative process, a *"transformation* through a process of thought."[23] Its outcome is *formed reality*. The form is called "concept," and there are two kinds: a "general" one which is used to establish knowledge of the elements common to all reality, and an "individual" or "historical" one with whose help the individual and characteristic features of concrete phenomena are described. The process of selection, therefore, can be viewed as a process of giving reality the form of concepts. When Weber says that "concepts are primarily means of thought for the intellectual mastery of empirical data"[24] he refers to concepts as forms into which reality is cast so that scientific investigators can achieve their goal, namely knowledge of empirical reality.

But Weber uses "concept" in a second sense. Here, a concept is "any thought-construct, no matter how individual, which originates through logical treatment of a concrete multiplicity for the purpose of acquiring *knowledge of that* which is essential."[25] Thus, the term designates the end-product of the selective process, a content which has a particular form.[26] The content consists of a number of facts. If they are the elements common to all reality, the form is general; if they are those which are characteristic of one phenomenon, the form is individual. Concepts in this sense *are* what scientists want to know, not *means* to what they want to know. Knowledge consists in having such concepts.[27] The process of selection is a process of concept formation, i.e., the combination of one of the two available conceptual forms with a particular content.

Where empirical science treats a given multiplicity as a "thing" and therewith as a "unity," there this object is indeed . . . a thought-construct which always and without exception contains something "concretely" empirical—nevertheless, it still is an absolutely *artificial* construct whose "unity"[28] is determined through the selection of that which is essential with regard to certain research purposes;[29] thus, it is a thought-product which is only "functionally" related to the "givens"[30] . . . which originate[s] through a transformation of the empirically given by the intellect, and which can be verbally designated.[31]

Weber does not properly distinguish between the two meanings of the term. Neither does Rickert. They occur even side by side in the same sentence. For instance, with reference to the natural sciences, there is the following statement: "Their specific logical *means* is the use of concepts with an always wider scope and, therefore, an always smaller *content*, their logical *outcome* is *relational* concepts of *general validity* (laws)."[32] Furthermore, there is yet another possible source of confusion. For Weber does not only say that concepts (in the sense of "conceptual forms") are the means which humans have to employ in order to reach a specific end, namely knowledge of empirical reality. He also says that *general* concepts are indispensable as a means for the establishment of *historical* knowledge.[33] But here "concept" refers to a form-content combination, and it is a means of *explanation*, not of formation. What exactly Weber is talking about in this case will be discussed later.[34] The point here is to show the necessity of properly distinguishing the different referents of "concept" and "means" in, e.g., statements like this one:

If one perceives the implications of the fundamental ideas of modern epistemology which ultimately derive from Kant, namely that concepts[35] are primarily means of thought[36] for the intellectual mastery of empirical data and can be only that,[37] the facts that precise genetic concepts are necessarily ideal types will not cause him to desist from constructing them. The relationship between concept[38] and historical research is reversed for those who appreciate this . . . the concepts[39] are not ends[40] but are means[41] to the end of understanding phenomena which are significant from concrete individual viewpoints.[42]

It is an obvious implication of Weber's theory that a concept is logically equivalent to a (set of) judgment(s).[43] For a concept is a particular organization, or formation, of facts, and facts in turn are judgments (i.e., form-content combinations). The factual content of a concept in its totality is an account of empirical reality. This account has the status of *objective scientific knowledge*, if it has been correctly formed. It is *objective* because it is a (methodological) form-content combination which everybody wants performed, which is, therefore, considered intersubjectively valid due to every scientist's acceptance of truth as a value. It is *scientific* knowledge because its content is facts and its form is conceptual (whereas the content of *factual* knowledge is ideas of sensations, and its form is categorical).

Weber's reasoning concerning concept formation is, it seems, identical with Rickert's arguments in which the latter shows how the adoption of either one of the aforementioned goals enables a scientist to overcome the infinite multiplicity of empirical reality.[44] However, with regard to the goals of science Rickert also tried to show that it is not only the result of an empirical and contingent consensus among scientists that those two goals are and have been guiding all scientific research. He made an effort to argue that they are the goals attainable to humans which most closely approximate the ultimate but humanly unreachable ideal, namely photographic knowledge of the whole world, and that, therefore, everybody who aspires to knowledge in the most ideal form accessible to humans necessarily must adopt these two goals.[45] Whether Weber accepted this derivation is hard to say, for clear statements relating to this matter are lacking. Throughout his essays in a pragmatic fashion he takes it for granted that in science humans have these two goals, and he quite flatly refuses to deal with the problem of their justification. Referring to history, he says:

For considerations which remain strictly within the limits of methodology proper, the circumstance that certain *individual* components of reality are selected as objects of historical treatment can be justified absolutely only by reference to this *factual* existence of a corresponding *interest*. Value-relevance cannot indeed mean more than that for such considerations in which the *meaning* of this interest has not been made the object of a question.[46]

But he also makes a statement which seems to express agreement with Rickert's argument:

The *objective* validity of all empirical knowledge rests exclusively upon the ordering of the given reality according to categories which are *subjective* in a specific sense, namely in that they present the *presuppositions* of our knowledge and are based on the presupposition of the value of those truths which empirical knowledge alone is able to give us. The means available to our science offer nothing to those persons to whom this truth is of no value. .... Those for whom scientific truth is of no value will seek in vain for some other truth to take the place of science in just those respects in which it is unique, namely, in the provision of concepts and judgments which are neither empirical reality nor reproductions of it, but which allow its *ordering in thought* in a valid manner.[47]

Thus, one encounters here a problem in Weber's reasoning. While attempting to limit himself strictly to questions within the area of methodology proper (i.e., the theory of concept formation), he nevertheless makes statements transcending its realm, and in doing so provokes the question whether the philosophical foundation of his methodology is identical with Rickert's. On the basis of the last quote alone, of course, no answer can be given. The proper place to deal with the problem is in the context of Weber's account of concept formation in history, and, therefore, no conclusions are drawn at the moment.[48]

Weber's argument establishing the methods which have to be used in the acquisition of scientific knowledge makes no reference to the nature of the facts with which a particular kind of science deals. The only relevant feature of reality in this respect is its infinity. But it is only of "negative" significance.[49] For it is merely the stumbling block of any kind of "mirror image" theory. It has its place in an argument which states that which does *not* and can *not* be the aim of science. The "positive"[50] determination of what is done in science is derived from the cognitive aims of scientists and the means at their disposal to reach these aims.[51] The nature of facts does not play any role in this derivation. Accordingly, the principles of concept formation are general. They apply to everything which is a fact in Weber's definition, i.e., a content in a categorical form. Thus, the basis of the validity of knowledge is also general. The fact that human investigators can "understand" certain events whereas others are meaningless to them does not make any difference in this respect. It is a

... rather trivial insight—which, in spite of everything, is questioned time and again—that neither the "substantive" qualities of the "material" nor "ontological" differences of its "being" ... decide about the *logical* meaning [of knowledge] and the conditions of its "validity." Empirical knowledge in the field of the "psychic" and in that of "outside" "nature," of the processes "within" us and those "outside" us, is always bound to the means of concept formation, and the logical nature of a "concept" is the same in both substantive "fields."[52]

Of course, this is not to deny that there *are* substantive differences between certain kinds of fact,[53] and that this may be important for certain purposes.[54] But for logical considerations they are indeed irrelevant.[55]

Before concluding this section it may be useful to comment briefly upon the relationship between the scope and content of concepts as postulated by both Rickert and Weber. It will be recalled that the latter described the process of the natural sciences as the successive formation of general "concepts with ever wider scope and, therefore, ever smaller content. . . ."[56] History, in contrast, uses relational concepts with "ever greater content and, therefore, ever smaller scope."[57] It must be indicated, however, that although there are cases in which this postulated reciprocity of scope and content exists, this is by no means always the case. Consider the following two statements, both of which are possible according to Rickert's and Weber's theory of concept formation: "Man is a featherless biped," and "Man is a featherless biped with a navel." It seems that in both cases the concept "man" has the same scope, although according to the theory the content of the latter is greater. A more crucial objection to the criticized assumption is that in its formulation the diversity of operations through which conceptual elements can be combined to form a conceptual content is completely neglected. The tacit assumption is that the combination is always through "and"; but other constructions are possible, e.g., "A government is a group of people ruling a country either on the basis of popular consent or on the basis of police power." In such cases the scope increases with the content. Finally, a look at their own special constructs—"individual concepts"—could have shown Rickert and Weber the incorrectness of their assumption. For, as the term itself indicates, the scope of an individual concept comprises one empirical case, no matter how elaborate the content. Thus, the unqualified doctrine of the reciprocity of conceptual scope and content in Rickert's and Weber's theory is not correct.[58]

4. THE CONCEPTS OF NATURAL SCIENCE

Empirical reality, i.e., the totality of facts, is the object of science. Each fact is the combination of a particular idiosyncratic content and a categorical form. Thus, empirical reality "without exception and everywhere is given and conceivable only as concrete, individual, and in qualitative particularity."[1] The goal of science is to establish knowledge of this reality. The logical difficulty inherent in this stems from the fact that for the observer reality represents an "extensively and intensively infinite multiplicity" of diverse phenomena.[2] For the limited human mind its complete description is an impossible task, not only practically but in principle.[3] It can contain only a limited number of facts, and, therefore, a selection from among their totality is required.

All efforts to acquire intellectual knowledge of the infinite reality through the finite human mind, therefore, rest on the tacit assumption that in each case only a finite *part* of this reality can be scientifically grasped, and that it alone is "essential" in the sense of "worth knowing."[4]

The task of methodology proper (as distinguished from epistemology, which deals with the problem of the constitution of facts) is to explicitly show the principles in accordance with which this part is determined, and their justification. The function of these principles is "to overcome the infinity of reality," to use Rickert's terms. It is fulfilled by reducing the amount of facts to be known to proportions which can be handled by the human mind. These principles are formal insofar as it is not possible without empirical research to determine just which particular facts will be included in a scientific account of reality.

The analysis of existing scientific research reveals that there are two such principles in use. This reflects the fact that scientific investigations can be guided by either one of two goals. Each principle makes use of a different criterion according to which certain empirical phenomena are selected in order to be incorporated into a scientific account of the world. The two possibilities are

... either the selection of the *generic* features as that which is worth knowing, and their subsumption under generally valid abstract formulas, or the selection of the individually significant phenomena and their ordering into universal—though individual—contexts. . . .[5]

The application of the former principle of selection is the logical procedure defined as that of natural science, and largely adopted in it; the application of the latter is defined as the logical means of the historical, or cultural, sciences, where it is in general use. This is not to say that in any science as it concretely exists, necessarily only one of these standards is used across the board. Only in pure mechanics and in certain parts of history is this so.[6] Rather, the exclusive application of either one or the other of these standards represents a logical ideal.

The process of selection is a process of concept formation. Depending on the standard used, its outcome is either a "general"[7] or an "individual"[8] concept. The knowledge of the natural sciences is presented in the form of general concepts, historical knowledge is in the form of individual, or "historical"[9] concepts. The formation of a concept, i.e., the process of selecting the essential phenomena from concrete reality is a process of *abstraction*.[10] For Weber, as for Rickert, "to abstract" quite literally means "to take away" parts of concrete reality by discarding, or eliminating, its nonessential parts. In this mentalistic conception, facts of reality *concretely* exist in the mind before being "treated" scientifically, i.e., before being formed. The formative process involves the elimination of the inessential parts of this concrete reality which is given in the human consciousness; they are not incorporated into scientific knowledge; they are not *thought*. On the level of knowledge, they are forgotten.

In science, the investigator does not have concrete reality in the mind, but abstract reality in conceptual form. Abstraction is involved in any kind of concept formation, in natural science[11] as well as in history.[12] The "analytic-discursive"[13] nature of human knowledge, i.e., the fact that humans can have knowledge only in the form of judgments about particular contents, "removes" them from the concrete empirical world "by disrobing reality of its full concreteness through a process of abstraction."[14] Such abstraction is an *irreversible* process. Once one has abstracted from reality its concreteness is lost and cannot be reconstituted. Since each method of concept formation discards and retains phenomena according to "entirely heterogeneous and disparate"[15] criteria, one kind of knowledge can in no way substitute for the other. "Neither of the two modes of ordering reality in thought has any necessary logical relationship with the other."[16] It may happen that the same empirical fact is included in a general concept as well as in an individual one, but this is coincidental from the logical point of view. As a result of the different principles underlying their formation there is a distinct difference in the relationships in which the contents of general and individual concepts stand to the concrete reality which they conceptualize. This difference is expressed by the easily misleading name given by Rickert and Weber to the sciences using individual concepts as the predominant form: "sciences of concrete reality" (*Wirklichkeitswissenschaften*).[17] What exactly this difference is will become clear in the course of the discussion of concept formation in natural science and history.

In logical terms, natural science is defined as the establishment of knowledge of the generic features of individual phenomena. Here an individual concrete phenomenon is worth knowing only in those aspects which it shares with other concrete phenomena, which make it an *instance of a class* of phenomena. For Weber, as for Rickert, every concrete phenomenon—be it a "thing" or a "process"—is a complex of component concrete phenomena. It is regarded as one "thing" or one "process" only because, and as long as, the human observer chooses to look at it this way, to view it as a unity. It may be very small or very large, this makes no difference. And rather than treating it as a concrete unity, scientists may analyze any concrete phenomenon as a particular complex of diverse concrete subunities. Every concrete phenomenon is made up of some subunities, or component parts, which are particular to it alone, and others which are of a kind also occurring in other phenomena. This is also the case with the causal relations in which these parts stand. In natural science, investigators abstract from the particular features of concrete phenomena. Thus they retain those component elements which are common to many phenomena. In the case of "things," they are smaller unities, in the case of "processes," they are component processes. Such processes are temporal series, and since temporal successions are given by the human mind the categorical form of causality, they are stated as causal sequences common to many concrete phenomena. In natural science scientists try to retain only those component elements and causal relationships which occur in (ultimately) all concrete phenomena. For here the ultimate goal is "a system of concepts and laws which approach as much as possible absolutely universal validity,"[18] i.e., a system of statements describing the elements, and the relations between them, which occur as component parts of every possible empirical phenomenon,[19] and the causal relationships holding for them (the "laws" of causality governing all phenomena).[20] This *logical* goal forces the scientist in the natural sciences

... to progressively dismantle the individual "accidentals" of everything concrete from the "things" and processes given in our consciousness in order to give their concepts the unambiguous content which necessarily is striven for. The never resting logical constraint toward systematizing subsumption of the general concepts thus acquired under others which are even more general, together with the striving for exactness and clarity, urges them to reduce the qualitative differentiatedness of reality as much as possible to exactly measureable quantities. Finally, if in principle they want to go beyond the mere classification of phenomena, their concepts have to contain potential judgments of general validity; if these judgments are to be *exact* and of mathematical evidence, they have to be in the form of causal equations. All this, however, involves an increasing removal from empirical reality.[21] . . . Its ultimate consequence is the creation of elements which are though as absolutely without qualities, and, therefore, absolutely unreal.[22] These elements carry out processes of motion which are only quantitatively differentiated, and whose laws can be expressed by causal equations.[23]

As this quotation documents, Weber accepts every major part of Rickert's account of generalizing concept formation:[24] in natural science, investigators strive for an exhaustive system of general concepts;[25] they try to eliminate all ambiguity of content;[26] concepts are equivalent to judgments;[27] general concepts ultimately occur in the form of mathematically formulated causal equations;[28] the empirical world is conceived as consisting of ultimate, nonconcrete elements governed by the laws of motion; all change is motion;[29] the assumption that there can be general concepts which are absolutely and universally valid, not just empirically general.[30]

In the process of concept formation in the natural sciences described by Weber, progressive generalization necessarily involves progressive abstraction.[31] In other words, the conceptual contents account for ever fewer particular details of the concrete phenomena of empirical reality. Since "reality" for Weber (and Rickert) always means "concrete reality in all its details," the kind of abstraction used in natural science for him constitutes a "movement away"[32] from reality toward unreality. Therefore, he can say that "the knowledge of social laws is not knowledge of social reality . . . ,"[33] for laws are general concepts, and concrete reality can never be the content of general concepts.[34] It is only an application of this idea when Weber contends that historical reality can never be deduced from laws even if scientists had a comprehensive system of such laws.[35] By "deduced" Weber does not mean the explanation of a constellation of facts with the help of initial conditions and nomological hypotheses. Rather, interpreting the contents of laws as factual descriptions of the common features of many empirical phenomena, Weber argues that such descriptions alone do not tell anything about the particulars of a specific situation. "This would be impossible, not only for practical reasons, but in principle due to the logical nature of 'nomothetic' knowledge. For establishing 'laws' —relational concepts of general validity—is identical with emptying the conceptual content through abstraction."[36] If against this it were argued that "deduction" from laws of course always means "deduction with the help of initial conditions," Weber would respond that knowledge of initial conditions is something entirely different from knowledge of general concepts. For, in the case of history, it is knowledge of the particularity of an individual situation, and the logical structure of such knowledge follows its own principles; "the reality *for* which the laws are valid always remains equally individual, equally *undeducible* from laws."[37] For laws are abstractions from it.

5. THE CONCEPTS OF HISTORY

The formation of general concepts is a valid way of overcoming "the extensively and intensively infinite multiplicity"[1] of empirical reality. For in the fields in which this method is used every scientist agrees that the results are worth knowing. However, in other fields of inquiry the knowledge which would result from a generalizing procedure is not considered to be essential.[2] Therefore, a different method of concept formation is employed "wherever the essential, i.e., those features of the phenomena which for us are worth knowing, is not exhausted by subsuming the phenomena under a generic concept, but concrete reality *as such* is of interest to us."[3] Accordingly, sciences where this is the case are the "sciences of concrete reality" (*Wirklichkeitswissenschaften*); they are the "historical," "cultural," or "social" sciences.

The social-scientific interest has its point of departure, of course, in the *real*, i.e., concrete, individually-structured configuration of the social-cultural life around us in its *universal* context which in itself is no less *individually structured*, and in its development out of other social-cultural conditions, which themselves are obviously likewise individually structured.[4]

But knowledge of this reality also involves abstraction. For of course concrete reality "as such" can never be known in a scientific fashion, since it is infinite. But within the limit which the requirement of concept formation sets to scientific knowledge, one can try to be as detailed as possible. Thus, history is a science of concrete reality not in the sense that it reproduces the totality of reality, but in the sense "that it fits elements of the given reality, which as concrete elements can only be relatively vague conceptual contents,[5] as 'real'[6] components into a concrete causal context."[7] the distinction between "sciences of the concept" and "sciences of concrete reality" is, therefore, a distinction indicating the direction into which concept formation goes: either away from or toward concrete reality.

It sounds, of course, paradoxical and is not altogether precise to say that in history scientists abstract in such a fashion that their concepts approximate concrete reality. For what is really involved is that in history they attempt to account for one overall feature of everything concretely existing which is entirely disregarded in the natural sciences, namely its individuality and uniqueness. The description of this individuality is possible in a way that is compatible with the necessity of concept formation, and knowledge of the individuality of a phenomenon is, therefore, used as a substitute for the knowledge of its concreteness which cannot be scientifically known. Weber nowhere states this consideration explicitly. But it is implied in his taking for granted that as a result of human interest in knowledge of reality as such there is the science of history, i.e., descriptions of the uniqueness of particular phenomena. For in history investigators do not describe empirical phenomena in so far as they are constellations of the same ultimate elements; it is their "qualitative coloration"[8] which they want to know. Accordingly, they describe the "individual particularities" and the "significance" of constellations of phenomena,[9] not their generic features.

 The standards according to which abstraction in the historical sciences takes place is the standard of *value-relevance*.[10] Its application results in the selection of those empirical phenomena as essential, i.e., worth knowing, in which for human observers cultural values find their expression. Consequently, history is a science "whose object, formulated in the terminology of the philosophy of history, represents [for human observers] 'the embodiment (*Verwirklichung*) of values in concrete phenomena' . . ." and which treats "the human individuals [who are part of the historical material] who themselves 'value' always as 'carriers' of that process."[11] This way the extensive infinity of reality is overcome as well as the intensive one, for cultural values for human observers are embodied in only a limited number of concrete phenomena and attached to only a limited number of their component elements.

Weber's acceptance of the principle of value-relevance is based on the same considerations as those put forward by Rickert. The first step of the derivation consists in the insight that through practical valuation certain constellations of empirical phenomena become the object of human attention. "Now, what interests us here . . . is . . . the fact that this 'valuation' is tied to the incomparable, unique, and . . . irreplaceable particularity of the object. . . ."[12] But, of course, valuation is merely a practical way of overcoming the infinity of reality and is not theoretically satisfying, although genetically most frequently the beginning of what is to become a scientific interest. Certain things are selected from reality because humans actually value them. These things, through the valuation, acquire a *subjective meaning* for those humans who value them. But in science, investigators do not want to practically value things; their aim is to *describe* them without making value judgments, for their objective in science is knowledge of reality, not its valuation.[13] What scientists need, then, is a principle of selection which allows them to select individual phenomena in order to describe them without having to value them.

A selective principle of the required kind can indeed be established. This principle prescribes the selection of those phenomena as objects of historical description in which for human observers general cultural values are expressed, without forcing the scientists to make value judgments.[14] These phenomena are *significant* for human investigators,[15] since for them they are "the concrete, individual, and, therefore, in the last analysis *unique* form in which 'ideas'—to employ for once a metaphysical phrase—are 'embodied,' or 'are effective' (*sich auswirken*) . . . in the . . . structures in question. . . ."[16] Thus, knowledge of an individual constellation of facts, due to the principle of selection involved, always is knowledge of meaningful, i.e., understandable, facts.[17] Their description fulfills the requirement demanded from a scientific account of empirical reality, namely to overcome the infinity of reality. For a certain cultural value is embodied only in a finite number of phenomena, and only in a finite number of their constituent elements.[18] Weber says that the "chaos"[19] of empirical phenomena can be ordered only due to the fact "that in each case only a *part* of individual reality is interesting and *significant* to us, because it alone is related to the cultural value-ideas with which we approach reality. Only certain sides of the infinitely complex individual phenomena . . . are, therefore, worthwhile knowing."[20] These phenomena are of general interest. This is so as long as the values embodied in them relate to a collective concern of the social group of which the investigating historian is a member. For in this case, in spite of the possible divergences among different persons' practical values—due to which in practical life their attention becomes focused on certain individual constellations of facts—the phenomena to which they are attached are of general interest; they are "cultural" phenomena.[21] Phenomena are cultural

... *only* because and *only* insofar as their existence and the form which they *historically* assume touch directly or indirectly on our cultural *interests*, as they arouse our striving for knowledge from viewpoints which are derived from the value-ideas which make that portion of reality ... *significant* for us.[22]

Of course, this implies that everyone, including the historian as a practical actor, has values relating to such common concerns. Otherwise he would not be interested in those phenomena in which other persons' values relating to collective concerns are embodied.

It is true that these considerations are not very explicit in Weber's essays. However, Rickert's work being widely known, it seems legitimate to assume that Weber treated them as known, and in any case it is only on the basis of this reasoning that the following statement of Weber's makes any sense:

"Culture" is a finite segment of the meaningless infinity of the world process, a segment which from the point of view of *human beings* has meaning and significance conferred upon it. This is true even for the human being who opposes a *concrete* culture[23] as a mortal enemy and who demands "return to nature." For even this position he can adopt only by *relating* the concrete culture to his value-ideas[24] and finding it "too soft." This is the *purely logical-formal* fact which is involved when we speak here of the logical necessity of anchoring all historical individuals to value-ideas. The transcendental presupposition of every *cultural science* does *not* at all lie in our finding a certain "culture" or any "culture" in general to be valuable but rather in the fact that we *are* cultural *beings*, endowed with the capacity and the will to adopt a deliberate [valuing] *attitude* towards the world and to lend it a *meaning*. Whatever this meaning may be, it will lead us in [practical] life to *judge* certain phenomena of human social existence in its light and to take a (positive or negative) position toward them as *significant* phenomena. Whatever may be the content of this position which we take—these phenomena have cultural *significance* for us, and on this significance alone rests their scientific interest.[25]

A description is objective when it describes those phenomena in which for human observers values are embodied which relate to a cultural concern of the collectivity of which they are members.[26] For everybody is interested in knowledge of such facts. The principle of value-relevance, therefore, means that only those phenomena are selected for scientific historical description in which for all human observers general cultural values are expressed. This kind of concept formation is, therefore, "anthropomorphic"[27] and "teleological."[28] It is only a different expression when Weber talks of "the conditioning of cultural knowledge through *value-ideas*."[29] It was seen that this does not involve value judgments on the part of the historian in his role as a scientist.

The "objectivity" of social-scientific knowledge depends rather on the fact that the empirical data are always related to those value-ideas which alone make them *worth* knowing, and that their significance is understood on the basis of these values, but that nevertheless they are never made the basis for the empirically impossible proof of the validity of these values.[30]

There are a great number of particular general cultural values which observers can find embodied in particular social phenomena, and additional ones are discovered all the time. Even those of which historians can be aware at any given time are too many to allow the description of all the constellations of phenomena to which they are attached, and the historical developments of all these phenomena, in one single historical account. A division of labor is, therefore, necessary. There are, however, no logical principles which prescribe to the individual historian on which particular value-embodiments he should focus his attention.

The historian is "free" as far as the choice of the guiding values is concerned which in turn determine the selection and formation of the "historical individual" . . . which is to be explained. From here on, however, he is absolutely bound to the principles governing the establishment of causal interdependences. He is "free" in a certain sense only as far as the inclusion of logically "accidental"[31] elements is concerned.[32]

It is the freedom of choosing a particular cultural value—and, of course, the specific subject matter whose description is to be guided by it—which Weber has in mind when he calls the value-ideas "subjective"[33] and then continues:

Between the "historical" interest in a family chronicle and that in the development of the greatest conceivable cultural phenomena which were and are common to a nation or to mankind over long epochs, there exists an infinite gradation of "significance" arranged into an order which differs for each of us. And they are, naturally, historically variable in accordance with the character of the culture and the ideas which rule men's minds. But it obviously does *not* follow from this that research in the cultural sciences can only have *results* which are "subjective" in the sense that they are *valid* for one person and not for others. Only the degree to which they *interest*[34] different persons varies. In other words, the *choice of the object* of investigation and the extent or depth to which this investigation attempts to penetrate into the infinite causal web are determined by the value-ideas which dominate the investigator and his age.[35]

The fact that in history only those phenomena are described which for human observers embody some general cultural value is referred to by the expression that history is always written "from specifically *particular viewpoints.*"[36] That historians adopt a viewpoint from which historical knowledge is established is only another way of saying that they describe only those phenomena in which for them as observers one or a few specific general cultural values are embodied, i.e., values relating to the collective concerns of the observer's society.[37]

When we require from the historian and the social research worker as an elementary presupposition that he distinguish the important from the unimportant and that he should have the necessary "points of view" for this distinction, we merely mean that he must understand how to relate the events of reality—consciously or unconsciously—to universal "cultural values" and then to select *those* relationships which are significant for us.[38]

When Weber says that the viewpoints necessary for the establishment of historical knowledge are "oriented to values,"[39] or "derived from values,"[40] he is stating that without the existence of values which are embodied in concrete phenomena historians would have no means of discriminating, no principle of selecting the essential parts of reality. It does not mean, as Henrich seems to think,[41] that in Weber's view there are values and that from each of them somehow—how exactly is not specified by Henrich—viewpoints can be derived, perhaps like theorems from axioms. That there is a "plurality"[42] of viewpoints only means that there is a plurality of general cultural values which for observers are embodied in the same concrete and complex reality, which therefore, can be described from several viewpoints. Since it is impossible to incorporate all possible viewpoints into one historical account, all historical knowledge necessarily displays a certain "onesidedness."[43] Not everything which it is legitimate to say about a particular concrete cultural phenomenon can be said in any one historical account describing its development.

The cultural phenomena which embody certain values were created and maintained as a result of the fact that historically human individuals held particular values which they attempted more or less successfully to embody in social arrangements. Those historical humans occurring in the description of a particular historical development who (more or less) consciously held values of the same kind as those which from the point of view of the investigator are embodied in the phenomena, i.e., which a historian decided to use as the viewpoint from which a particular historical investigation is undertaken, are at the center of the description of the historical development of these phenomena. Therefore, they are called "historical centers."[44] The core of every historical account of empirical reality are those historical developments which were the direct result of the actions of these human beings. Their actions and thoughts in relation to their social and physical environment[45] constitute the "primary"[46] historical individual. Those phenomena which are also included in historical accounts because they are causally related to the primary development—either as its consequences or its mediate causes—constitute the "secondary"[47] historical individual. The historical humans occurring in it did not pursue those general cultural values in whose embodiments the historians are interested when they have adopted a certain point of view. Finally, there are those elements which are included in order to enliven the description and make it more reality-like.[48] They defy any attempts of finding a logical criterion for their selection.

The general viewpoint to be adopted by the articles published in the *Archiv fuer Sozialwissenschaft und Sozialpolitik*, according to Weber's plans, is that of *"the economic conditioning and ramifications"* of cultural phenomena.[49] In other words, the published articles are to deal with those constellations of social phenomena which are the result of the economic ideas and values held by people, that is, with the properly "economic" processes and institutions and with their causal impact on other parts and sectors of the concrete culture of which they are part,[50] with those things "which *consciously* were created or are used for economic purposes."[51] Also to be included are descriptions of " 'economically relevant' phenomena,"[52] i.e., those which were not created to economic ends, but had effects affecting the economic phenomena proper. Finally, the *Archiv* is to contain accounts of "economically *conditioned*" phenomena"[53] which are causally influenced by economic processes without being themselves of an economic nature. Such an "economic *interpretation* of history,"[54] or "economic interpretation of reality,"[55] offers "a partial picture, a *preliminary contribution* to the complete historical knowledge of culture."[56]

Unfortunately Weber never spells out his conception of "complete" historical knowledge. If one wants to speculate on what he might have had in mind, it seems that there are three possibilities that are open. One is that "complete" knowledge is knowledge from all possible viewpoints; another is that "complete" knowledge is knowledge from absolutely valid viewpoints to which those which are in use stand in some relation. The latter interpretation has the drawback that correctly Weber should have called this knowledge "ultimate" rather than "complete." The former interpretation contradicts Weber's explicit statement:

Life in its irrational reality[57] and its content of *possible* meanings is inexhaustible. The selection of values for the *actual* establishment of particular value-relevances (*die konkrete Gestaltung der Wertbeziehung*) remains, therefore, in flux, ever subject to change into the hidden future of human culture.[58]

It is this eternal possibility of discovering new general cultural values to which human history can be related which precludes the establishment of a system of *historical* concepts in analogy to the ultimate system of general concepts in natural science.[59]

The immeasurable stream of events flows unendingly towards eternity. The cultural problems which move men emerge ever anew and in different colors, and the boundaries of that area which in this always equally infinite stream of individual events acquires meaning and significance for us, i.e., which becomes an "historical individual," are constantly subject to change. The contexts in which it is thought, from which it is viewed and scientifically conceived, change. The points of departure of the cultural sciences therewith remain changeable into the infinite future as long as Chinese ossification of intellectual life does not render mankind incapable of posing new questions to the always equally inexhaustible life. A system of cultural science, if only in the sense of a definitive, objectively valid, systematizing fixation of the *questions* and *areas* with which they are supposed to deal, would be nonsense in itself.[60]

It may, therefore, be assumed that Weber has the following idea: at any given time period, certain aspects of concrete phenomena are of historical interest from a great but finite number of value-viewpoints which do not change during this period. "Complete" historical knowledge then would be "complete" knowledge relative to the actually available viewpoints during this period, if world history had been written from all these viewpoints. However, there is no proof that this is indeed Weber's conception. It is merely a reasonable possibility which is not contradicted by any of Weber's statements.

Although, as was shown, the values which are used as viewpoints guiding historical descriptions occur in the historical material itself as the practical values of some humans whose actions are described, this does not mean that logically the historical material "prescribes" particular viewpoints from which it is to be described.

If the opinion that those viewpoints could be "taken from the material itself" continually recurs, this is due to the naive self-deception of the specialist who is unaware that due to the value-ideas with which he unconsciously has approached his subject matter, *a priori* he has selected from an absolute infinity a tiny portion as *that* part with whose study alone he *concerns* himself.[61]

For logical considerations, the selection of a value to which empirical reality is to be related has priority. Genetically, the situation is mostly different. In this context, the choice of the guiding value is a function of the investigator's own practical outlook on life, the meaning which he gives it.

To be sure, without the investigator's value-ideas there would be no principle of selection of facts and no meaningful knowledge of reality in its individuality. Just as without the investigator's *belief* in the *significance* of some cultural contents any attempts to establish knowledge of reality *in its individuality* is absolutely senseless, the refraction of values in the prism of his mind gives direction to his work.[62]

This enables him to become aware of heretofore unrecognized possibilities of describing particular phenomena from particular viewpoints.

And the values to which the scientific genius relates the object of his inquiry can determine the "conception" (*Auffassung*) of a whole epoch, i.e., decide not only what is regarded as "valuable" but also what is significant or insignificant, "important" and "unimportant" in the phenomena.[63]

Historical phenomena are not described as entities existing in isolation from the rest of the world. Rather, they are descriptively placed into an individual, i.e., unique, but general, i.e., comprehensive, context.[64] Its components constitute the secondary historical individual. Its inclusion in an historical account is a result of the conception of history as a science of concrete reality. If one would merely describe the primary historical individual one would write "formal" history, i.e., trace the development of particular social institutions without making any attempt to establish the impact which their emergence and existence had on the rest of the concrete culture in question. In contrast, history as a science of concrete reality describes this impact, i.e., the *cultural significance* of these phenomena. This is not a minor difference, as Weber illustrates with an hypothetical example:

The cultural *significance* of normatively regulated legal *relations* and thus the norms themselves can undergo fundamental revolutionary changes even though the formal identity of the valid legal norms is entirely preserved. Indeed . . . one might theoretically imagine, let us say, a situation in which the "socialization of the means of production" has come about unaccompanied by any conscious "striving" towards this result, and without the disappearance or addition of a single paragraph of our legal code. Of course, the statistical frequency of each legally regulated relationship would be radically changed, in many cases reduced to zero. A great number of legal norms would become *practically* insignificant; their whole cultural significance would be changed beyond recognition.[65]

Since in history scientists deal with facts, i.e., categorically formed contents, they describe them as caused and causing.[66] Historical knowledge is, "of course, purely causal knowledge."[67] The fact that among its contents there are understandable motives does not change this in the least.[68] The causal relationships which are established in history are not general,[69] but describe individual relationships between concrete phenomena.[70] Any concrete phenomenon "represents, from the point of view of the 'nomological sciences,' an individual constellation of an infinity of distinct causal sequences...."[71] In scientific history, of course, this infinity is reduced to a finite amount. Since historians are interested in individual developments, an historical explanation consists in finding that individual constellation of elements which, due to the operation of causal laws, has to be considered as the total and individual cause of the historical individual to be explained.[72]

Every individual constellation ... of course, is causally explicable only as the consequence of another equally individual constellation which has preceded it, and however far we may go back into the gray obscurity of the most distant past—the reality *for* which the laws are valid always remains equally individual, and it is always equally *impossible to deduce* it *from* the laws.[73]

The procedure is to determine the individual cause of each element of the total effect and then to treat all these causes as a unity, i.e., *the* individual cause of the total effect. Often, common-sense knowledge is sufficient to establish the component causal relationships;[74] but in logical terms, as becomes apparent in cases in which common sense is not enough, what takes place is the application of nomological knowledge to individual constellations of facts.[75] This is what Weber refers to when he calls general concepts "means" for the establishment of historical knowledge. Thus, he states that

...the availability of unambiguous concepts and the knowledge of ... laws would obviously be of great value as a *means* for the acquisition of knowledge[76]—although *only* as such. Indeed, for this purpose they would be absolutely indispensable.[77]

6. THE VALIDITY OF HISTORICAL KNOWLEDGE

Historical knowledge is possible only as value-relevant knowledge. It is apparent that this state of affairs poses the problem of the validity of this knowledge in a specific way. For the validity of knowledge is a direct result of the general acceptance of the principle of selection in accordance with which it has been abstracted. In history, however, the principle which is in use always needs substantive specification before it can be applied, i.e., a particular value viewpoint has to be selected. Numerically, however, these specifications are not subject to any limitation. As was stated earlier, the cultural values by which an historical investigation can be legitimately guided are infinite in number insofar as it is not possible to rule out the possibility that new ones will emerge. Of course this possibility is very much compatible with the availability for historical investigation of only a limited number of such values *at any specific moment or period in time.* The question which must be asked, however, is whether this situation reduces historical knowledge to merely *empirical* validity, as Rickert calls it, or whether in some sense *absolute* validity can also be claimed for it. Rickert, as was documented in the previous chapter, argues in favor of the latter assumption.[1] As for Weber, however, this is the first instance in which there seems to be good reason to doubt his conformity with Rickert. At least this is the opinion expressed in virtually all of the secondary literature. With the notable exception of Henrich[2] there is unanimous agreement on the opinion that Rickert postulated the existence of absolutely valid values which can serve as viewpoints for historians, whereas Weber maintained that they are "subjective,"[3] thus allowing "a far-reaching subjectivism of the view of history,"[4] a "psychological, sociological, and historical 'relativization' of these value-ideas."[5] Fleischmann even says that for Weber the attempt to found history on absolutely valid values was an "absurdity."[6] However, the situation is not nearly as unambiguous as this near-unanimity might lead one to suppose.

(1) Concerning the formation of general concepts in the natural sciences, Weber says: "Finally, if in principle they[7] want to go beyond the mere classification of phenomena, their concepts have to contain potential judgments of general validity...."[8] Rickert and Weber use the term "classification" for a system of general concepts which refers to all the phenomena which are empirically known, i.e., an empirically limited number of facts only. There can be no doubt, therefore, that

Weber—at least for the natural sciences—accepts the idea of absolutely universal knowledge. He characterizes the natural sciences as those sciences which strive "to order the extensively and intensively infinite multiplicity through a system of concepts and laws which approach as much as possible universal validity."[9] Considering the systematic character of Rickert's theory which cannot have escaped Weber's attention, it would be strange if Weber had accepted the idea of absolutely valid knowledge for general concepts only. For, as this theory is built, it is possible to altogether "bracket" that part of it which deals with the problem of absolute validity (in both sciences). Rickert himself points this out and adds that this problem (i.e., absolute validity) is of no concern to the empirical scientist anyway.[10] However, it does not seem possible without being inconsistent to accept one half of this part and to reject the other.

(2) Indeed, the discussion of concept formation in history in Weber's essay on "Objectivity" is opened with a statement which rather clearly implies agreement with the notion of absolutely valid historical knowledge.

By separating "value judgment" and "empirical knowledge" on reasons of principle, we have presupposed so far that in the field of the social sciences there is indeed a kind of knowledge, i.e., an intellectual ordering of empirical reality, which is absolutely valid. This presupposition now becomes problematic insofar as we have to discuss what objective "validity" of the truth for which we strive can mean in our field.[11]

(3) Unfortunately, after having posed the question so squarely, Weber never gives an equally square answer, neither a positive one nor a negative one with respect to the relevant problem. But again, there seems to be a statement which implies such an answer.

There is no absolutely "objective" scientific analysis of culture—or put perhaps more narrowly but certainly not essentially differently for our purposes—of "social phenomena" *independent* of special and "one-sided" viewpoints according to which—expressly or tacitly, consciously or unconsciously—they are selected, analyzed and organized for expository purposes.[12]

Seemingly, Weber accepts the idea of absolutely valid historical knowledge, although with the qualification that it must always be tied to special viewpoints, and must therefore be one-sided.

(4) The following statements, which are usually taken as document-

ing the divergence between Rickert and Weber, and which were already interpreted above,[13] do *not* prove what they are supposed to
prove:

> Now, without any question are all those value-ideas "subjective." Be-
> tween the "historical" interest in a family chronicle and that in the de-
> velopment of the greatest conceivable cultural phenomena which were
> and are common to a nation or to mankind over long epochs, there exists
> an infinite gradation of "significance" arranged into an order which dif-
> fers for each of us. And equally, of course, they change historically with
> the character of the culture and the thoughts themselves which dominate
> men. But naturally it does *not* follow from this that the investigations in
> the cultural sciences can also only have *results* which are "subjective" in
> the sense that they are *valid* for one person and not valid for another. What
> changes is rather the degree to which they *interest* one and not the other.
> In other words: *Whatever* becomes the object of investigation ... is de-
> termined by the value-ideas dominating the scientist and his time; but as
> to the "How?" ... the scientist, of course, here as everywhere is bound
> to the norms of our thinking. For scientific truth is only what *wants* to
> be valid for everybody who *wants* truth.[14]

What Weber claims here is the objectivity of those historical accounts which are written with the help of "subjective" (note that
Weber himself puts "subjective" between quotation marks) value-
viewpoints. Since for Weber the objectivity of a scientific description is based on the use of an intersubjectively accepted standard of
selection, and since in history the standard of selection involves reference to value-ideas, the "subjectivity" of these value-ideas in the
present context obviously has nothing to do with a lack of objectivity
in Weber's sense. Rather, what Weber means when he calls such value-
ideas "subjective" is that it is not the material of history, the *object*,
which determines what is essential for an historical account, but the
historian, the *subject*. Unfortunately, however, he invites confusion
by talking in the same breath about two other related but different
things: the fact that different people are attracted to different topics
and viewpoints, and the fact that viewpoints change over time. Thus,
whether somebody studies his own pedigree or the Protestant Reforma-
tion in Holland is a matter of individual psychology. Not everybody
may want (psychologically) to investigate a certain topic. But if the
correct method (of forming individual concepts) is used by those who
do investigate it, this results in valid knowledge, i.e., knowledge whose
establishment is *logically* justifiable. Therefore, what Weber expresses

here in somewhat misleading terms is this: The establishment of historical knowledge is an unending undertaking, since new cultural values emerge all the time. There are a great number of things which humans want to know, whose knowledge is logically justifiable. But what part of this task is tackled at any given time is a function of the psychological make-up of the investigators, which in turn has been influenced by their cultural environments. Clearly this reasoning does not contain anything incompatible with Rickert's argument about the absolute validity of historical knowledge, but neither does it show Weber's acceptance of such a position.[15]

(5) Another statement which is adduced in support of the contention that for Weber there is no absolutely valid historical knowledge is this:

It is not the determination of the "historical" causes of a given "object" which is to be explained which is "subjective" in a certain sense which we shall not discuss here again—rather is it the delimitation of the historical "object," of the "individual" itself, for in this value-relevances are decisive whose "conception" is subject to historical change. On the one hand, it is, therefore, incorrect when Eduard Meyer asserts that we are "never" able to attain an "absolutely and unconditionally valid" knowledge of anything historical. This is not correct for the "causes" [of a selected historical individual]. On the other hand, it is equally incorrect when he then asserts that the situation is "no different" with respect to the validity of knowledge in the natural sciences from what it is in history. The latter proposition is not true for the historical "individuals," i.e., for the way in which those "values" play a role in history, nor does it hold for the modality of those "values" (regardless of one's opinion about the "validity" of those "values" as such—the "validity" of the "values" is in any case something which is different in principle from the validity of a causal relationship which is an empirical truth, even if both should in the last analysis also be conceived of philosophically as normatively bound). For the "points of view" which are oriented towards "values" ... change. ... This way of being conditioned by "subjective values" is, however, entirely alien in any case to those natural sciences which take mechanics as a model, and it constitutes, indeed, the distinctive *contrast* between the historical and the natural sciences.[16]

Obviously, as Weber states himself, this argument is compatible with an opinion in favor of, as well as with one against, the assumption of absolutely valid values. The fact that only the establishment of a phenomenon's cause is called "absolutely and unconditionally valid"[17] is here misleading. For, as becomes clear from the context in which the above statement appears, it merely refers to the fact that their establishment does not involve directly "subjective" viewpoints, since at the stage of investigation which is in question they are being taken for granted.

(6) It seems now that Weber's statements allow either one of two inferences: one is that their implications provide a sufficiently solid basis for the assumption that Weber is in agreement with Rickert in his answer to the question of the absolute validity of historical knowledge. The other, more cautious one, is that Weber deliberately refrained from taking a stand, either because he was not quite sure, or because he thought it irrelevant.

The *belief* which we all have in some form or another in the meta-empirical validity of ultimate and highest value-ideas to which we tie the meaning of our existence, does not at all exclude the incessant change-ability of the actually used viewpoints from which the empirical reality receives its significance; rather, it includes it. Life in its irrational reality and its content of *possible* meanings is inexhaustible. The selection of values for the actual establishment of value-relevances remains, therefore, in flux, ever subject to change into the hidden (*dunkel*) future of human culture.[18]

Here, it might be argued, Weber would have taken a position had he wanted to. However, except for the absence of any explicit and unambiguous statement to the contrary, there is nothing on which the assumption of a disagreement between Rickert and Weber can be based. It is, therefore, not a very strong hypothesis. It seems wisest, therefore, to stick to Weber's statement that "the epistemology of history[19] establishes and analyzes the significance of the relevance to values for historical knowledge, but it is not its task to *provide a foundation* of the validity of the values,"[20] and to assume that Weber did not *want* to take a position which in any case would have no significant consequences as far as the methodological procedures of empirical sciences are concerned.

(7) Those of the interpreters who claim that Weber did not believe in the existence of absolutely valid values have usually drawn two conclusions from this.

(a) In Weber's view, they argue, the objectivity of history cannot be based on the nature of the viewpoints in use, and, therefore, there is no objective history.[21] Tenbruck, for instance, argues that the adoption of the principle of value-relevance in Weber's framework implies an abandoning of the objectivity of history, since viewpoints are subjective. In his opinion, the argument in Weber's essay on "Objectivity" amounts to the rejection of the claim to objectivity for history.

Cultural science . . . is not objective because it is an arbitrary selection and combination of phenomena into an object which does not refer to anything objectively existing. Therefore . . . there is not even in the problematic sense a cultural science of a kind which validly represents a knowledge of culture. Within the limits of elementary facts phenomena can be arbitrarily selected, arbitrarily combined, and their causes can be arbitrarily traced. Science of culture is this unending series of possible combinations of reality.[22]

(b) Whereas the choice of the historical individual is subjective, according to the interpreters, Weber claims objectivity for the causal relationships which are established once the subject matter is determined.[23] Aron, for example, thinks that in Weber's opinion "after the subjective choice, scientific results must be obtained by procedures that are subject to verification by others."[24] He continues: "Analysis of causal determinations is one of the procedures by which the universal validity of scientific results is insured."[25] And he concludes: "If the objective of universal truth is to be attained, therefore, the subjectively conditioned frame of reference must be followed by procedures of universal validity."[26]

Alexander von Schelting, whose analysis is similar, tries to account for this alleged difference between Rickert and Weber and has to conclude that it is impossible to find out whether Weber correctly understood Rickert and rejected his reasoning, or whether he never had an adequate understanding of Rickert's thought.[27] Von Schelting tries to resolve a nonexisting problem, though. First of all, even if it were certain that Weber rejected the idea of absolutely valid values, this would still not mean the "abandoning of history as a science."[28] It would merely imply that there can be no absolutely and universally valid historical accounts. It would not imply that there cannot be empirically generally accepted historical accounts, that is, accounts which are objective in the sense that every existing historian thinks that they are worth knowing. It is this empirical objectivity alone with which the natural scientist and the historian are concerned. The problem of absolute objectivity (which concerns the epistemologist) transcends methodological considerations, and Weber speaks only as a methodologist. As a methodologist he is merely concerned with empirical objectivity. That this empirical validity of historical descriptions does indeed exist, however, Weber believes to have shown. Secondly, with regard to Weber's methodological premises, it is completely non-sensical to think that the establishment of causal relationships can be objective in Weber's sense although the selection of the historical in-dividual to be causally explained cannot. The problem of objectivity, for Weber, is one of the proper selection of a limited number of facts from empirical reality, and nothing else. It is not at all the problem of finding out what facts are causally interrelated, but the problem of deciding *what* causal relationships to describe. The assumption that Weber views whatever objectivity history has as founded on the proper use of methods for the establishment of causal interdependences, therefore, goes counter to every premise of his methodology. It is safe to say, on the basis of the discussion presented in this section, that there is no good reason to make this assumption.

The tenets of Weber's epistemology and methodology that have been presented in this chapter make up that part of his writings on the logic of science which deals with the same problems as those raised by Rickert. It seems justified to conclude that his solutions are the same, too. There is no reason, therefore, to doubt the identity of the two men's opinions on those issues with which both of them dealt. Tenbruck's claim that it is "inadequate to trace back Weber's methodo-logical efforts . . . to the influence of Neo-Kantianism. . . ."[29] must be rejected. Of course, both Rickert and Weber also treated problems to which the other paid no attention, at least in written form. As far as Rickert, these parts of his work are not of interest in the present con-text. With regard to Weber, the whole of the next chapter is devoted to their discussion.

CHAPTER III. WEBER'S ELABORATION OF RICKERT'S METHODOLOGY

1. VALUE-ANALYSIS

The previous chapter documented the extent of Weber's indebtedness to Rickert's theory of concept formation and its epistemological premises. It showed that a great number of statements, dispersed throughout Weber's essays on the logic of science, when brought into a systematic order amount to an argument which is practically identical with that of Rickert's. It was also argued that Weber—although not entirely successfully—refrained from giving a metamethodological justification of his methodology. However, this is not all there is in Weber's essays, as far as the problems of concept formation are concerned. Weber enriched and elaborated on Rickert's account. These additions concern problems which Rickert either did not discuss at all or which he did not treat systematically and in detail. But they remain within Rickert's theoretical framework, i.e., they do not involve any modifications of the assumptions on which it is built. Thus, these elaborations go beyond Rickert only in the sense that they concern problems with which for some reason Rickert did not deal, not in the sense that they introduce implicitly or explicitly altered premises.

A beginning may be made with some of Weber's considerations concerning the genetic aspect of historical investigation. It was said[1] that history is not possible without specific viewpoints from which empirical reality is differentiated into essential and inessential parts. It was also said[2] that there is no logical principle prescribing the choice of any particular of all possible viewpoints. Rather, from the point of view of logic the historian is free to choose whatever general cultural value he wants to choose. Psychologically, the situation is somewhat different. It may be remembered here that, according to Weber, the choice of viewpoints is a function of the practical values (the value-ideas) "dominating the investigator and his age."[3] This touches on the fact that, genetically, the direction taken by a scientist's historical interest typically is related to his practical pursuits as actor in everyday life. "*Because* the 'historical individual' ... in the *logical* sense can only be a 'unity' which is artificially produced through *value*-relevance, therefore, 'valuation' is a normal psychological intermediary step on the way to the 'intellectual understanding.' "[4]

The valuations of those phenomena with which historians are concerned are attached to their particular, incomparable, and unique features. "Now, without being able here to deal somewhat more closely with the nature of 'value judgments,' for our considerations in any case one point has to be emphasized: it is *the clearly determined content of the judgments* (*die Bestimmtheit des* [*Urteils-*]*inhalts*) which removes the object to which they refer from the sphere of mere 'feeling.' "[5] Through valuation, certain features of the experienced reality (sensations) become prominent, through value *judgments* they become clearly defined; their communication allows everybody to focus his attention on the same content.[6] This is how the overwhelming ambiguity of mere experience is overcome. "For in contrast to a mere 'content of feelings' we call a 'value' just that, and only that, which can become the content of a position which we take, of an articulate, conscious, positive and negative 'judgment'. . . ."[7]

The formation of an historical concept usually is not a step which immediately follows valuation. There is an intermediary level which Weber calls "value-interpretation"[8] or "value-analysis."[9] He says that

... valuation of the object in its individual particularity supplies the reason that the phenomenon becomes an object of *reflection* and of—at this point we will deliberately avoid saying "scientific"—intellectual treatment, that is, it becomes an object of *interpretation* (*Interpretation*). . . . Interpretation can and does become first "value-interpretation" (*Wertinterpretation*), i.e., it teaches us to "understand" the "meaningful" (geistig) content of [the phenomenon in question] . . . ; it develops and raises to the level of articulate "valuation" that which we "feel" dimly and vaguely. For this purpose, interpretation is not at all required to enunciate or to "suggest" a *value judgment*. What it actually "suggests" in the course of analysis is rather various *possibilities* of *relating* the object to values.[10]

This "value-analysis",[11] i.e., the establishment of all the values to which it is possible to relate a given phenomenon,[12] does not yield scientific historical knowledge as it is defined by Weber. For it is not the account of the causal historical development of an individual culturally significant phenomenon.[13] This does not mean, though, that such attempts "to uncover the *possible* 'value-viewpoints' and 'aspects' (*Angriffspunkte*) to which 'values' can be attached"[14] do not result in any knowledge whatsoever. But such knowledge is philosophical rather than scientific. A value-analysis provides knowledge for a person

... in the sense that it, as we say, extends his own inner "life" and his "mental and spiritual (*geistig*) horizon," and makes him capable of comprehending and thinking through the possibilities and nuances of life-style and to develop his own self intellectually, aesthetically, and ethically (in the widest sense) in a differentiated way—or, in other words, to make his "psyche" more "sensitive to values," so-to-speak—. . . . Here, however, we reach the outermost edge of what can still be called "treatment of the empirical world in thought"; there is here no longer a concern with "historical work" in the logical sense of the word.[15]

For the purpose of logic, the function of value-analysis lies in the fact that through it possible value-relevances are brought to the attention of the investigator. It provides him with a choice among several different individual constellations of facts, selected from the same concrete phenomenon in which several different cultural values can be found embodied.

And obviously, that type of "interpretation" which we have here called "value-analysis" functions as a guide for this other "historical" i.e., causal type of "interpretation." The former type of analysis reveals the "valued" components of the object, the causal "explanation" of which is the problem of the latter type of analysis. The former creates the points of attachment from which there are to be regressively traced the web of causal connections and thus provides causal analysis with the decisive "viewpoints" without which it would indeed have to operate, as it were, without a compass on an uncharted sea.[16]

Once the historian has decided to make a particular constellation of facts, the embodiment of a particular value, the object of his investigation, i.e., once he has adopted a particular point of view, the realm of value-analysis is left altogether. The task now is the description of the empirical causal development of the selected constellation of facts which embodies, for the scientific observers, a particular value. The meaning which, for the purpose at hand, the concrete phenomenon has for them, that is, the values which they find embodied in it, is taken for granted. It provided the justification for its selection. The description of the historical development considers solely what the historical actors themselves had in their minds when they contributed to the creation and maintenance of the phenomenon in question. Partly these were values identical with those to which the observing scientists in each case relate concrete reality,[17] partly these were different values. What they were, of course, has to be empirically established in each case. Substantively, this begins as a means-end analysis. "All thinking reflection about the ultimate elements of meaningful human conduct is at first required to use the categories 'end' and 'means.' Concretely, we want something either 'for its own sake' or as a means of getting what we ultimately want."[18] Empirical analysis begins with this schema because what fits into it empirically is easiest to establish. From there the investigation proceeds to the other empirical elements.

2. CULTURAL SIGNIFICANCE

The discussion of value-analysis is not the only context in which Weber makes mention of the genetic aspect of concept formation in history. It is also referred to in several statements in which he talks of the "(cultural) significance" of the phenomena which are described by historians. Thus he says that history "concerns itself with the question of the *individual* consequences which the operation of . . . laws in a *unique configuration* produces, since it is these individual configurations which are *significant* for us."[1] It must be indicated here that in Rickert's argumentation such considerations concerning the cultural significance of phenomena are rather more implicit than explicit. Approaching methodology in terms of a means-end analysis, he develops the principles of concept formation as means to reach certain goals; the means are justified as long as the goals are legitimate. It is not the task of methodology proper to investigate the legitimacy of the goals themselves, though. The factual consensus of all those concerned, that the goal of, e.g., history, is the establishment of knowledge of phenomena in their uniqueness is sufficient for the purposes of methodology. It is possible to go beyond this and to provide a philosophical, i.e., *meta-methodological*, justification of the goals of science taken for granted in methodology itself by showing that the conception of perfect knowledge makes the particular goals of history and natural science necessary (as the closest humanly possible approximations to perfect knowledge). Rickert does so;[2] Weber, in contrast, does not want to deal with this problem at all. With reference to history, he says:

For the reasoning which remains strictly methodological, the fact that certain *individual* components of reality are selected as the objects of historical treatment can be justified absolutely only by pointing to this *factual* existence of a corresponding interest; indeed, for such a reasoning which does not ask the question of the *sense* (*Sinn*) of this interest, the 'relevance to values' cannot mean anything else. . . ."[3]

He is satisfied with the factual agreement of the scientists in each field on the goals of their respective sciences, as far as the logical aspects of this situation are concerned. Nevertheless, he does not treat these goals as ultimate data. However, their formal philosophical derivation is replaced by a reference to their *origin*: humans are interested in knowing individual constellations of facts because they are significant for them.

Weber was probably not aware of the fact that he gave his logical argument a genetic twist at the end. For "(cultural) significance" designates not only the *psychological cause* of the selection of a particular phenomenon for the purpose of historical description. It also refers to the *logical reason* for the validity of this description as a scientific account of empirical reality. In many cases, as in the quotation at the beginning of this section, it is impossible to decide what the referent really is. But this is not all. For whereas, according to some statements, it is *due* to their significance that humans want to know the individuality of certain phenomena, there are other instances in which Weber declares that knowledge of the (cultural) significance of phenomena is the *goal* of historical investigation.[4]

The kind of social science in which *we* want to engage, is a *science of concrete reality*. Our aim is the understanding *in its particularity* of the reality of the life around us in which we move—on the one hand, the interrelations between, and the cultural *significance* of, its individual phenomena in their contemporary manifestations; on the other hand, the causes of their having become historically *so* and not *otherwise*.[5]

For the sake of clarity in the following exposition, let "cultural significance" in its latter meaning be designated by the superscript G (for "goal"), in its psychological meaning by the superscript P, and in its logical meaning by L. It is easy to distinguish "significance^G" from the other two, but often impossible to decide whether in a particular instance Weber has "cultural significance^P" or "cultural significance^L" in mind. When the term is given the latter meaning, the argument in which it occurs assumes logical character; "significant" equals "essential" in the logical sense. Thus, humans want to know individual configurations of phenomena since they are essential components of an account of the world, since they are worth knowing. When "significant" is interpreted as "significant^P," then the argument in which it occurs has to be taken as psychological or anthropological: men want to know unique constellations of facts as a consequence of their (psychic) dispositions.

The fact that Weber does indeed use the term in both meanings, "significant^L" and "significant^P" can be documented by a few unambiguous statements. Thus, "significant^L" occurs in the following quotation: "Sometimes every historical event which is *not* explicable by the invocation of economic motives is regarded *for that very reason* as a scientifically insignificant 'accident.' "[6] "Significant^P" occurs in the following statement:

> The quality of an event as a "social-economic" event is not something which it possesses "objectively." Rather, it has this quality as a result of the direction which our *interest* in knowledge takes. This direction is derived from the specific cultural significance which we attribute to the particular event in a given case. Wherever an event of the cultural life, in those parts of its individuality on which its specific *significance* for us is based, is related to the production and distribution of scarce goods, it can involve a problem for the social sciences.[7]

Or elsewhere, Weber says that

> ... knowledge of *cultural* events is inconceivable execpt on a basis of the *significance* which the concrete constellations of reality have for us in certain *individual* concrete situations. In *which* sense and in *which* situation this is the case is not revealed to us by any law; it is decided according to *value-ideas* in the light of which we view "culture" in each case. "Culture" is a finite segment of the meaningless infinity of the world process, a segment on which *human beings* confer meaning and significance.[8]

In the great majority of all instances it is impossible to decide which meaning—"significant^L" or "significant^P"—Weber has in mind. This lack of discrimination on Weber's part is rather easy to understand. One only has to remember that, on the one hand, those phenomena whose individuality is interesting to everybody are always cultural phenomena which have a meaning for humans. On the other hand, cultural phenomena are those which in practical life have values attached to them, are valued by practical actors. Humans, therefore, are existentially involved in them, and this is the (psychological) cause of their efforts to establish knowledge of them. Weber says that "those highest 'values' underlying the *practical* interest [of human actors] are and always will be decisively significant[9] in determining the *direction* into which the ordering activity of our thinking in the sphere of the cultural sciences goes in each case."[10] As long as the values embodied in the phenomena are general cultural values of the community of which the historian is a member, the description of these phenomena in their individuality inevitably constitutes valid historical knowledge. For these phenomena are value-relevant from the point of view of the value embodied in them, and, therefore, essential. Thus, whatever is "significant^P" also is—from some value-viewpoint—essential ("significant^L") and *vice versa.* Weber fails to analyze this relationship, and due to the fact that he can use the same word for different purposes, he creates a terminological and logical chaos. Take this example:

The concept of culture is a *value-concept.* Empirical reality *becomes* "culture"[11] for us because and insofar as we relate it to value-ideas. It includes those—and *only* those—components of reality which have become *significant* to us because of this value-relevance. Only a miniscule portion of the individual reality under consideration in each case is colored by our interest which is derived from those value-ideas; this portion alone is significant to us. It is significant because it reveals relationships which are *important* to us due to their connection with value ideas. Only because and to the extent that this is the case is it worthwhile for us to know it in its individual particularity. We cannot discover, however, *what* is significant for us by means of a "presuppositionless" investigation of empirical data. Rather, the establishment of what is to be significant [by selecting a point of view] to us is the precondition for something to become the *object* of investigation. Of course, that which is significant as such does not coincide with any law as such, either. . . .[12]

In view of such statements it is indeed fortunate that the two arguments involved, the logical one and the anthropological one, are complementary and not contradictory. Often it does not make much difference whether "significant" means "logically essential" or "emotionally interesting" ("significant^P").[13] The simple idea behind the terminological confusion becomes apparent. According to Weber, humans as cultural beings are existentially involved in the creation, maintenance, and destruction of particular concrete phenomena and their consequences. Humans, therefore, develop a particular interest in these phenomena as a result of which they undertake to establish knowledge of them and their development through the course of history.[14] This knowledge is objectively valid since it is about phenomena which everybody wants to know due to his involvement in his culture. These phenomena are significant in both senses. In the light of these considerations it seems that Dieter Henrich's contention, that Weber has replaced Rickert's logical foundation of methodology in the cultural sciences by an anthropological one, is exaggerated.[15] For Weber's argument is complementary, not alternative. Furthermore, Rickert's own theory requires anthropological assumptions of the same kind. The discussion of the problem of value-relevance in chapter one has made this rather obvious.[16]

Humans are induced to investigate historical phenomena because these are cultural phenomena to whose existence, or to the existence of whose consequences, men are positively or negatively committed. Because of their existential involvement in the creation of culture as humans, and, therefore, as cultural beings, they want to know them *as meaningful phenomena, as* embodiments of values. These phenomena do not exist in isolation but are causally related to other meaningful phenomena; they are caused by some, and they are also causes of others. Meaningful phenomena, as cultural phenomena, exist only because humans want to implement certain values. The description of the origin and maintenance of such phenomena, therefore, involves reference to human "motives." Since motives belong to that part of empirical reality which can be "understood," the desired causal explanations of history require "meaningful interpretation" of what motivated actors.[17] Furthermore, every historical account which includes the description of the causal relationships of which the events under consideration are part, involves an assessment of the impact which the efforts to implement certain values have had on other phenomena. This is what Weber calls the description of the "cultural significance G" of phenomena. It is an account of their significance for the wider culture of which they are part[18] and its development, of their causal importance in modifying or perpetuating other phenomena, and of the degree to which they characterize the spirit of the culture as a whole. Weber gives an example:

The *generic features* of exchange, purchase, etc., interest the jurist—as far as we [historians] are concerned, our task is the analysis of just that *cultural significance* of the *historical* fact that today exchange exists on a mass scale. When this is to be explained, when we wish to understand what *distinguishes* our social-economic culture from, e.g., that of antiquity, in which, of course, exchange showed precisely the same generic traits as it does today, in other words, when we raise the questions as to where the *significance* of "money economy" lies, logical principles of quite heterogeneous derivation [from those used in the natural sciences] enter into the investigation.[19]

There is yet another usage of "significant," namely when it occurs in the combination "causally significant."[20] Its meaning cannot be understood without some knowledge of Weber's notion of "adequate causation." This notion—which Weber took over from the physiologist von Kries—was developed in response to the problem of determining the historical causes of a concrete phenomenon. The question is: Which ones of the infinitely many events occurring at the time t_1 were necessary for a particular event to occur at t_2? To answer this question, it must be asked in the case of each event occurring at t_1 whether the particular event at t_2 would have occurred even if the event in question at t_1 had not occurred, or occurred in a different way. E.g., did the American Revolution happen because of the Boston Tea Party in conjunction with a certain number of other factors, or would it also have happened without it? An event at t_1 whose occurrence is thus necessary for the subsequent existence of the concrete event in question at t_2 is "causally significant," the event at t_2 is "adequately caused" by it in conjunction with all the other causally significant events at t_1. This means

... that certain components of the reality which preceded the result in time *thought* in isolation, in accordance with empirical generalizations *generally* "favor" a result of the type in question. This means, however, as we know, that this result is usually brought about by these components in the majority of the conceivably possible combinations with other conditions, while certain other components *generally* do not cause this result but a different one. When Eduard Meyer, for example, says of cases where ... "Everything *pressed* toward a certain result" ... what is meant ... is simply that we can observe causal "factors," and can isolate them in *thought*, to which the expected result has to be thought as being *adequately* related, since we can *conceive* of only relatively few combinations of these factors with other causal "factors" from which—in accordance with *empirical generalizations*—another result could be "expected." [21]

3. *VERSTEHEN*

Weber's theory of concept formation in the historical sciences depends on the fact that humans embody cultural values in certain phenomena. Without this, there would be neither a desire nor a logical possibility for the establishment of historical knowledge. Those phenomena to which humans attach values thereby become "meaningful." It is immediately obvious from everything that was said about individual concepts, that every historical description necessarily contains such meaningful elements. For only those phenomena validly become the object of historical investigation in which general cultural values are incorporated.[1] This is so because everybody is interested in knowing them, and as was just seen, the source of this interest is the nature of human involvement in the collective cultural concerns of the social group. Therefore, everybody is interested in knowing them *as* embodiments of cultural values, as meaningful phenomena. Since this interest is an historical one, everybody wants to know their historical development and cultural significance.[2]

The knowledge which scientists are striving for in history thus involves knowledge of human actors' "inner states." For it is these "inner states" of actors, i.e., their motives, plans, affects, emotions, etc., which *cause* their actions and thereby give these actions their *subjective* meanings.[3] Knowledge of such "inner states" and therewith the meanings of actions and objects in conjunction with which such inner states occur has usually been called "understanding" (*Verstehen*).[4] In contrast to understanding stands the "grasping" (*Begreifen*) of meaningless facts, i.e., those which are not, or cannot, be treated as having some human actor's inner states concerned with their creation or maintained existence.

The distinction between meaningful and meaningless contents of consciousness coincides with that between events going on "within" humans, in their minds, and those occurring "without" them, outside their minds.[5] The former are thoughts, emotions, ideas, feelings, etc., the latter are physical things and processes, i.e., "nature." In this context, the opposite of nature is "culture" as a *concrete* phenomenon, i.e., the sum total of all meaningful events. "Culture" in this sense must be distinguished from "culture" in the logical sense, i.e., that part of reality which is subjected to the formation of individual concepts.

Since the scientific interests of historians have their focus on the embodiment of cultural values in concrete phenomena, meaningful, i.e., understandable, elements make up a prominent part of any historical description. According to Weber, therefore, understanding is the specific aim[6] of the historical sciences.[7] For the principle of value-relevance leads the researcher to focus on social groups and the actions of their members, whose significance can be shown only through an understanding of the values held by the individuals.[8] Acknowledging thus the necessity of *Verstehen*, the problem to which Weber addresses himself is the clarification of its "logical status,"[9] the clarification of the relationship between interpretive knowledge and meaningful concrete reality. He asks how a meaningful content of the consciousness is *known* and states: "How this is done, however, is the only thing which is relevant for the assessment of the logical nature of knowledge gained in an 'interpretive' way, and it is this alone with which we shall here continue to deal."[10] His reason for undertaking this was that time and again the fact that meaningful elements are understood had been used as a basis for claims to the extent that there is a difference between historical and natural sciences as far as the *methodological principles* are concerned which govern the establishment of knowledge in each of these fields. Weber radically opposed any such arguments which postulated a special *method* of understanding. Pragmatically, he pointed out that meaningful phenomena can be treated, and indeed are treated, in a generalizing fashion, i.e., in a way which supposedly fits only "natural" phenomena. But the crucial point is that within the framework of his methodology and, more specifically, his theory of concept formation, there is no reason to accord meaningful phenomena a special status with regard to logic.[11] For his argument is entirely formal and, therefore, applies to all kinds of contents of consciousness, whether meaningful or not.[12] "Understanding" is merely the phenomenologically distinct mode in which one "has" meaningful contents in the mind, whereas "grasping" is the phenomenologically distinct mode in which humans have meaningless contents in the mind.[13] This is *not* a logical operation; it is not a *method of abstraction.*

Weber's refusal to view *Verstehen* as a special method of abstraction shows arguments like Georg Weippert's to be completely unfounded. Weippert, noting that Weber acknowledges the special quality of the objects of history,[14] claims that as a result, Rickert's doctrine experiences a significant alteration. "Only as long as he adhered strictly to Rickert's standpoint could Max Weber say that the particularity of history is derived from the individual's interest in knowledge. At the moment at which understanding receives a leading role, however, the particular quality of the object cannot be denied any longer."[15] Weippert overlooks the facts (1) that *Verstehen* for Weber is not a logical procedure, is not a method of abstraction, and, therefore, cannot yield a characterization of the logical particularity of history, and (2) that a subject matter which is meaningful characterizes history *only* due to the historian's interests in the particularity of phenomena, *not* because a meaningful object arouses only historical interests. He is, therefore, mistaken in contrasting Rickert's formal-theoretical approach (which neglects the qualities of the object under study) and Weber's "objectivism" (which takes them into account).[16] For Rickert as well as for Weber *Verstehen* has no *logical* significance. (Rickert's later statements on the topic were made after Weber's death and are without significance in the present context.[17]) The elements of reality which are to go into an historical account are determined by a different principle, derived from the *aim* of knowledge. Von Schelting and Andreas Walther claim that the postulate of *Verstehen* does have logical significance since it requires the establishment of understandable causal links in history, and thereby prohibits explanations other than those referring to the motives of individuals.[18] This is not correct, though. The limits in these cases are imposed by the historian's desire to know the meaningful parts of reality. Of course, they can be known only since they can be understood. However, not everything that *can* be understood also *is to be* understood. Only what is value-relevant, and thereby worth knowing, is to be understood. Only in this sense is *Verstehen* the specific aim of history. Its justification is entirely based on the presence of a particular interest, and the nature of the principle of abstraction connected with this interest (as von Schelting himself realizes).[19] Theodore Abel, therefore, errs when he says that Weber's postulate of *Verstehen* "could only be rejected if the proof were given that the subjective side of human behavior, i.e., the motives and intentions of actions, could be dispensed with and the explanation of behavior still complete. But such a proof has not been forthcoming."[20] *Verstehen* is necessary because historians are not interested in nonmeaningful events. In this sense, *Verstehen* may be seen as a directive to look for certain substantive aspects of action.[21]

Whenever Weber, in his essays on the logic of science, deals with understanding, the thrust of his argument denies it any special methodological status.[22] It is, therefore, entirely unjustifiable to count Weber among the champions of a special method of *Verstehen*, as Tenbruck and Freund do.[23] The opposite is true. The fact that Weber called his sociology "interpretive" (*verstehend*) must not be misinterpreted. It was primarily intended to indicate that its concepts always make reference to actors' subjective meanings which are connected with the phenomena designated by the concepts. It does *not* imply that *Verstehen* is a method.

It is undoubtedly the case that Weber attaches more significance to *Verstehen* than Rickert does. The question is whether this can be explained as a differential relative emphasis of the practical researcher and the philosopher, respectively, or whether it has systematic significance. Dieter Henrich has advanced an interesting argument in favor of the latter assumption. His starting point is that history as a science, according to Weber, exists, and is possible at all only because it is a basic characteristic of human individuals that they can adopt values as valid guides for their own practical conduct,[24] and also have the potential to consistently act in accordance with them, that is, to be *rational*.[25] They are not helplessly subject to irresistible affects, but with some effort they can overcome them.[26] Orienting their actions toward their values they create cultural phenomena, that is meaningful phenomena. These phenomena become the object of history because the historian, as a human being himself involved in cultural concerns, can adopt value-viewpoints and can understand cultural phenomena. In short: he can have knowledge of the meaning of cultural phenomena. In Henrich's view, Weber, struggling to establish the possibility of history, finds it in the possibility of understanding. "Justification of the objectivity [of history] for him is the demonstration of the possibility to acquire knowledge of reality, in the case of methodology, to name and analyze methods by which one can get access to the given reality."[27] Understanding is such a method. "That acquisition of knowledge of reality which is based on the identity of the subject and the object of knowledge, Max Weber calls 'understanding.' "[28] The essential precondition for any possible understanding is the feature of human action, to be oriented toward values, and thus a certain anthropology. According to Henrich, therefore, the foundation of Weber's methodology of the cultural sciences is really an anthropology. This is why Weber does not explicitly deal with the problem of the absolute validity of values: for him, the objectivity of history is not endangered by the possible absence of such absolute validity.

It is true that Max Weber's methodology has as its starting point a logical distinction between natural science and cultural science. This logical distinction, however, has its foundation in an anthropological characterization of human existence in contrast to nature: Man is essentially rational. He has the necessary tendency to actualize his reason in culture.[29]

The anthropology underlying the doctrine of *Verstehen* and the whole methodology is presented in terms of Rickertian concepts and also is not necessarily opposed to Rickert's logical argument. It is Weber's original intention, however, and not taken over from Rickert. For Henrich, then, this anthropology is the single principle in which the theoretical unity of Weber's essays lies, which establishes the originality of his methodology, and its break with Rickert and the whole Neo-Kantian tradition.

With regard to the fact that underlying Weber's methodological arguments there are certain assumptions about the nature of man, Henrich is undoubtedly correct. As a matter of fact, his insight is one of the few valuable contributions toward a better interpretation of Weber's work which has emerged from the vast secondary literature. But whether this fact has the methodological significance attributed to

by which "quality" (....
 or otherwise) i,
3. VERSTEHEN 107 comh f

it by Henrich seems doubtful. The core problem of Weber's methodology is not the analysis of methods by which one can get access
to the concrete reality, but the analysis of procedures of abstraction.
Understanding is *not* such a method of abstraction. Therefore, it cannot be the basis of the objectivity of historical knowledge. Weber
does not deal with the problem of absolute values, *not* because he
separates methodology from its epistemological connections and bases
it on an anthropology, as Henrich claims.[30] Rather, the reason is that
from the methodological point of view—and this is the one adopted by
Weber—the only thing that is important is the *empirical* validity of
the values guiding historical research, not their absolute validity. It is
true that the methodological argument presupposes a particular image
of man, but it does so in Rickert's theory as well as in Weber's, as the
discussion of Rickert's conception of value-relevance in the first chapter of the present essay has made obvious.[31] The only difference seems
to be one of relative emphasis. As to the originality of Weber's anthropological considerations, this impression to a degree seems to be a
result of the fact that Rickert has been relatively neglected by interpreters and nobody has ever bothered to spell out the anthropology
implied in his methodological and philosophical writings.

It is safe to say, as a matter of fact, that Weber did not pay much
attention to understanding at all. He took it as a fact that historians
are able to understand—within certain limits and to different degrees, of
course. It also was his conviction that history to a large degree had to
report meaningful phenomena which historians had to understand.
But there is no indication that the problems of a theory of understanding were of much concern to him. For although he noted the absence
of such a theory,[32] he himself in no way made any attempts in this direction. His few remarks on this topic cannot be considered such.
Furthermore, from the statements which Weber does make, his conception of understanding cannot be easily inferred.[33] It is the task of
this section to piece this conception together, as far as possible. The
approach thereby cannot be in doubt. For if interpretive knowledge,
as it was claimed, is merely a phenomenologically distinct mode of
knowledge of a certain kind of facts, that is, not a special way of abstracting, but a special way of *having* a particular kind of mental content, then everything which Weber said about knowledge in general
must also apply to interpretive knowledge.

Knowledge, for Weber, is having formed contents in the mind. It
has been shown that in his epistemology he distinguishes between the

level of sensations (unformed contents, immediate experiences), facts (categorically formed ideas of sensations), and methodologically formed facts (concepts). It has also been noted that he is not all too concerned in his formulations with the proper distinction between facts and science, so that it sometimes sounds as if in his conception scientific knowledge results from giving a conceptual form to sensations. A reading of his statements on understanding shows that the same ambiguity reigns here, too. But this must not become a cause of confusion in the solution of the problem as to how understanding fits into, or is related to, this tripartition. The question which must be asked, then, is whether *Verstehen* for Weber refers to forming a content of one's consciousness, or whether it refers to a particular mode in which a content—formed or not—is in the consciousness. It seems that Weber uses the term in the latter sense. When he states that *Verstehen* is "re-experiencing" or "having empathy,"[34] this does not refer to a formative process, a process of abstraction. It describes phenomenologically the particular mode in which humans have meaningful contents in the consciousness, as it is contrasted to the *Begreifen* of meaningless contents.[35]

In view of Weber's general theory of knowledge, one should then expect to encounter understood contents not only on the level of scientific or factual knowledge, but also as still unformed sensations. This is indeed the case. There are places where Weber talks of " 'immediately' understandable" psychic events.[36] This, of course, raises the question as to how humans acquire these contents when they are not their own "inner" states but those of other persons, i.e., when they do not understand themselves, but others. They can certainly not perceive them through their sensory apparatus. An answer to this question requires finding out what is taking place, in Weber's conception, when humans "re-experience" another person's inner states, or have "empathy" with him.

Human "inner states" and events Weber calls ("inner") "experiences" (*Erlebnisse*). "Experiences" in this sense must not be confused with the "experiences" in the epistemological meaning of the term: the undifferentiated, formless sensations. In the present context, "(inner) experiences" are meaningful contents of the human psyche, in contrast to the physical reality "outside" humans. As such, they may be either formed, i.e., be known, or unformed, on the level of sensations. Thus, Weber seems to make a subdivision within consciousness: One —unnamed—part in which occur those contents which are identified as the physical "outside" world, the other—the "psyche"—which contains a person's "inner," meaningful experiences, i.e., that which he feels himself.[37] This psyche, however, not only contains a person's own "inner" states, but also those of others, which the person "re-experiences."[38] To "understand" another person, therefore, is to have this person's "inner" states as contents in one's own psyche. In a literal sense, however, this is impossible. For a person's inner states are private, they are not directly accessible to others. Thus, they themselves cannot be the content of anybody else's psyche.

In this situation, the only available alternative is to assume that a person, when understanding another, uses his own private inner experiences as substitutes for those of the other person which are not directly accessible to him. This process may occur without any reflection and remain on the level of sensation; it may also be more or less conscious and deliberate. In this case it is an aspect of a process of formation and best called "interpreting" (deuten).[39] Weber's general position can be inferred from statements of his declaring that certain inner states of another person cannot be understood by somebody who is not accessible to such inner experiences himself.[40] The problem thus becomes gaining a clear idea of the particulars of this conception. The greatest difficulty here is immediately obvious: the statement that a person's psyche has a certain meaningful content, e.g., ire or a multiplication of two numbers, means that this person is irate or is computing. Thus, when the observer substitutes his own inner states for those of the observed individual, it seems that the observer would have to be irate or computing, in this example. This, of course, is not Weber's opinion.

For we undoubtedly "understand" the irrational dynamics of the most unrestricted "affects" as well as we "understand" the occurrence of rational "considerations;" when it is adequately "interpreted" (gedeutet), we are able in principle to re-experience the actions and feelings of the criminal and the genius just as the actions of the "average man," although we are aware that we were never able to experience them ourselves.[41]

In other words, one can understand, e.g., that somebody feels extremely hostile toward a person, although he himself would never be able to feel as hostile, or hostile at all, toward this person.

It seems that this last statement contradicts the earlier one, that one can understand certain inner states of other persons only when one himself is accessible to them. But disregarding this for the moment, it can be said on the basis of this last consideration that the following idea appears to underlie Weber's statements: a person's psyche contains events which are this person's own subjective inner experiences; his own being is involved. This is the case, e.g., when he wants to do something, or when he is sad, etc. When he understands another individual who, for instance is sad, the observer's psyche also contains sadness. However, it is not the sadness of the individual who is understood, but the sadness which the understanding person feels when he himself *is* sad, only this time *not felt as his own*, but *imputed to the other person*. His own being is not involved. In this sense the understanding person's inner states, dissected from his own existence, function as a substitute for those occurring in the person who is understood. This is what Weber seems to mean by "re-experiencing" and "empathy"[42] or " 'inner' *re*creation"[43] of somebody else's subjective states.[44]

This interpretation is compatible with the statement that a person's capacity for understanding is a function of the inner experiences which he can have himself. But now that other statement of Weber's has to be fitted in, namely that one can understand a genius or a criminal without himself being able to *be* a genius or a criminal. This task can be accomplished by a slight modification and elaboration of the previous argument. So far, inner states have been treated as wholes, but it is entirely in line with Weber's general theory of knowledge to consider them as complexes of elements, and Weber himself does just this. So it now has to be said that, in order to be able to understand a (complex) inner state of another person, one must have experienced its *constituent elements* himself. This provides the solution to the problem of understanding a genius.

That a constellation of psychic "elements"—whatever we may understand by this last term—whose quality and intensity is extremely variable and which due to innumerable complications and relations among each other and to the always individually structured external situation occur in an absolutely infinite variety of combinations as far as their *meaning* is concerned, constitutes for us something unique which in its uniqueness is valued by us as "genius," but nevertheless does not contain any absolutely unknown "elements," in itself does not appear to be particularly difficult to explain at all. In any case this does not seem to be more difficult to explain than the fact that each of us continuously shows himself capable of "experiencing" inside something qualitatively "new."[45]

Weber's theory of understanding as re-experiencing—as far as it can be extrapolated and reconstructed from his few dispersed remarks

—of course has many loose ends. Before the interpretation is continued, it may be useful to mention the two most important questions which remain open within Weber's own framework. The first concerns the status of the emotions, affect, feelings, etc., which a person attaches to his actions, making them thereby meaningful. What is their kind of existence? Weber does not give an answer.[46] It may be that he conceives of them in analogy to the way in which he conceives of values, thinking that humans accept them as valid and try to embody them in concrete reality. But this is only a speculation. The second question concerns the way in which a person's own inner experiences are used for the purposes of understanding and interpretation. Are they separated from his own self, disassembled into elements, and kept in a psychic memory bank, something like an armory of inner states, in order to be activated when they are needed for the purposes of understanding? Again, an answer to this question could only be a speculation; Weber himself is silent on that matter.

So far understanding has been treated only as it is re-experiencing, the constitution of a particular kind of content in the human consciousness. Now its scientific treatment has to be considered. Giving a meaningful content the form of a judgment Weber calls "interpretation" (*Deutung*), or also "interpretive understanding" (*deutendes Verstehen*). An interpretation is "the imposition (*Zumutung*) of a judgment in the sense of the acknowledgement of an *empirical* interrelationship as a validly 'understood one' "[47] Unfortunately, Weber often uses the terms "interpret" and "understand" synonymously, with the inevitable result of terminological and theoretical confusion on the part of the reader. Thus, he equates "empathy" and "re-experiencing" with "interpretive understanding,"[48] calls "interpretation" an "absolutely secondary category which has its home in the artificial world of science,"[49] calls "understanding" an "interpretive grasp" (*deutende Erfassung*),[50] but also says that there is understanding whose purpose is not to produce a "theoretical interpretation."[51] In this situation it is necessary to realize that "understanding" denotes the mode in which humans "have" meaningful contents on any level of consciousness, whereas "interpreting" always refers to the "having" of such contents in form of a judgment.[52] For a correct assessment of Weber's ideas about understanding it is, therefore, vital to determine in each case in which there is reference to understanding whether it is used to denote the constitution of meaningful contents, i.e., "inner" states, in the consciousness, or whether it is used to denote the formulation of judgments, whose contents are ideas of such meaningful contents, given on the level of sensations.

The insight that the meaningful interpretation of empirical facts in history involves the same process of forming reality as the acquisition of knowledge of facts which do not have meanings attached to them means that the same categorical and methodological forms are applicable to everything empirical. Understanding (in the form of judgments, that is, interpretation) and causal knowledge, therefore, are not mutually exclusive, as has sometimes been claimed. On the contrary, Weber argues, the former requires the latter, for the principle of causality is "the precondition of all science."[53] For instance, when the occurrence of certain events is ascribed to certain motives of human actors, understanding takes the form of an interpretation establishing causal knowledge.[54] Interpretive understanding in history, for Weber, always is causal understanding, the understanding of meaningful mental events occurring in human individuals as the results of previous (mental or nonmental) events, and as the causes of later ones. It is not the understanding of meaning alone, detached from the things and processes in conjunction with which it occurs, but always of meaning as a spatio-temporal event, as attached to a "substratum." Von Schelting criticizes Weber for limiting the role of interpretive understanding in history to such causal understanding and insists that an understanding of pure complexes of timeless meaning-structures plays an important role in history.[55] He asserts that such meanings, abstracted from the concrete thought-acts in which they occur, have nothing to do with causality.[56] Since Weber himself in his substantive works deals with such meaning, according to von Schelting, Weber's theory of understanding is too restrictive.[57] This argument, although repeated by many interpreters, is not very insightful. For it seems that Weber, when he describes such complexes of meaning as parts of historical accounts, intends to describe them as a set of actual spatio-temporal mental occurrences, and *not* as pure structures of meaning divorced from the minds in which they exist. To interpret them otherwise, as von Schelting does, is not correct.

Naturally, descriptions of meaningful events are not possible without methodological forms. Interpretive *knowledge*, like all knowledge of a scientific nature, *has to* be in the form of *concepts*, and it *can* be in individual as well as in general form. This is explicitly stated by

Weber.[58] The following statement, therefore, does not postulate the incompatibility of understanding and generalization:

The interpretation of the historian, however, does not appeal to our ability to order "facts" as instances into general class concepts and formulas, but to our familiarity with the task which confronts us daily, namely to "understand" individual human conduct in its motives. Of course, the hypothetical "interpretations" which our empathic "understanding" offers us, are verified by reference to "experience."[59]

The only things which are contrasted in this quotation are the *historian's* understanding and the formulation of general concepts. For by definition, the historian's interpretation concerns unique events. It is in accordance with this that the following statement has to be interpreted:

. . . in the social sciences[60] we are concerned with the fact that among the relevant events there are *psychic* (*geistig*) processes whose "*understanding*" through re-experiencing naturally is a task which is specifically different from the one which the formulas of the exact natural sciences can or try at all to accomplish.[61]

The presentation of Weber's ideas about understanding is complicated by the fact that he states them in connection with considerations concerning the "certainty" (*Evidenz*) of interpretative knowledge.[62] "Each interpretation, like all science in general, strives for 'certainty.' "[63] In order to understand how this statement fits in with what has been said so far, it is necessary again to go back to the earlier discussion of Weber's general theory of knowledge. It must be remembered that for Weber, knowledge consists in having formed ideas of sensations, i.e., judgments, in the mind. In this conception, "having" has to be taken quite literally. It is really thought as a state of having absorbed or incorporated a content, namely sensations. The pure "stuff" or material of knowledge has been grasped by a receptive agent. The feeling of certainty in an observer results when he "has" the stuff.[64] In an epistemology which does not ascribe an active role to the mind in the acquisition of knowledge, the feeling of certainty might, therefore, be treated as an indicator of the presence of the "stuff" in the mind, that is, of knowledge. Weber, however, insists that knowledge involves giving forms to contents in response to the acceptance of the value of truth. Thus, the feeling of certainty, for him, cannot function as a reliable indicator of knowledge.[65] Weber is very clear about this and emphasizes that "this 'certainty' of the 'meaningfully' understood

event must be carefully kept separate from any connection to 'validity.' "[66] For "validity" refers to the general acceptance of a form-
content combination. It depends on the use of the proper methodological means and has nothing to do with a subjective feeling of certainty
concerning the grasp of a mental content. Thus, the following statement is in full agreement with the foregoing interpretation of re-
experiencing": "The ability to completely 're-experience' (*volle Nach-
erlebbarkeit*) is important for the feeling of certainty of the understanding, but it is not absolutely necessary for the interpretation of
meaning."[67] For "re-experiencing" designates the constitution of a
content in the mind, namely another actor's inner states. Those (complex) inner states, however, all the elements of which a human observer
has experienced himself on some occasion, and possibly in the same
constellation (or a similar one) as the person who is to be understood,
he can "have" in the mind with the greatest ease and clarity.[68] He can
"see" how these elements belong together. The more elements—and
the combinations in which they occur—that are unfamiliar to him
(i.e., are not available in his psyche), the greater his difficulty to have
understanding knowledge. The highest degree of evidence usually
accompanies the understanding of rational means-end relationships.[69]

Due to the nature of concept formation in history, the certainty of
understanding is not entirely without function in methodology. "Its
indirect *logical* significance for history lies in the circumstance that
another person's inner states, with which we can have 'empathy,' also
include those 'valuations' in which the sense and meaning of our 'historical interest' is anchored. . . ."[70] For without the feeling of certainty,
the conviction that certain values are embodied in certain phenomena,
these phenomena would never become the object of historical investigation.[71]

Understanding knowledge, as it appears to be obvious by now, involves some kind of inferential process. Since another person's inner
states are not directly accessible to the observer, he has to depend on
clues and indicators. Weber does not deal with the structure of this inferential process by which the observer arrives at a particular interpretation in a given instance, and the assumptions underlying such inferences. He merely refers to "our own imagination, schooled by the
experiences of everyday life. . . ."[72] As especially Alfred Schuetz has
shown, this process is far from simple. Weber does not analyze it.[73]
This problem lies quite outside the realm of his interest. His concern is
to show that within his epistemology "understanding" has to be con-

sidered as having knowledge, when it occurs on the level of "interpretation." It would be fallacious, however, to infer from this that he ignored
the difficulties involved in establishing an empirically correct interpretation. All he wished to establish was the status of interpretive understanding as knowledge in the same sense as any other kind of empirical
knowledge, i.e., the combination of a form and a content. It is unjustified to impute anything else to his statements.

4. THE LOGICAL STATUS OF THE IDEAL TYPE

The objective of the theory of concept formation in history, as it was
developed by Rickert, was to establish a principle of abstraction whose
application allows the valid selection of facts for the purpose of forming individual concepts. As a result, the principle of value-relevance
was formulated. When the content of an historical concept is selected
in accordance with this principle, objective scientific knowledge is
established. It is knowledge of a unique constellation of phenomena.
The account of this constellation *as a whole* is an individual, or historical concept. The problem which has not been treated so far in this
presentation of Rickert's and Weber's methodology concerns the methodological status of the conceptual *elements* of individual concepts. In
relation to this, Rickert made only one short comment. He said that
the conceptual elements of historical concepts are *general* concepts.[1]
The *individuality* of any historical concept as a whole derives from the
unique constellation in which these general elements occur.
    Weber did not question this general position. As a matter of fact, it
has been shown that he is quite emphatic about the role played by
these general elements in the description of causal interrelationships in
history.[2] But whereas Rickert apparently never examined whether *all*
the conceptual elements of historical reports could without difficulties
and adequately be given the status of general concepts, Weber did. He
immediately ran into difficulties. To understand their source, it must
be recalled in what fashion, according to Rickert's and Weber's theory,
general concepts are formed. It has been shown that this is done by
selecting those component elements of concrete phenomena which
each of them has in common with many—and ultimately all—other
empirical phenomena. This must be understood quite literally. Thus,
the conceptual content of, e.g., "tree," consists of those empirical parts
which can be *equally* found in all trees as identical components. Turn-

ing now to the component parts of historical descriptions, it is easily realized that many of them cannot be called "general" concepts in this sense. These are concepts like "bureaucracy," "conflict," "Catholic," etc. For although their *form* is general, i.e., although they refer to many phenomena, their contents do not contain elements which all these phenomena have *strictly* in common. Rather, some of the definitional characteristics are present *in different degrees* in different instances. Thus, such concepts are not general in the sense in which the term has been used here. When a person has these concepts in mind, he does not know what many or all things have in common. He only knows what occurs to a greater or lesser extent in many instances.[3]

The occurrence of such concepts in historical descriptions is not accidental. For in history there is a concern with those phenomena which embody cultural values. The "carriers" of the processes of embodying such value in phenomena, to use Weber's expression,[4] were humans who tried to implement their values. They acted because they had certain things in mind, and a large portion of historical research is concerned with the establishment of particular events which happened due to the ideas which certain actors had in their minds. The important point, as far as the problems of concept formation are concerned, is that these ideas may be *more or less* present in different actors' minds, i.e., some may be consciously aware of them, others not, some may be exclusively guided by them, some may entertain additional considerations, etc.[5] In each case, the resulting concrete actions and their meanings are different. Therefore, if one wants to form general concepts of these phenomena, he is confronted with a situation in which some of the components which he wants to include in the definition (because the historical interest is focused on them), i.e., the inner states of actors, are not present to the same exent in each relevant instance. Thus it seems that it is impossible to form properly general concepts of these phenomena. Yet it is undoubtedly the case that concepts of such phenomena exist, and that they have at least the *form* of general concepts. The question then is: How can such concepts be fitted into a methodological theory like Rickert's or Weber's (or, for that matter, any theory in which general concepts are treated as representations of the general features of many phenomena)? The contention here is that this is the problem which Weber attempted to solve with his conception of "ideal type." If this is correct, then the ideal type is neither "a synthesis of his epistemological doctrine," as Aron thinks,[6] nor the "fundamental concept of his methodology,"[7] but merely the specific

solution to a very specific problem arising from his methodological
theory. This insight into the true nature of Weber's problem is the key
to any interpretation of his statements concerning this construct. For
only in this frame of reference do every one of Weber's statements concerning ideal-typical constructs make sense, and become compatible
with all the others. With one single exception, nowhere in the existing
secondary literature, as far as it has come to the attention of this author,
has it been clearly realized that it was the above question which Weber
tried to answer *with the means provided by Rickert's theory itself.*
It seems that of all the interpreters only von Schelting[8] was aware of
this when he realized that the necessity of value-viewpoints in history
influences the logical structure of the general concepts which, as a
means of exposition and explanation, have to be used in historical accounts. Specifically, he realized that they become ideal-typical. Due
to other confusions, however, von Schelting could not profit from
this insight. Therefore, every interpretation thus far has encountered
severe problems, manifesting themselves usually in the inability to
provide an account in which all of Weber's statements were consistent
with each other.

Weber opens his discussion of the ideal type by asserting that he
intends to clarify "the relationship between 'theory'[9] and 'history'
which is still problematic in our discipline."[10] The pages following this
quotation show that he refers to the controversy raging at his time in
the field of economics between the proponents of "abstract" theory[11]
and the German historical school.[12] The issue here clearly was the one
that was just mentioned, namely whether the so-called "laws" of
classical economics are something like the laws of nature, i.e., general
concepts, established in the natural sciences.[13] According to Weber,
they are not.

The naturalistic prejudice that every concept in the cultural sciences
should be similar to those in the exact natural sciences has led in consequence
to the misunderstanding of this theoretical thought-construct (*theoretische
Gedankengebilde*). It has been believed that it is a matter of the psychological isolation of a specific "impulse," the acquisitive impulse, or of the
isolated study of a specific maxim of human conduct, the so-called economic principle.[14]

This is an error, however, argues Weber. It is committed as a result
of a wrong conception of the relationship between "law and reality,"[15]
or "the concept and the conceptualized"[16] in the scientific analysis of
historical processes.

In the establishment of the propositions of abstract theory, it is only apparently a matter of "deduction" from fundamental psychological motives. Actually, the former are a special case of a kind of concept construction which is peculiar and to a certain extent, indispensable, to the cultural sciences.[17]

This kind of concept Weber calls "ideal type."[18] But unfortunately, whereas he states his opinion with all desirable clarity, the underlying reasoning on which this opinion is based is not made explicit at all; to call it "lucid," as Freund does, is a gross distortion of the situation.[19] This section will attempt to show that the considerations mentioned at the beginning of this section indeed were shared by Weber, and that the ideal type, as conceived by him, is his solution to the problem of determining the conceptual status of certain elements of historical descriptions within the premises of Rickert's theory of concept formation.

Weber's discussion of ideal types is contained in the last twenty-five pages of the essay on "Objectivity" which was written in 1904. Preferably, what is said in this essay *about* ideal types should be confirmed by—or at least be compatible with—what is presented *as* ideal types in, roughly, the first three hundred pages of Weber's *Economy and Society*, which were written between 1918 and 1920. Precisely this, however, has emerged in the secondary literature as one of the main difficulties. For the ideal types presented in *Economy and Society* are a mixture of definitions, classifications, and specific hypotheses seemingly too divergent to be reconcilable with Weber's statements. Since most interpreters have started with the analysis of Weber's methodological writings, their lack of success suggested to some writers[20] that it might be better first to investigate what Weber actually did rather than what he said he did. This does not seem to be a promising idea, though. The problem is not to find out what Weber did, in this context, but how he *conceptualized* what he did. This cannot be found out by the analysis of his formulated types and some kind of inductive procedure based upon this analysis. For instance, an attempt to find the common denominator of all ideal types leads to the following somewhat forced one-sentence summary: in *Economy and Society*, the term "(ideal-) typical" is applied to categorizations of, and statements about, relationships between actions or action elements in terms of, or by reference to, the presence of one or a few maxims in the minds of actors according to which they orient their thoughts and actions. This is as far as an attempt to establish the common features of all ideal types will lead, and it is quite apparent that this approach is a dead end street as far as useful insight into Weber's argument about the nature of ideal types is concerned.

Whatever the approach, no existing interpretation has succeeded in reconciling Weber's statements with his actual practice or even in reconciling his many statements with each other. To avoid this situation, it has been suggested that one should distinguish between different kinds of ideal type. One may then try to make sense out of Weber's statements on the topic by arguing that each of them, although it may not be compatible with every kind of ideal type, is reasonable at least in relation to one. The first and most widely acknowledged attempt in this direction is Alexander von Schelting's, which said that all attempts to eliminate the "obscurities, contradictions, and ambiguities"[21] contained in the conception of the ideal type have to remain fruitless unless distinctions are made. Practically everybody has agreed with him in this. Many of these later interpretations attempt to reconcile Weber's statements in the essay on "Objectivity" with the types presented in *Economy and Society* by postulating a shift in the conception of "ideal type" from the historicist's interest in historical wholes —"historical individuals"—to the sociologist's interest in the analytical elements of a general theory.[22] Unfortunately, it is hard to see how the assumption of a shift in Weber's conception can be justified. In any case, nobody has ever come up with a reason for the change and "flux"[23] in which Weber's conception of the ideal type supposedly was. It also has to be emphasized that already in his methodological essays, i.e., before the alleged shift took place, Weber talks about "generic ideal types," and doing this he has the "fundamental concepts"[24] of economics in mind. Furthermore, as will be seen later on,[25] there is no difference in the ways in which an individual ideal type like "city economy" and a generic ideal type like "bureaucracy" are formed. Finally, Weber states:

Naturally, however, also those *generic* concepts which we constantly encounter as elements of historical descriptions and concrete historical concepts can be formed as ideal types through abstraction and exaggeration of certain conceptually essential elements. In practice this is indeed a particularly frequent and important instance of the application of ideal-typical concepts, and every *individual* ideal type comprises conceptual *elements* which are ideal-typically constructed.[26]

It seems that drawing such distinctions is side-stepping the whole issue, anyway. For everything indicates that from the very outset Weber consciously attributed a common ideal-typical feature to things with otherwise very divergent characteristics. Therefore, if one wants to discover what Weber had in mind when he introduced the conception of ideal type, it does not seem to lead very far to argue that the term is applied to seemingly heterogeneous things which must be distinguished if one wants clarity. Rather, one must discover the reasons Weber had to treat them as the same. One must discover why it apparently was entirely natural for him (as one must assume, for otherwise he would have felt the need to make himself more explicit) to call all these things "ideal types."

The first problem which must be solved in such an approach, is presented by the fact that Weber applies the term "ideal type" indiscriminately to two things which are usually treated as entirely distinct, namely definitions of general concepts and empirical statements.[27] The solution to this is that for Rickert and Weber definitions of concepts *are* statements about empirical reality.[28] Thus, from this point of view there are no differences, and it may be said that all ideal types are empirical statements about interrelations between elements. A survey of the types occurring in *Economy and Society* shows that they are statements connecting particular actions and particular inner states of individual actors, generally action-maxims.

The fact that Weber sees no distinctions of a logical kind between the things he calls "ideal types" has now been accounted for. But if the explanation given is correct, one can see that Weber is in a dilemma. For the statements which are the equivalent of general concepts have to be interpreted as true universal statements. They are supposed to state what empirically all things which are designated by them have in common. But ideal-typical general concepts do not qualify as such. Consider one of Weber's examples: classical economic theory. When the propositions of the theory which are usually interpreted as economic laws are viewed as descriptions of the common features of all the concrete empirical phenomena to which they are taken to refer, they are only approximately correct. *Undoubtedly for this reason,* and only for this reason, did Weber refuse to grant them the status of genuine general concepts and "laws of nature"; instead, he called them "ideal types."[29] It may seem now that as statements about empirical reality, ideal types are not too useful. However, Weber argues that they are "to a certain extent indispensable"[30] in two respects: they have heuristic as well as expository functions. "The ideal-typical concept will help to develop our skill in imputation in *research*: it *is* no 'hypothesis,'[31] but it offers guidance to the construction of hypotheses. It is not a *description* of reality but it aims to give unambiguous means of expression to such a description."[32] Weber's claim of the indispensability of ideal types for historical *descriptions* is the core of the whole problem, and if this can be solved, the heuristic function is easily explained.

Weber gives the following reason for the indispensability of ideal types:

Every conscientious examination of the conceptual elements of historical exposition shows however that the historian as soon as he attempts to go beyond the bare establishment of concrete relationships and to determine the *cultural significance* of even the simplest individual event in order to "characterize" it, *must* use concepts which are precisely and unambiguously definable only in the form of ideal types.[33]

And elsewhere he says:

The contrast between simple class, or generic, concepts (*Klassenbegriffe*) which merely summarize that which *empirical phenomena* have in common, and generic (*gattungsmaessig*) *ideal types* . . . of course varies with each concrete case. But no class, or generic, concept as such has a "typical" character, and a purely generic "average" *type* does not exist. . . . The more we are concerned with the simple classification of events which in empirical reality occur as mass phenomena, the more it is a matter of *class* concepts. However, the more we are concerned with the conceptualization of complicated historical interrelationships with respect to those of their components in which their specific *cultural significance* is contained, the more the concept—or system of concepts— will be *ideal-typical* in character.[34]

In other words, in history scientists describe those parts of concrete phenomena which are *significant*, or *characteristic*. These must be distinguished from the *common* elements. It is necessary "to eliminate the common notion that in the sphere of cultural phenomena the abstract type is identical with the abstract *class*. This is not the case."[35] Thus the description of the characteristic elements of cultural phenomena requires ideal types. Von Schelting saw this with great clarity: "The 'ideal type' is a type since it expresses in thought facts which are significant for the particularity of *many* cultural phenomena, although to different degrees."[36] Examples are provided by terms like "feudal," "charismatic," "capitalistic," "bureaucratic," "Christian," etc.

It is now possible to assert that Weber calls certain concepts "ideal types" because they are neither truly general concepts nor individual ones. "Or can concepts such as 'individualism,' 'imperialism,' 'feudalism,' 'mercantilism' . . . as far as their contents are concerned . . . be defined as the abstracting synthesis of that which several concrete phenomena have in common?"[37] And later: "The goal of ideal-typical concept construction is always to make clearly explicit *not* the class or average character, but rather the unique particularity of cultural phenomena."[38]

It does not require elaboration that ideal types are not individual concepts (which have been described as accounts of unique historical developments), for they refer to a plurality of similar phenomena. It is, however, only a logical consequence of Weber's premises that ideal types are not genuinely general concepts, either. For according to Weber, general concepts are formed by stating a combination of component parts common to many phenomena. However, as the foregoing quotations have made explicit, historians by definition are generally not interested in the common constellations of elements, but in the characteristic (typical) ones of a number of particular historical phenomena. These typical elements are shared by many phenomena, *but not to the same degree*.[39] Some exhibit them in a more pronounced way than others. Therefore, a true general statement which predicates all these features of all the phenomena in question cannot be formulated. In terms of the class logic which Weber uses this is possible only when the predicated properties do not occur in degrees but are either equally present or equally absent. Thus, the concepts used by historians cannot properly be said to be general concepts.[40] Weber gives an example:

The concept of "exchange" is for instance a simple class concept (*Gattungsbegriff*) in the sense of a complex of traits which are common to many phenomena, as long as we disregard the *significance* of the component parts of the concept and simply analyze the term in its everyday usage. If however we relate this concept to the concept of "marginal utility" for instance, and construct the concept of "economic exchange" as an economically *rational* event, this concept then contains—as does every concept which is logically fully elaborated—a *judgment* concerning the "typical" *conditions* of exchange. It assumes a *genetic*[41] character and becomes therewith ideal-typical in the logical sense, i.e., it removes itself from empirical reality which can only be *compared* or related to it.[42]

In simple words, the analysis of a number of economic exchanges reveals that they are motivated *in varying degrees* by the desire to maximize individual utilities, a situation which cannot be handled properly in terms of the presence or absence of certain absolute properties and, therefore, requires concepts of a particular kind.[43]

This analysis shows that Weber is struggling with a problem which is inherent in his logic, since within his class logic the things which he wants to say cannot be said.[44]

Let us take for instance the concepts "church" and "sect." They may be broken down purely in a classificatory fashion into complexes of elements (*Merkmalskomplexe*) whereby not only the distinction between them but also the content of each concept must constantly remain fluid. If however, I wish to conceptualize "sect" in a *genetic*[45] fashion, e.g., in reference to certain important cultural significances which the "sectarian spirit" has had for modern culture, certain characteristics of both become *essential* because they stand in an adequate causal relationship to those effects. However, the concepts thereupon become ideal-typical, i.e., in full conceptual purity these phenomena either do not exist at all or only in single instances. Here as elsewhere it is the case that every concept which is not *purely* classificatory diverges from reality.[46]

The reason that for Weber certain concepts are neither general nor individual is now clear. So they must be accorded a special status. Given his starting point, however, it is not possible for Weber to conceive of other methodological forms than either general or individual ones. Therefore, since he has no appropriate conceptual forms available for what he wants to say, *Weber has to change the reality to which the concepts refer.* Thus, ideal types are general concepts which do not describe the elements which the instances of a class of phenomena have in common in the empirical world,[47] but the elements which they have in common in an imaginary world, a utopia.[48] This utopian world is so constructed that what are "characteristic" and "significant" elements, existing in gradations in the empirical world, become common elements in the imaginary one. There they are shared by all relevant phenomena to the same degree. The concept of ideal type thus denotes by no means a residual category, as Parsons argues,[49] nor does it lack a positive characterization. Nor, finally, is it true that the utopian character of its content—"the 'fictional' nature of social science concepts," as Parsons says[50]—is due to the diversity of possible value-relevances to which the historical material may be subjected.[51] Rather, it is the only solution available to Weber trying to determine, with the tools provided by his methodology, the logical character of particular and not at all residual concepts.

Since Weber describes the conceptual content of ideal types as exaggerated, sometimes existing nowhere in empirical reality, and as utopian, the question has arisen whether or not Weber is justified in calling such pictures of a nonexisting world "concepts," i.e., formed presentations of facts. Von Schelting, for instance,[52] asks how an ideal type can be constructed according to the principles of objective possibility and adequate causation, as Weber says it can. For these principles can be applied only to empirical phenomena, not things which only exist in the imagination of thought. Weber's reply would probably be that by calling the contents of ideal types "unreal" he did not want to convey the idea that they are free inventions of the imagination but merely that they describe phenomena which in principle are empirically possible but have failed to materialize as a result of factual circumstances. Whether or not he would have given this answer, though, depends on whether or not he regarded knowledge of the empirically possible as empirical knowledge. Since he regarded economics and sociology as empirical sciences, it seems that a positive answer must be given. Direct pronouncements on the problem do not exist.

Weber deals in rather great detail with the way in which ideal-typical contents are abstracted from reality, i.e., with the derivation of an ideal, utopian world from the real, empirically existing one. It has been declared that Weber "does not derive the ideal type from a series of empirically existing cases. Rather, he imposes it as a . . . measuring device."[53] This is not correct, however. Empirical science, for Weber, proceeds inductively, and he views types as inductively abstracted from reality.[54] This reality from which ideal types are abstracted is always human cultural reality (for ideal types occur only in the cultural sciences), and it is helpful for an understanding of Weber's description of "idealizing abstraction," or "exaggerating abstraction," as this procedure may be called, to recall some of the earlier remarks concerning Rickert's and Weber's conception of culture. Cultural phenomena, it was said, are phenomena which are created or maintained because the acting humans find their own practical values embodied in them. Empirical analysis of these processes of culture creation and culture maintenance encounters the elements "means" and "ends" as the ultimate constituents of human actions.

For *our* considerations [as historians] "purpose" is the conception of an *effect* which becomes the *cause* of an action. Since we take into account every cause which contributes or can contribute to a *significant* effect, we also consider this one. Its *specific* significance consists only in the fact that we not only *observe* human conduct but can and desire to *understand* it.[55]

Human conduct is understandable because, in this case, the conception of an effect in a person's mind, as a result of which an action occurs, gives it a meaning. Reference to the meaning of an action is always at least an implicit reference to an actor's inner states which were the cause of the action. Empirically it now so happens that many actions occur in similar situations as a result of similar inner states. Thus, there are similar actions, but they are not similar enough for Weber to be able to form generic concepts of them. The source of this dissimilarity is to be found in the fact that the situational conditions vary and that the inner states which are treated as the motives of the relevant actions are complex; that is, empirical actions are often the result of a variety of considerations in an actor's mind. Therefore, any single consideration motivates the resulting action only to a certain degree.

In this situation, in order to be able to form general concepts, Weber relies on the device of constructing a course of action as it would take place if only one or a few clearly specified considerations of the many which are in operation in any concrete instance governed an actor's (actors') conduct, occasionally specifying under what situational conditions they are assumed to occur.[56] Such a construct he calls an "ideal picture" (*Idealbild*), for its content does not represent what numerous empirical phenomena have in common, but what they *would* have in common without the causal influence of what—*for the purposes of concept formation*—are disturbing influences in the sense that they disallow the construction of genuine general concepts.

This thought-image (*Gedankenbild*) brings together certain relationships and events of historical life into an internally consistent cosmos of interrelationships existing in thought [of the scientist]. As far as its content is concerned, this construction has the character of a *utopia* which has been arrived at through an exaggeration (*Steigerung*) *in thought* of certain elements of reality.[57]

"Exaggeration" means that of the complex meaningful considerations within the minds of the empirical actors to whose actions an ideal type refers, only one or a few elements are assumed to operate, and that the actions which are thought as resulting from them, therefore, embody certain meanings more purely than the empirically existing actions. This does not require any intuition, contrary to Georg Weippert's assumption, nor does this mean that the "pure" meaning of an action is presented in perfection.[58] It is merely assumed that an actor has only one action-plan clearly in his mind which he single-mindedly pursues. The ideal-typical construct contains both the actor's plans and the actions following from them.

Hans Oppenheimer has thrown some doubts on the adequacy of Weber's account.

Of the fact that in a human being whose conceptions frequently contain meaningful elements of Puritanism, all of a sudden elements of the complex of meaning "capitalism" become actual, any science working with the causal methods of natural science can grasp and explain only what for history is irrelevant, namely the common features of all the psychic acts of which conceptions consist as far as their *existence as nature* only is concerned.[59]

Ideal types, therefore, cannot be described merely as a kind of generalizing concept, according to Oppenheimer, since their contents represent *meaningful* interrelationships, not just "natural" ones.[60] Interrelationships of meaning, however, are not causal interrelationships.[61] From Weber's point of view it would have to be answered that meanings are embodied in things and conduct, and that the historian is interested in meanings as embodied meanings, and that it is possible to conceive of phenomena at the same time as causally and meaningfully interrelated. For thinking causally is to give categorical forms to immediate experiences, and methodological forms to facts, whereas understanding meaning is not giving a form to anything. It cannot be denied that even the causal methods of the natural sciences— the establishment of causal laws—can grasp meaningful content. Oppenheimer's claim that they can handle only phenomena insofar as they are physical—"nature"—is without any foundation.

The demand that an ideal type has to be "internally consistent" means that it must contain only those actions which would exist as a causal result of the exclusive influence of the "exaggerated" inner states. Thus, in an example Weber describes an "economic organization based on handicraft principles" which is arrived at "by one-sidedly exaggerating, as far as their consequences are concerned, certain features which are diffusely found among craftsmen of the most diverse times and countries, combining them into an internally consistent ideal picture, and relating them to an *idea* (*Gedankenausdruck*) which one finds manifested in it ."[62] Because of the reference to such inner states as the *causes* of the action phenomena—which at the same time give these phenomena their *meanings*—which are described in ideal types, Weber calls the definitions of ideal types "genetic definitions,"[63] i.e., definitions through reference to the way in which the defined phenomena originate. Since the complexity of these causes—the motives—is one source of the impossibility to form properly general concepts of action phenomena, Weber says: "When a genetic definition of the content of the concept is sought, there remains only the form of the ideal type. . . ."[64] Henrich's comments on this are completely erroneous. He declares that class concepts, or "classificatory concepts," defined by *genus proximum* and *differentia specifica*, in Weber's opinion are mere nominal definitions (!) which cannot provide any knowledge of the actual conditions under which certain phenomena are possible. Only real definitions are suited to this purpose. Since in the cultural sciences knowledge of reality in its particularity is desired, real definitions are required through which given facts are explained by showing the causes of their existence. Such real definitions, says Henrich, are called "genetic definitions" by Weber. They are explications of phenomena from the context of reality which has made their concrete existence possible.[65] "Real-explications in cultural science are ideal types."[66] Ideal types are "explanations—accomplished in the form of a concept—of historical events by reference to the circumstances which made their existence possible."[67] As against Henrich's reasoning it must be asserted that it is simply not true that in Weber's view class concepts are nominally defined. Ideal types are genetic concepts because reference to a cultural phenomenon's meaning automatically indicates the meaningful cause of its existence, and vice versa.

The exaggeration which is necessary in the construction of an ideal type is called "one-sided" since it is equivalent to the disregard of the causal influence of certain empirically operative factors. The latter are certain motives in the minds of the relevant actors which may conflict with other co-existing motives in the sense that the enactment of all of them would require several mutually incompatible courses of action. Empirically, such a conflict of motives is often resolved through a compromise, so that some actions do not happen although they would be compatible with at least one of the different motives in the actor's minds.[68] Therefore, when an ideal type is constructed on the basis of the assumption that only one or a few motives which are compatible with each other are operative in an actor (actors), the description of the resulting phenomenon, the utopia, may have to include elements which in the empirical world, due to the presence of conflicting considerations and desires in the minds of the concerned actors, do not exist anywhere in this combination.

An ideal type is formed by the one-sided exaggeration (*Steigerung*) of *one* or *several* viewpoints[69] and by the combination of a great many *single* phenomena (*Einzelerscheinungen*) existing diffusely and discretely, more or less present and occasionally absent, which are compatible with those one-sidedly emphasized viewpoints, into an internally consistent *thought-picture* (*Gedankenbild*). In its conceptual purity this thought-picture cannot be found empirically anywhere in reality, it is a *utopia*. . . .[70]

What is exaggerated depends, of course, on the viewpoint from which the historian who uses ideal types writes history, and accordingly each ideal type is "a theoretical and hence 'one-sided' viewpoint from which light can be thrown upon reality, to which it can be related, but which proves obviously inadequate as a schema in which it could in its totality find its place."[71]

Walter Eucken criticizes Weber for thinking that stages of economic development, like "handicraft" or "capitalism," are conceptualized in the form of ideal types. Rather, he maintains, they are *real* types, since they are intended to portray the real conditions of the economy of a country at a particular time.[72] They are constructed by generalizing abstraction.[73] Ideal types, in contrast, are created by isolating abstraction.[74] The purpose of this procedure is "to derive from economic life the basic forms of which it is made up. These basic forms are and always have been strictly limited in number. . . ."[75] Weber confused the two kinds of concept, and, therefore, his reasoning "contains serious defects."[76] Obviously Eucken has not at all understood why Weber called his types "ideal." His distinction between ideal and real types ignores the source of Weber's logical difficulties. Eucken's conception is that concrete economic phenomena are particular combinations of "pure"[77] economic forms. Whereas real types describe such combinations, ideal types describe the pure forms which constitute

. . . a comprehensive morphological scheme. . . . These types do not purport to be pictures of actual economic life, that is, they are not real types . . . but purely ideal types each representing one single aspect of a group of cases. That does not mean that they are "utopian," as Max Weber mistakenly called them, for a "utopia," is something to be contrasted and compared with actual economic conditions. These ideal types are got from the actual economic world and help us to understand it.[78]

Clearly, Eucken here misses Weber's point in calling his ideal types "utopian."

The fact that ideal types are one-sided exaggerations for Weber implies the possibility that many ideal types can be constructed of what is to be considered the same concrete phenomenon. For such a phenomenon is the concrete result of a whole complex variety of inner states. Many meanings can be found manifested in them.

It is possible, or rather it must be accepted as certain that several, indeed in each case very numerous utopias [of, e.g., capitalism] of this sort can be worked out, of which *none* is like another, of which *none* ever can be observed in empirical reality as the actually existing organization of the [capitalistic] society, but *each* of which, however, claims that it is a representation of the "idea" of capitalistic culture. *Each* of these indeed can claim this insofar as each has actually taken certain features of our culture, which are significant in their particularity, from reality and brought them together into a unified ideal picture. . . . Just as there are . . . the most diverse "viewpoints" from which we can look at phenomena as being significant for us, the most varied principles can be applied in the selection of the interrelationships which are to enter into the construction of an ideal type of a particular culture.[79]

Thus, *what* elements of the empirical phenomena are used to construct the ideal type depends on the viewpoint from which an historian writes an historical account. Different viewpoints require different ideal types. Since the points of view from which history is written change, and since new ones are constantly emerging, it is not possible to construct an exhaustive system of ideal types which would be analogous to the system of general concepts established in the natural sciences.

For none of those systems of thought[80] without which we cannot do if we want to conceive of those parts of reality which are significant in each case, can possibly exhaust the infinite richness of reality. None is anything else than the attempt . . . to bring order into the chaos of those facts which in each case we have included within the horizon of our *interest*.[81] . . . The history of the sciences of social life, therefore, is and remains a continuous alternation between the attempts to order facts in thought through the formation of concepts—the dissolution of the thought-pictures so constructed through the expansion and shift of the scientific horizon—and the formation anew on the foundation thus transformed . . . this process shows that in the sciences of human culture the formation of concepts depends on the setting of the practical problems,[82] and that this setting varies with the content of culture itself. The relationship between concept and reality in the cultural sciences [i.e., the necessity of value-relevance] involves the transitoriness of every such synthesis. . . . The greatest advances in the field of the social sciences are substantively tied up with the shift in practical cultural problems [i.e., the emergence of new cultural values causing a new way of looking at things] and take the guise of a critique of concept formation [i.e., of the value-relevance of the concepts].[83]

Of course, those ideal types which describe ultimate or near-ultimate elements of all cultural phenomena—like "traditional action" or "social relationship"—are not affected by such changes to the same degree as more complex constructions—like "capitalism" or "feudalism"— since as (near-) ultimate parts they have to occur in any historical account, no matter what the viewpoint from which it is written. But the smaller the scope of an ideal type, the more is its construction bound to particular viewpoints.

The more inclusive the interrelationships which are to be represented, and the more many-sided their cultural *significance* has been, the *more* their comprehensive systematic exposition in a system of concepts and thoughts approximates the character of an ideal type, the *less* is it possible to be satisfied with *one* such concept, the more natural and inevitable is it, therefore, to constantly repeat the attempts to bring to light ever *new* aspects of its significance through the new formation of ideal-typical concepts.[84]

5. THE DIFFERENT KINDS OF IDEAL TYPE

After the reconstruction of the considerations which guided Weber when he claimed that historical descriptions require concepts with a special status, namely ideal-typical concepts,[1] there remains the examination of the application of this analysis to everything which in Weber is given the status of ideal type. In this respect its compatibility with the so-called "individual ideal type"[2] is especially problematic. Weber states: "We have purposely considered the ideal type essentially—if not exclusively—as a thought-construction for the scrutiny and systematic characterization of *individual* complexes of interrelationships which are significant in their uniqueness, such as Christianity, capitalism, etc."[3] Since in such cases the ideal type appears to refer to a single—though complex—phenomenon, not only the interpretation given in the previous section seems to collapse, but it is also necessary to ask what sense it makes to construct an ideal type of an individual phenomenon. Why not just form an individual concept?[4] Weber provides no answer to this question although it seems unavoidable that it be posed. As a matter of fact, it seems that from Weber's position no sensible answer can be given. There plainly is no reason to prefer, for the purposes of historical exposition, an individual ideal type to an individual concept. However, the question which has never been asked anywhere in the secondary literature is whether the individual ideal type actually refers to just one phenomenon. Rather, a positive answer was always taken for granted.[5] This has created unsurmountable difficulties to all interpreters. It, therefore, has to be realized that the correct answer is negative, for concepts like "feudal," "individualistic," etc., which exemplify individual ideal types, are used to characterize many phenomena and not just one. Weber himself says in an example that one constructs the individual ideal type of a medieval city economy and then looks to establish the degree to which the economic situation in *each* particular city is that of a city economy.[6] An individual ideal type, therefore, is *an account of numerous instances*. The concept "capitalism," for instance, refers to a particular ("individual") constellation of elements which would be common to a number of phenomena if the world were governed by particular principles *only*, namely those called "capitalistic." What is defined as "capitalistic" is not a conventional decision, though. Weber asks the rhetorical question: "Or are all concepts such as 'individualism,' 'imperialism,' 'feudalism,' 'mercantilism,' [so-called] 'conventional' [definitions]. . . ?"[7] They are not, of course. Ideal-typical definitions are not "nominal definitions" but "real definitions," namely "genetic" ones. To be sure, what is defined as "capitalism," etc., depends on the viewpoints from which the historian looks, e.g., at the age of capitalism as a *concrete* historical epoch. But this does not mean that he can arbitrarily decide about a convenient definition. Rather, from the point of view from which he approaches the empirical material certain elements empirically appear as the unique and distinct characteristics which distinguish this epoch treated as a whole from all others, namely certain values which dominate peoples' minds and induce them to commit certain actions. This constellation occurs, although in different degrees, in many phenomena. There is, for instance, British, French, and German capitalism. The ideal type of the class constituted by such phenomena, e.g., the many existing capitalistic systems, describes these phenomena as they exist in an imaginary world. This world is so constituted that the phenomena in question all have the constellation of elements given in the definition of the ideal type in common. As already mentioned,[8] several such imaginary worlds can be constructed of the same empirical phenomena through an appropriate change of viewpoints.

The considerations involved in the construction of individual ideal types are now clear. These types are "abstract concepts of interrelationships."[9] As far as the label is concerned, this type of ideal type is not called "individual" because it refers to one individual phenomenon, but because the occurrence of the constellation of elements described in it characterizes, from the point of view adopted by the historian, a class of phenomena occurring in a distinct, unique, i.e., individual, historical epoch.

A second kind of ideal type which Weber mentions he calls "generic ideal types."[10] As far as their logical status is concerned, there is no difference between individual and generic ideal types. If the above analysis of the individual ideal type is correct, they are both general, i.e., state what happens in a multitude of instances. The existing difference between them is one of the relative complexity of the phenomena to which they refer as well as one of the extent to which the occurrence of these phenomena is limited to certain historical periods. Individual ideal types state ". . . individual complexes of interrelationships which are significant in their uniqueness, such as Christianity, capitalism, etc. . . ."[11] Generic ideal types state their component elements. "Every individual ideal type comprises generic conceptual elements which are ideal-typically constructed."[12] What Weber has in mind when he speaks of generic ideal types are, for instance, ". . . all the so-called 'fundamental concepts' of economics. . . ."[13] Almost all the ideal types presented in *Economy and Society* are generic.

Weber lists a third kind of concept which is formed in ideal-typical fashion: those constructs which describe the (alleged) "essence" of complicated systems of ideas, such as "Communism" or "Christianity."[14] Weber's point here is that those constructs which are usually presented as descriptions of the "essence" of phenomena do not describe *the* essence at all, but are ideal types, i.e., exaggerations from a particular viewpoint.[15] Weippert is completely mistaken when he says:

We see here that Max Weber—by declaring it to be the task of ideal types to present the essence of historical phenomena—does *not* want *the understanding of meaning and the clarification of the essence* interpreted *as the conceptual picturing of something that exists in empirical reality.* Rightly so.[16]

Weber does not think that essences—if there are any—can be known. To him, for example, the Christianity of the Middle Ages empirically consists of thoughts and ideas in the minds of individuals. These ideas are infinitely differentiated and highly contradictory among each other.

If we raise the question as to what in this chaos was *the* "Christianity" of the Middle Ages (which we must nonetheless use as a stable concept) and wherein lay those "Christian" elements which we find in the institutions of the Middle Ages, we see that here too in every individual case, we are applying a pure thought-construct created by ourselves. It is a combination of articles of faith, norms from church law and custom, maxims of conduct, and countless concrete interrelationships which *we* have fused into an "idea": a synthesis which without contradiction we would not be able to attain without the use of ideal-typical concepts.[17]

It describes a world in which all people think along those lines which lead to the ideas which are selected and incorporated into the ideal type, so that in this world "Christian of the Middle Ages," for instance, is a general concept. Weber emphasizes the ideal-typical nature of these concepts because it is often possible that what is described in the ideal type was the practical ideal of the majority or an important segment of the people in the period considered. This has often led to the erroneous confusion of historical reality and the historian's abstracted scientific account of it.

This confusion expresses itself firstly in the belief that the "true" content and the essence of historical reality is portrayed in such theoretical constructs or secondly . . . in the hypostatization of such "ideas" as real "forces" and as a "true" reality which operates behind the passage of events and which works itself out in history.[18]

Finally, there are ideal types of developments.[19] They do not require any new considerations; their construction follows the principles already established. A development is a causal sequence; the statement describing a causal sequence is ideal-typical when it states what only approximately or partly happens in a number of cases, and, therefore, cannot be given the status of a causal law of nature. Ideal-typical causal sequences, then, are those which would be causal laws of nature if the world would function according to certain specified principles.

One can, for example, arrive at the theoretical conclusion that in a society which is organized on *strict* "handicraft" principles, the only source of capital accumulation can be ground rent. From this, perhaps, one can . . . construct a pure ideal picture of the shift, conditioned by certain specific factors . . . from a handicraft to a capitalistic economic organization.[20]

In other words, wherever empirically a handicraft society existed or exists, its main but not exclusive source of capital accumulation is ground rent, and, therefore, the transformation into a capitalistic society occurs more or less as described in the type.

As a result of the whole discussion of the ideal type it is now possible to indicate the special feature of everything which, in *Economy and Society*, is given ideal-typical status. *Ideal types are statements of general form asserting the existence of certain constellations of elements which are empirically only approximated by the instances of the class of phenomena to which each type refers;* they are elements of meaningful action and thought. To make it possible to retain their general form, these concepts are, therefore, interpreted as accounts of an ideal world in which the relevant phenomena equally share these constellations of elements. For example, the instances of the particular class of concrete actions called "traditional action" are not all to the same degree "determined by habituation."[21] Therefore, "traditional action" is an ideal type whose definition is a general statement which lists what the instances of a class of phenomena in an imagined world have in common.

On the basis of the interpretation put forward in this essay it is apparent that Max Weber, from his point of view, was justified in calling all the above-mentioned concepts "ideal types." Within this system, all the constructs to which the term is applied seem to exhibit the same logical structure. Critics have consistently failed to recognize this, either due to a faulty interpretation of Weber's own premises,[22] or because they argued from methodological positions differing from Weber's.[23] Thus, Weippert accuses Weber of not properly distinguishing between two kinds of construct, namely (a) those expressing the meaningful essence of cultural phenomena, and (b) rational schemes which are auxiliary constructions for the purpose of establishing causal relationships.[24] According to Weippert, only the first kind should be properly called "ideal type." Here the special nature of the subject matter is acknowledged, its existence as meaningful reality is recognized. "*Verstehen*" is necessary for its grasp. Rational schemes, however, do not conceptualize the meaningful quality of phenomena but rather allow one to find out how things are related to each other when total rationality is assumed.[25] What Weippert seems to have in mind is this: the basis of economics has to be an ontology of economic phenomena. Since the subject matter of economics consists of phenomena of a meaningful quality, such an ontology has to establish the meanings which economic phenomena *as* economic phenomena *necessarily* have. A theory like classical economics does not provide an insight into the essence, the nature of the meaningful phenomenon "economy." It is not an "ontology of economics."[26] It provides only "rational schemes" without regard for the inherent meaning of the phenomena. The proper procedure for the establishment of the essential meaning is the formulation of ideal types stating pure meanings. Weber's basic fallacy, in Weippert's opinion, consists in denying the special quality of the subject matter of economics—although in a fashion inconsistent with this he emphasizes the necessity of understanding. Therefore, he does not distinguish between abstractions resulting in ideal types of pure meaning and abstractions resulting in rational schemes.[27]

The answer to all this is that Weippert assumes that it is possible to determine the "essence" of economic phenomena whereas Weber does not. Why else would he introduce the principle of value-relevance? Weippert never discusses the question on this level but presupposes an answer in his favor. He takes for granted that the essence of cultural phenomena consists of pure meanings of a certain kind. But for Weber there are no absolute and objective differences in the pureness of meanings; rather, what is "pure" can be established only in relation to a point of view. Weippert's distinction between phenomenological ideal types and rational schema is also rather dubious on other grounds. If it is true that the former give in pure form the meanings embodied in phenomena, then the latter can merely be useful fictions.[28] Weippert's opinion that phenomenological ideal types abstract from the material which is given whereas logical schemes are imposed on it, can only mean, it must be supposed, that logical schemes explain empirical reality in terms of a meaning which is not there. Weber, however, wants to use ideal types of rational behavior only when there is some correspondence in empirical reality.

From this discussion, then, it must be concluded that contrary to a practically universal belief it is not necessary to distinguish between certain kinds of ideal types in order to save the internal consistency of Weber's arguments. As far as the substantive content of ideal types is concerned, and not their logical character in the sense in which Weber understands it, it is of course possible to distinguish different types, as Weber himself did. Within the framework of his argument, however, this has no methodological significance.

6. THE USE OF IDEAL TYPES

If the above interpretation is correct, then the obvious question is: What good are general statements about the phenomena of an imagined, utopian world when the aim is to find the general concepts, or laws, of the empirical one? The first part of the answer is that, for the reasons which have been explained, it is impossible for Weber to formulate general concepts of the empirical *social* world and at the same time to retain those elements which are historically interesting, or significant. In this situation ideal types are the most feasible solution. For the goal of scientists is clear knowledge, and this is possible only in conceptual form. "If the historian (in the widest sense of the word) rejects an attempt to construct such ideal types as a 'theoretical construction,' i.e., as useless or dispensable for his concrete heuristic purposes, the inevitable consequence is . . . that he remains stuck in the realm of the vaguely 'felt.' "[1] This is the reason behind Weber's undertaking the definition of the "hundreds of words"[2] occurring in the historian's vocabulary. It is an entirely logical consequence of his theory of knowledge. For without clear definitions, these words would be "vague thought-images created to meet the unconsciously felt need for adequate expression whose meaning is only concretely felt but not clearly thought out."[3] To be sure, when reading historical descriptions, in many cases it is sufficient just to "feel" what the historian has in mind.[4]

However, the more it is our endeavor to produce a clear awareness of the significance of a cultural phenomenon, the more imperative is the need to work with clear concepts which are not only partially, but completely defined. A "definition" of those syntheses of the historian's thought according to the schema of *genus proximum* and *differentia specifica* is nonsense, of course. To see this, you only have to give it a try. . . . Also, a simple "descriptive analysis" of those concepts into their components does not exist, or exists only in the illusion, for the crucial point is exactly *which* ones of these components should be regarded as essential.[5]

A clearly defined concept representing the significant parts of a cultural phenomenon is possible only in ideal-typical form.

The second part of the answer is that such ideal types adequately fulfill the function which they are supposed to fulfill, namely, allow the conceptually clear description of *individual* historical developments, whenever this is necessary and a merely felt mental picture is too unprecise for a particular purpose in question. In the cultural sciences laws are formulated *only* to facilitate the establishment and description of individual relationships. If ideal types are sufficient for the purpose, it makes no sense to object that they are not laws of empirical reality, but describe merely an imaginary world. It would be a reasonable objection only if the establishment of the laws governing cultural phenomena were the ultimate goal of the cultural sciences. But this is not the case. History "is oriented to the causal analysis and explanation of individual actions, structures and personalities possessing cultural significance."[6] Generalizations have only instrumental character.

And indeed, *whether* it is a purely intellectual play or a scientifically fruitful formation of concepts can never be decided *a priori*. Here, too, there is only one criterion, namely that of success in the establishment of knowledge of cultural phenomena in their interrelationships, causal origin, and their *significance*. Accordingly, the formation of abstract ideal types must not be considered as the goal, but as a means.[7]

The implication of all this, of course, is that sociology and (classical) economics, to the degree to which they formulate ideal types, are auxiliary sciences of history.

Due to his conception of the goal of cultural science, the question of the usefulness of ideal types for the knowledge of empirical phenomena poses itself for Weber not as the problem of the relationship between ideal types and whole *classes* of concrete empirical phenomena, but between ideal type and individual concrete instances.

In *all* cases, however, the relationship between such rational teleological constructions and that reality which is the subject-matter of the empirical sciences, is of course not at all that of "law of nature" and "constellation" [of empirical facts], but merely that of an ideal-typical concept which serves to facilitate the empirically valid interpretation by providing a possible interpretation—an *interpretive schema*—with which the given facts are compared.[8]

The relationship between an ideal type and concrete reality is such that ". . . where relationships of the kind as abstractly described in the construct . . . have been observed or are assumed to exist in reality to some degree, we can make the *particularity* of this [empirical] relationship pragmatically clear and understandable to ourselves by reference to an *ideal type*."[9] The exact nature of this relationship between ideal type and empirical reality "is problematical in every single case."[10] However, when it has been established that in a particular instance ideal world and real world—or parts of them—coincide, then the ideal type —or elements of it—can be used as a description of the empirical world. It is irrelevant whether the two worlds coincide generally. For instance, it may be said that the phenomenon X is a rational bureaucracy with the exception of the traditional elements a and b. This is the descriptive use of ideal types which Weber has in mind. Therefore, when he says that ". . . sociology seeks to formulate type concepts and generalized uniformities of empirical process,"[11] this does not mean that the task of sociology is the formulation of universal laws and their subsequent testing in order to confirm or falsify them. The task is the construction of as many ideal worlds (or rather, parts of ideal worlds) to which ideal types refer as are necessary to yield the number of concepts sufficient to describe the historical developments in which historians are interested.

Since the function of ideal types is described by Weber as that of a means to an ulterior end, it is apparent that for him sociology is an auxiliary science to history. As Antoni correctly states: "In relation to history, this sociology might be viewed as a kind of terminology."[12] The difference between sociology and history is not just one of degree. Weippert is wrong in his opinion that it depends on the context whether a concept is an ideal type or an historical concept.[13] For the task of sociology is the construction of a special kind of general concept whereas the goal of history is the formation of individual concepts. Von Mises is equally mistaken in stating that in Weber's view "economics and sociology were historical sciences. He considered sociology a kind of more highly generalized and summarized history."[14] Weber did not consider sociology a kind of history, nor, for that matter, did he consider it an autonomous theoretical science *in its own right*. He, therefore, never was in danger of committing the fallacy of mosaic atomism of which Parsons accuses him, saying that Weber in his approach "tends, by hypostatization of ideal types, to break up in a sense not inherent in analysis as such, the organic unity both of concrete historical individuals and of the historic process. In its reification phase it issues in what may be called a 'mosaic' theory of culture and society, conceiving them to be made up of disparate atoms. (Defined as ideal type units.)"[15] Parsons's objection is based on the assumption that Weber wanted to construct a comprehensive and systematic theory in the sense of a nomological deductive system. He declares that

. . . it is one of Weber's basic theorems that while there is a plurality of possible ultimate value systems [i.e., of concrete viewpoints from which history can be written], their number is, in fact, limited. From this it follows that on Weber's own principles there is a limited number of possible constructions of historical individuals from the same concrete objects of experience, on the one hand, and of systems of theoretical concepts, on the other.[16]

As the present interpretation shows, these statements are unfounded. Parsons has not understood at all that it was precisely the seemingly unlimited number of concrete viewpoints which constituted one of Weber's and Rickert's main problems. So he declares that

. . . however different from each other the conceptual schemes are . . .
if valid, they must be "translatable" into terms of each other or of a
wider scheme. This implication is necessary to avoid a completely relati-
vistic consequence that would overthrow the whole position.[17]

This indeed misses the whole point of Weber's efforts.

The analysis of the descriptive use of ideal types has made it easy to
see why Weber thinks that they are also heuristically indispensable.
Since the terms which scientists have to use in historical descriptions
refer to an ideal world, it is a preliminary task in each instance to
determine in what respects the empirical and the ideal worlds coincide.
Before historians can describe something as "bureaucratic" they have
to find out whether, and to what degree, it has the features of a bureaucracy. The ideal type tells them where to look, i.e., it lists the things
which should be there if certain motives had been operating. If only
some of these things are there, the scientist has to infer that other motives also had an influence.[18] This is what Weber means when he says
that the ideal type, "if it leads to this result, fulfills its logical purpose
just *by* manifesting its own *unreality*."[19] The implicit assumption, of
course, always is that the type has been correctly constructed, i.e.,
that its content is objectively possible and that the motive(s) to which it
refers is (are) an adequate cause of the actions described as resulting
from it (them).[20] "Historical research faces the task of determining
in each individual case the extent to which this ideal-construct approximates or diverges from reality. . . ."[21] In the frame of this interpretation, one of Weber's examples which has puzzled the interpreters
indeed makes perfect sense.

Thus in attempting to explain the campaign of 1866, it is indispensable
both in the case of Moltke and Benedek to attempt to construct imagina-
tively how each, given fully adequate knowledge both of his own situation
and of that of his opponent, would have acted. Then it is possible to
compare with this the actual course of action and to arrive at a causal
explanation of the observed deviations, which will be attributed to such
factors as misinformation, strategical errors, logical fallacies, personal tem-
perament, or considerations outside the realm of strategy. Here, too, an
ideal-typical construction of rational action is actually employed even
though it is not made explicit.[22]

The ideal type used implicitly is, of course, that of "military battle."
This is not an ideal type of an individual battle, but a generalizing
concept of ideal-typical character which is applied to a specific situation.

It is now apparent what Weber means by postulating the indispensability of ideal types in historical research both for heuristic and expository purposes. And it is also clear what he means when he says that the ideal type

. . . is a thought-picture (*Gedankenbild*)[23] which *is* neither the historical reality [i.e., its content is not a complete reproduction of concrete reality] nor even perhaps the "true" reality [i.e., it does not present, in an absolute sense, the "essence" of reality], whose purpose is even less to serve as a schema *in* which a part of reality should find its place as an *instance* [i.e., it is not a true general concept] but it has to be interpreted as a purely ideal *limiting* concept for the *comparison* with and *scrutiny* of reality for the purpose of emphasizing certain significant parts of empirical reality.[24]

When the empirical situation seems to have all the features described in a type, then the assumption underlying its construction can be used to explain this situation. The type becomes what Weber calls a "hypothesis." In other cases it is used as a heuristic device in order to *find* the correct hypothesis.

Those interpretive schemas, therefore, are not *only*—as has been said—"hypotheses" analogous to the hypothetical "laws" in natural science. They can *function* as hypotheses when we heuristically interpret concrete processes. But in contrast to the hypotheses in natural science, the fact that in a concrete instance they do *not* contain a valid interpretation does not negate their value for the acquisition of knowledge. . . .[25]

The only event which can lead to the abandoning of an ideal type—if it has been correctly constructed—is the becoming obsolete of the value-viewpoint which provided the impetus for its construction, i.e., when history is "rewritten" from a new point of view. "The light of the great cultural problems moves on. Then science too prepares to change its standpoint and its conceptual apparatus. . . . It follows those stars which alone are able to give meaning and direction to its labor."[26]

7. WEBER AND THE *METHODENSTREIT*

It was argued in chapter one[1] that it was the *Methodenstreit* which "forced" Weber into methodological studies.[2] There can be little doubt that Weber intended his conception of the ideal type as an answer to the crucial question raised in this controversy, namely that concerning the methodological status of the generalizations of classical economics.[3] "Methodological status," it must be reiterated, refers to the way in which scientific statements (concepts) have been abstracted from concrete empirical reality. The whole discussion, thus, centered around the problems, (1) just how classical economic theory was abstracted from empirical reality, i.e., what the relationship was between the theoretical statements and the concrete data about which they were intended to inform, and (2) whether or not this way of abstracting was scientifically justified, that is, whether or not it contributed to the aim of science. The opponents in this controversy were Carl Menger, the founder of the Austrian school, on the one hand, and the various German economists constituting the so-called German Historical School, on the other, especially Wilhelm Roscher, Karl Knies, Bruno Hildebrand, and Gustav Schmoller. The various adherents of the Historical School had by no means a common methodological position; as a matter of fact, there were rather wide divergences among them. It is, of course not possible in the present context to give an exposition of all these varying positions and of the various stages of the discussion. Rather, the presentation here must be limited to just a few of the arguments put forward by Menger and Schmoller (who at the time of Weber's writings most vigorously advocated the historical position).[4] For the purposes at hand Schmoller is the most relevant representative of the Historical School, since he was the one who was most directly involved in the often rather vicious argument with Menger.[5]

In order to properly understand the reasons, claims and objections put forward by the two opponents, it is necessary to be aware that, for both of them, scientific knowledge constituted a mental picture of the empirical phenomena in question; it was conceived as a replica of the object in the mind.[6] Consequently, the question which was fundamental to the whole controversy was: What counts as a satisfactory replica? Since (in Menger's and Schmoller's views) it is the task of methodology to establish the procedures through which such a mental replica can be achieved[7] (i.e., the correct methods of abstraction), it is obvious that there can be no methodological agreement unless there is agreement on the answer to the question of just what constitutes a satisfactory replica. It was this agreement which was lacking between Menger and Schmoller, and it is this lack of agreement which was at the root of the whole *Methodenstreit*.

What was the cause of this disagreement? Basically, it seems it was the adherence to different presuppositions about the subject-matter under consideration. When knowledge is viewed as a mental picture, or replica, of the phenomena which are the object of this knowledge, then there arises necessarily the question of the adequacy of this picture. Now, this question can be answered through recourse to some idea concerning what in empirical reality is important, or "essential." Menger as well as Schmoller relied on such a notion; the former talks of the "forms" of economic phenomena, the latter claims that a science of economics presupposes a correct definition of the national economy.[8] Of course, each held a different opinion with regard to what is "essential" in concrete economic phenomena, and thus it is not surprising that there was no agreement on methodological questions. If the foregoing considerations have any validity, then it might be said that the *Methodenstreit* was the manifestation in a specific field and problem area of the clash between two conceptions of, or outlooks on, human history. One of these had come to the forefront with natural law thought, the Enlightenment, and related movements. Its central characteristic was that it viewed the events of history as the varying manifestations of something which essentially always remains the same. In Eucken's words,

> It was not so much the grasp of what was individual and changing . . . but rather the grasp of what was always the same, . . . the historical forces which are and were always everywhere the same. . . . The Enlightenment very overwhelmingly held on to the basic conception which had also dominated all older history including Machiavelli: The conception of the everlasting sameness of all historical being which on the surface perhaps changes, but essentially remains the same. Accordingly it is the task of history to penetrate to what is permanent in history, to the nature of acting man and to the essence of institutions, to the forces which build, and to the forces of destruction.[9]

This was the dominant view of history when the foundation of classical economics was laid, and it was in this spirit, then, that the formulation of the classical doctrines was an endeavor to capture what was essential in the segment of historical reality with which they dealt.

The other view of history originated and came to prominence in the Romantic reaction against Individualism and Rationalism. It stressed the uniqueness of historical events as well as their organic interdependence within larger "wholes." It insisted that historical events had to be viewed within their larger context since it was their interconnectedness with other events which accounted for their uniqueness and significance. What was essential in history, therefore, could not be captured by the formulation of such laws which state only what is recurrent in empirical phenomena. This is the foundation on which the claim arose that economics as a science dealing with historical events must be something rather different from the classical conceptions.[10]

The Romantic movement was particularly strong in Germany where political and economic thought (the latter without the benefit of the practical success which the classical doctrines had enjoyed in England) came under its influence. The German Historical School drew from the Romantic heritage, and it is with this in mind that its opposition to the classical doctrines must be understood.[11] Classical economic theory was interpreted by this school as an attempt to depict the processes making up empirical economics. It was judged unsuccessful as not conveying an adequate account of what was going on in reality.[12] The cause of its shortcomings, it was diagnosed, was the failure of its advocates to realize (1) that human individuals, in their economic pursuits, were not driven exclusively by economic considerations, but by many others as well, which may conveniently be called "ethical," and (2) that these considerations were different in different historical epochs.[13] In short, the charge was that the classical economists had abstracted from some essential features of empirical reality. The suggested remedy was to give systematic recognition to the ethical factors and their historically changing content and influence. Schmoller's ideas in this respect amounted to the view that in their economic pursuits individuals are imbued with a unitary national spirit, a national spirit which changes through time following a law of development.[14] Just how ethical considerations influence economic pursuits, and how they change over time, he intended to establish through detailed historical research. Menger, of course, was at pains to show (1) that the methods and results of classical economics were entirely justifiable, (2) that the objections of the Historical School were based on faulty premises, and (3) that the alternative suggested by the Historical School was not realizable. The arguments against or in favor of the classical style of theorizing concentrated on three specific interrelated points: (1) the universality of the classical doctrines, i.e., their validity for all times and all places; (2) their assumptions about human behavior, i.e., rationalistic hedonism; (3) the use of the "deductive" method, i.e., reasoning from first principles rather than generalization on the basis of empirical investigation. Briefly, the arguments confronting each other on each issue were the following:

(1) The problem of the universal validity of the classical theory centered around the question, whether the interrelationships between certain kinds of economic phenomena, which the theory asserts, exist

at all times and all places, or only in a particular historical period. Schmoller supported the second alternative, arguing that the economic activities going on within a group, nation or society are influenced by its institutions, legal systems, political organizations, religions and moral beliefs, etc., that these change, and that the economic activities conditioned by them therefore change too. Economic theory, if it is to give an adequate account of what is going on in empirical reality, has to consider this historical character of all economic phenomena and must not hypostatize the economic system of a particular historical period as *the* economy. [15] Menger countered this argument by stating that, of course, all economic behavior takes place in different historical circumstances, but that this cannot be an objection to the classical theory. To see in this theory, he reasons, an attempt to provide a picture of concrete economic reality, is to misunderstand it. Economic theory deals only with one *aspect* of empirical social reality, namely the economic one; that is, in Menger's view, it deals with the interrelationships between human needs, the available goods, and the striving to satisfy these needs as completely as possible, not as they concretely exist anywhere, but as they exist under certain conditions, i.e., undisturbed by any possible interfering factors.[16]

(2) The problem of the adequacy of the classical school's "psychology" concerned the assumptions that, in economic affairs, individuals are guided by self-interest, that they undertake to satisfy as many of their personal needs as they possibly can, given their resources. Schmoller reasoned that empirically people do not behave egoistically in this sense but, in their economic pursuits, are guided by a mass of additional considerations (which change historically) and that therefore the classical theory is faulty.[17] Menger responded by arguing that economic theory deals with only one "side" of human behavior, namely the individual's drive to satisfy his needs in the most "economical" (*wirtschaftlich*) fashion; that this was not to deny the empirical existence of other considerations in the acting individuals' minds, but that abstraction from "ethical" and other noneconomic elements in men's conduct was merely a device adopted in order to establish in an undistorted fashion the purely economic interdependences.[18]

(3) The issue of "deductive" versus "inductive" procedure, finally, involved the question whether the fundamental premises of classical economic theory were adequate to allow the derivations of theorems accounting for what was going on in empirical reality. After what has been said in (1) and (2) it is clear that Schmoller had to deny this,

and had to demand that on the basis of comprehensive historical research and through subsequent induction more adequate generalizations be formulated. Menger, of course, argued that the rejection of
these premises as empirically inadequate was based on the failure to
understand that they were intended to represent one aspect of human
conduct only, and that it could not be their purpose to account for
economic behavior in all its concreteness.[19]

These arguments clearly show that the *Methodenstreit* revolved
around the problem of the "representational" adequacy of the classical
theory. The central question was whether classical theory could provide a satisfactory picture of empirical economic phenomena. However, it was not formulated in these terms. Rather, it was posed as a
problem of abstraction: How was economics to abstract from concrete empirical reality? The adherents of the Historical School did not
have identical answers to this question. Some, e.g., Knies, argued that
the task of economics was to describe and explain economic behavior
in all its concreteness, and that only economic history was adequate to
this task. Others did not go so far; all were united, however, in the
belief that reference to the individual's rational pursuit of his self-
interest was not enough to explain actual economic phenomena. Thus,
Schmoller argued for the inclusion of "ethical" factors in economic
theory, which he visualized as an evolutionary theory.

Menger, now, by no means denied that, concretely, individuals in
their economic pursuits were not exclusively driven by self-interest.
He denied, however, that this invalidated classical economic theory
and argued (1) that every theory has to abstract from concrete reality
and that for theoretical purposes "ethical" and other motives could be
disregarded in economics, (2) that history and theory have diametri-
cally opposed aims and therefore cannot replace each other, and (3)
that an historical theory, as advocated by the Historical School, is a
contradiction in terms.[20] This he supported by the following reasoning.

All concrete phenomena can be considered from two different viewpoints;[21] the scientific interest can focus either on their concrete individuality or on the recurrent forms ("types")[22] in which they appear (*Erscheinungsformen*), i.e., their generic character. Accordingly,
there are historical sciences dealing with the concrete particularity of
phenomena and theoretical sciences, which attempt to generalize.[23]
Historical sciences try to understand a phenomenon by investigating
its individual process of development, "by becoming aware of the
concrete relationships under which it has developed and, indeed, has

become what it is, in its special quality."[24] Theoretical sciences try to understand a concrete phenomenon "by recognizing it to be a special case of a certain regularity (conformity to law) in the succession, or in the coexistence of phenomena."[25] The historical and the theoretical understanding of phenomena thus are two completely different, although equally justifiable, modes of grasping them scientifically. As such they must not be confused with each other. Menger charges that the adherents of the Historical School, by criticizing classical theory for neglecting the influence of "ethical" and other noneconomic factors which obviously empirically influence economic action, criticize a theoretical science for not being a historical one.[26] They do not realize that what they want to put in the place of the classical theory is not a better theory, but either a history of economic phenomena or an explanation of concrete phenomena with the help of the existing theory.[27] Through this they believe to contribute to the development of economic theory proper. "By having so failed to recognize the formal nature of theoretical economics . . . a large number of the German economists have fallen into . . . grievous error. . . . This is, to be sure, the most fundamental error of which a school can be the victim, for they have bypassed the very science which they thought to develop."[28]

Having thus argued in support of a theoretical economic science as an autonomous branch of inquiry, Menger attempts to justify the particularities of classical economic theory. He begins by stating that a theory can never be about phenomena in their total concreteness, but must always deal with only one particular "side" of the phenomena. A theoretical understanding of phenomena in all their concreteness can be yielded only by all theoretical sciences in their totality.[29] Economic theory deals with one side of human conduct only, namely the economic one, and it is nonsensical to accuse it of not taking other factors into consideration.

But those who perceive one-sidedness in this and want to sublimate pure economics into a theory of social phenomena in their totality also confuse here the points of view of historical and theoretical understanding. They overlook the fact that *history*, to be sure, has the task of making us understand all sides of *certain* phenomena, but that exact *theories* have the task of making us understand only *certain* sides of *all* phenomena in their way.[30]

Next, Menger draws a distinction between realistic-empirical theories and exact theories. The former state empirical regularities ("real types") [31] as they can be established in an inductive fashion. The regularities of coexistence or succession thus established can only be of an approximate kind since all concrete relationships of coexistence and succession in empirical reality are distorted and interfered with by disturbing influences.[32] Furthermore, there is nothing in induction which could justify the assumption that the established regularities are universal.[33] For this reason, it is not possible ever to formulate exact laws, or laws of nature ("strict types") on an inductive basis. They can be found only through a different procedure, one that permits an abstraction from all accidental disturbances and is a secure foundation of their universality:

> ... it seeks to ascertain the *simplest elements* of everything real. ... It strives for the establishment of these elements by way of an only partially empirical-realistic analysis, i.e., without considering whether these in reality are present as *independent* phenomena. ... In this manner theoretical research arrives at ... results ... which, to be sure, must not be tested by full empirical reality (for the empirical forms here under discussion, e.g., absolutely pure oxygen, pure alcohol, pure gold, a person pursuing only economic aims etc., exist in part only in our ideas). ... Exact science, accordingly, does not examine the regularities in the succession, etc., of *real* phenomena either. It examines, rather, how more complicated phenomena develop from the simplest, in part even unempirical elements of the real world in their (likewise unempirical) isolation from all other influences. ...[34]

To these two tenets—(1) that a theory deals with one aspect of phenomena only, and (2) that exact statements, or laws of nature, must not be rejected just because, due to disturbing influences, no empirical instance ever exactly conforms to them—Menger adds a third and very particular conception, namely that, from the point of view of a particular theory, those sides of concrete phenomena with which it is not concerned constitute the disturbing influences which prevent the empirical phenomena from ever conforming to the laws established by this exact theory.

Anyone who wants to understand the phenomena of nature as experience offers them to us ... in an exact way, i.e., as an exemplification of the strict regularity in all natural things, must not seek this understanding, for instance, merely in the laws of chemistry, of mechanics, or exclusively in those of physics, etc., but can attain them only through the totality, or at least a majority of the exact sciences. For only in this way will he reach an exact understanding of those phases and sides of real phenomena which from the point of view of a *single* exact science would perhaps present themselves to him as *irregularities*, as exceptions to the strict regularity of the world of phenomena.[35]

From all these considerations, Menger draws the following conclusion with regard to classical economic theory: social phenomena, or "human phenomena" (*Menschheitserscheinungen*), as Menger calls them, are composed of human actions which occur due to certain "propensities" or "drives."

The exact orientation of theoretical research . . . has . . . the task of reducing human phenomena to the expression of the most original and the most general forces and impulses of human nature . . . of hereupon examining to what formations the free play of each individual basic propensity of human nature leads, uninfluenced by other factors (especially by error, by ignorance of the situation, and by external compulsion).[36]

This must lead to a variety of (exact) social theories, each of which deals with only one side, or aspect, of the social phenomena, that is, deals with the manifestation of one propensity only, abstracting from the influence of the others.[37] Classical economic theory is the exact theory dealing with the most important human propensity, namely each individual's drive to strive for his material well-being, and the phenomena resulting from it. In doing so it abstracts from all other, noneconomic propensities as well as error, ignorance, etc. This procedure is intrinsic to the construction of any exact theory; complaints about the disregard of these factors are, therefore, unjustified.

As emerges quite unambiguously from Menger's reasoning, he views concrete empirical phenomena as being composed of elements belonging to different spheres or realms each of which is governed by laws of its own. Concretely and historically these spheres are intermixed and interpenetrate each other in various ways, the specific intermixtures creating specific sets of conditions under which the laws of each sphere operate; that is, the presence of phenomena belonging to any one sphere prevents the laws of some or all other spheres from operating in an undisturbed fashion. It is this conception against which Schmoller's main criticism is directed. By and large he agrees with Menger's distinction of historical and theoretical sciences, and he accepts in principle the necessity of abstracting from distorting influences.[38] He insists, however, that there is no such thing as an economic sphere with laws of its own which empirically is constantly interfered with by the intrusion of other spheres. This is the meaning of his reiterated postulate that human economic conduct must not be isolated from the social context in which it occurs (this context having an influence on individuals' motives), and that a more adequate theory of motivation be formulated.[39] He states that ". . . of course all thought and knowledge is based on abstraction; the important point is, however, to abstract correctly . . . ;"[40]

. . . certain isolations may be absolutely wrong. The chemist may dare to abstract from the physical properties of a chemical object; if, however, he analyzed the air of the atmosphere and said, in accordance with Menger's method of isolation: I consider only nitrogen, since it predominates, he would be immediately ejected from the laboratory.[41]

For Schmoller, the pursuit of individual self-interest is not a "side" of human conduct which can be isolated from other pursuits, since all of the individual's motivations are integrated into a unifying psychic system. The elements of this system and their relative importance change through time as the result of changes in the nation as a whole, of which the individuals are part. The most fundamental laws governing an economy therefore, are the laws of societal development.[42] From these conceptions issued his objections to Menger's claims for the universality of classical economic theory, its psychology, and its disregard for (inductive) empirical evidence, i.e., the use of the deductive method. In one way or other, all these objections are an argument against certain ontological assumptions about economic reality; this argument obviously amounts to more than a mere emphasis on the triviality that under different historical conditions the laws of economics entail different consequences. What is at stake is the very legitimacy of a peculiar conceptualization of a set of social phenomena as conditions to a somehow existing economic sphere. The option for the inductive method, accordingly, is the option for the idea that all social phenomena belong to the same ontological level of social reality and must therefore all be part of one unified theory. This is clearly recognized by Othmar Spann, a sympathizer with the Historical School who may therefore be quoted extensively:

Economics is only a province, a department, of society, existing side by side with State, law, religion, etc. This brings us up against the basic problem of method. . . . Can the laws of the internal structure and the evolution of political economy be studied as if they existed "by themselves," as if they formed a closed and self-determining system, originating out of purely economic causation (individual self-interest); or should we, rather, regard economics as inseparably interconnected with the other provinces of society, and therefore not subject to laws peculiar to itself, but participating in the historically conditioned structure and development of society as a whole—which, for the very reason that they are historically conditioned, are individual, and therefore not in strict conformity with law. If we adopt the former alternative, if (as did Ricardo and Karl Menger) we assume economics to exist apart, pure, and disconnected from the historical process, we shall choose a method which ignores social and historical configurations. It will be isolative or abstract; . . . If we adopt the latter alternative, after the manner of the historical school, which is concerned only with concrete historical realities, we shall choose a method directed towards the study of these. It will not only be historical, statistical, and realistic, but it will endeavor to understand the present as an outcome of the past. Necessarily it will renounce any attempt to comprehend economics in terms of theory. . . . Whatever regulative principles . . . it is possible to observe, will merge into evolutionary trends or other uniform successions.[43]

The "inductive" approach to economics, then, basically was to involve detailed historical research. This collected historical material ultimately was to provide the basis for generalizations, at least as far as Schmoller was concerned;[44] they were to be laws of evolution and the development of total societies, sequences of societal stages, and stages of progress. In fact, no such generalizations were ever established. Most importantly, Schmoller never clarified unambiguously the methodological status of these laws; he never clearly stated how they had to be abstracted from empirical reality. In practice the requirements of the tenet, that the basis for any induction must be the establishment of the economic facts in all their historical interrelatedness with the rest of the societal phenomena, led to ever more detailed historical research. Economists of a historical persuasion never got around to the precise formulation of generalizations, so that Menger could mockingly say that by the Historical School

. . . the art of abstract thinking, no matter how greatly distinguished by depth and originality and no matter how broadly supported empirically —in brief, everything that in other theoretical sciences establishes the greatest fame of scholars is still considered, compared to the products of compilatory diligence, as something secondary, almost as a stigma.[45]

This is how the lines were drawn between Menger and Schmoller when Weber felt compelled to devote his attention to methodological problems. At the end of his reflections, what he arrived at was a position which conformed with neither Menger's nor Schmoller's, but which incorporated many elements found in one or the other. That this was not the result of eclecticism, but achieved by systematic argument from certain premises, was shown in chapters two and three. Weber credits Menger with the fundamental insight that both an historical and a theoretical treatment of social reality are possible and that neither one can take the place of the other.[46] With this, he accepts two major criticisms directed against positions taken by adherents of the Historical School.

(1) Economic theory cannot be replaced by economic history. Neither is the presentation of the historical development of economic phenomena a theoretical undertaking nor can there be such a thing as an historical theory, i.e., a theory of economic phenomena in all their concreteness.[47] (2) The adequacy of economic theory must not be assessed by standards which are applicable to historical research only. The complete reproduction of historical phenomena in all their concreteness cannot be a measure of the theory.

With the Historical School, Weber shared the misgivings concerning the cognitive status of the classical formulations. But whereas the adherents of the Historical School objected to their establishment as such, Weber was dissatisfied merely with the methodological self-interpretations given by the supporters of the classical approach. He agrees with Menger who, in his polemic against Schmoller, triumphantly declares[48] that Schmoller himself admits the necessity of theoretical knowledge when he states that to be perfect, history "presupposes a perfect classification of the phenomena, a perfect concept formation, a correct subsumption of the individual instance under the observed types, a complete overview over the possible causes."[49] In Weber's opinion, history cannot be written without general concepts, and all objections to theory-construction as such are therewith pointless.[50] However, Weber is in total disagreement with Menger's methodological interpretation of these concepts.

In spite of the fundamental methodological distinction between historical knowledge and the knowledge of "laws" which the creator of the theory [of marginal utility] was the *first* and only to draw, he now claims empirical *validity*, in the sense of the *deducibility* of reality from "laws," for the propositions of abstract theory. It is true that this is not meant in the sense of empirical validity of the abstract economic laws as such, but in the sense that when equally "exact" theories have been constructed for *all* the *other* relevant factors, all these abstract theories *together* must contain the true reality of the objects, that is, whatever is worth knowing of reality. Exact economic theory deals with the operation of *one* psychic motive, other theories have the task to develop in a similar fashion doctrines of hypothetical validity about all remaining motives. . . . This claim fails to observe that in order to be able to reach this result even in the simplest case, the *totality* of the existing historical reality under consideration, including every one of its causal relationships, must be postulated as "given" and presupposed as *known*. But if *this* type of knowledge were accessible to the finite mind of man, abstract theory would have no cognitive value whatsoever.[51]

As the source of Menger's error Weber identifies "the naturalistic prejudice" that the "laws" of economics "were to be something similar to the ones formulated in the natural sciences...."[52] This led him to misunderstand their methodological status.

It was believed that the task was to isolate a specific "drive" in man, the acquisitive drive, or else to observe in isolation a specific maxim of human action, the so-called economic principle.[53]

However,

The formulations of abstract theory only superficially appear to be "deductions" from basic psychological motives; in reality, they are special cases of a kind of concept formation which is peculiar and to a certain extent indispensable to the sciences of human culture. [Rather, they are ideal types.][54]

Weber's solution to the *Methodenstreit* thus involves a vindication of theoretical research in the style of the classical economists. It must be borne in mind, however, that this vindication is based on premises which are rather different from Menger's. Menger, although he introduced the distinction between theoretical and historical pursuits, did not view them as corresponding to different human cognitive interests, but as corresponding to different features of concrete empirical reality. He justified theory as an attempt to find the "forms" which are inherent in phenomena. Weber, in contrast, argued on a subjectivist basis. It was this epistemological foundation, different from both Menger's and Schmoller's, which enabled him to find a way out of the dead-end street of the *Methodenstreit* and to come to the following conclusions:

(1) Economic phenomena in their (relative) concreteness can be grasped only through an historical treatment. The assumption made by the Historical School, that through the proper use of induction laws can be established which conceptualize the historical character of social phenomena, is a contradiction in terms.

(2) Economics can only be an historical science, since its task is to grasp conceptually a particular part of cultural reality—economic phenomena—*in its quality as cultural reality*. Cultural reality *as such* can be conceptualized only in an historical fashion. A generalizing procedure as it is used in the natural sciences would with logical neces-

sity lead to the disregard of, i.e., abstraction from, the very cultural elements of reality whose knowledge is the aim.

(3) No historical account of anything is possible without the (at least implicit) use of generalizations. This may sound like a compromise argument, settling the dispute by acknowledging the necessity of both historical treatment and "abstract theory." It must be emphasized, however, that this is not so. The reason simply is that the generalizations required by historians must concern the interrelationships of *cultural* phenomena as such. These laws cannot be established by a generalizing treatment of empirical reality in the same way as it is practiced in the natural sciences, since this treatment would eliminate the particular cultural features of the segment of reality under consideration. The classical economists' self-interpretation of their generalizations as laws of nature therefore is completely erroneous. The laws required by historians must hold between phenomena in their quality as *cultural* phenomena. Such generalizations can be established by limiting the generalizing procedure to cultural phenomena alone. This is plainly at variance with the method of the natural sciences whose generalizations encompass *all* of reality. By artificially limiting generalization to only a part of concrete empirical reality, the "laws" used by historians clearly cannot have the same status as "laws of nature."

(4) The generalizations used by historians have, for the reasons stated above,[55] a peculiar cognitive status, i.e., they stand in a peculiar relationship to the empirical phenomena to which they refer and about which they are intended to inform. They are ideal types, referring to, and informing about, an ideal, constructed world, not the empirically existing one. For this reason the self-interpretation of the classical economists, that their generalizations are laws of nature, is mistaken. They do not refer to a particular level or component of empirical reality taken in isolation from others with which it is empirically intermingled. Rather, these generalizations refer to an ideal world in which everything conforms to certain meaning structures, an important insight which Weber credits to Gottl. Thus, economic theory is not empirical in the sense that its generalizations are intended to give correct information about empirical (concrete) reality.

(5) Economic theory, i.e., generalizations about economic phenomena, is an auxiliary science to history, just as political science is auxiliary to (political) history, and sociology to (social) history.[56]

CHAPTER IV. IDEAL TYPES, MODELS, AND SOCIOLOGICAL THEORY

1. THE METHODOLOGICAL STATUS OF IDEAL-TYPICAL CONSTRUCTIONS

The conception of the ideal type has been regarded by many as the crowning achievement of Weber's efforts in the field of methodology. It is the task of this last chapter to inquire whether it has now become obsolete, or whether some of the ideas underlying its formulation have retained their validity. To this purpose it is useful first to give a summary of the most important and relevant results achieved in chapter three. As the analysis presented there has shown, there are three interrelated aspects of ideal-typical constructs which must be taken into account. These are (1) their *logical character*, as Weber sees it, i.e., their form and the relationship between their contents and the part of empirical reality which they are intended to conceptualize; (2) the particularities of the substantive *content* of ideal-typical statements, and (3) the *function* of ideal types *in research*. All three must be taken into account in a complete answer to the question, "What is an ideal type?"[1] It may be stated, then, (1) that with respect to its logical character an ideal type is a concept (a formed mental representation) of several relatively similar, complex phenomena. For the purpose of conceptualization it is pretended that each of these phenomena is constituted by an identical combination of component elements, although empirically there are considerable differences of degree between them in the relevant respects. For instance, the (ideal-typical) concept "bureaucracy" refers to a set of empirical phenomena which to varying extents exhibit "bureaucratic" features, as they are listed in the definition of the concept. Thus the form of an ideal type is general, its content is "ideal." This does not mean that it refers to something desirable. Rather, "ideal" means that the conceptual content is abstracted from empirical reality in an idealizing or exaggerating fashion. It means that the constellation of facts described in the definition of an ideal type would characterize to an equal degree the phenomena to which the type refers, if empirically certain—ideal—conditions were fulfilled. (2) With respect to its substantive content, an ideal type describes the particular kinds of norms and plans which human individuals decide to follow in a particular kind of social situation, and the types of acts and thoughts which follow from these decisions. (3)

As to its function in research, an ideal type is a heuristic device for—among other things—finding out in a specific empirical case by what motives the actors in question were guided in their actions. It describes a situation which has resulted from actions conforming to a particular kind of motive or action maxim, which alone is assumed to be operative in the minds of the relevant individuals. It is intended to refer to a class of complex empirical phenomena—named by the label of a particular ideal-typical construction, e.g., "conflict," "domination," "social relationship," etc.—and formulated as a description of the configuration of their component parts. This is done with the tacit assumption that they may not all have the same components (or the same configuration), since in addition to the assumed plans and motives empirically in all relevant cases (or almost all of them) other as yet unknown motives are also influencing the conduct of the actors in question. Thus an ideal type gives the impression of being a description of a number of empirically existing identical states of affairs, whereas it actually describes the state of affairs like which the existing phenomena would be if the relevant actors had been able to pursue consciously and exclusively certain clearly defined goals or plans of action in clearly defined ways. When this construct is compared with an empirical instance to which it is applicable, the divergence between the empirical situation and the type gives clues to what extent other motives than the ones mentioned in the construct actually existed as causes of certain actions which are a part of the concrete situation under consideration.[2]

In discussing the ideal type, Weber above all wanted to clarify the logical status of certain concepts occurring in historical writings, like "city," "bureaucracy," or "state." The specific solution at which he arrived directly followed from the presuppositions with which he approached the task. Clarifying the logical status of a concept for him meant analyzing the relationship between conceptual content and that part of empirical reality to which the concept refers, i.e., establishing a principle in accordance with which the concept has been abstracted from reality. The concepts in whose logical status he was interested could not be treated as genuine general concepts, as he conceived of them. He found this impossible due to the fact that genuine general concepts in principle cannot describe these phenomena. Another way of stating this is to say that the phenomena in question do not allow the formulation of class concepts. This is so because they do not exhibit to equal degrees the combination of characteristics which must be mentioned in the definitions of such concepts. This, of course is a result of the fact that the phenomena which are conceptualized are selected according to their cultural significance, and not because they exhibit the same constellation of parts which many other phenomena also exhibit. In fact, those of their component parts on which their significance rests, and in which historians are interested, are empirically not equally shared by a whole set of phenomena, but occur to different degrees in different instances. In order to emphasize the fact that the concepts he was dealing with are not genuine general concepts, although their form gives them this appearance, Weber called them "types." In order to point to the specific relationship between the contents of these concepts and the empirical phenomena which they are intended to grasp, he called them "ideal."

Ever since the publication of Weber's essays in 1904, the notion of ideal type has played a role in methodological and theoretical discussions in sociology. There are few authors who have not criticized Weber's position. Unfortunately, there are even fewer whose insight into the sources of Weber's concerns and difficulties was sufficient to make their contributions worthwhile. Were it not for two or three notable essays[3] it would hardly be an exaggeration to say that in 60 years practically nothing has been achieved as far as the clarification of the methodological status of the ideal type is concerned. The question, of course, is whether this is so because Weber, in his discussion of the ideal type, did not deal with a genuine problem, but with a dilemma which was self-created by an untenable methodological approach. As one author says: "The exact logic of science, which is recognized as valid also for the social sciences, understandably cannot make sense out of Max Weber's concept in a way that is logically justifiable." Strangely enough, this same author nevertheless does not want to abandon the concept.[4]

Weber argued that ideal-typical concepts are indispensable in the cultural sciences since—in addition to their heuristic function, which is of no concern in the present context—they are needed to describe phenomena which, in those aspects which interest the historian, cannot be subsumed under regular class concepts.[5] This argument rests on the idea that the linguistic expressions referring to observable phenomena are connected with concepts, i.e., formed mental contents, in such a way that the understanding of the expression evokes formed representations or images of empirical reality in the human mind, and that in a scientifically valid way humans can have reality in the mind only in the form of either general or individual concepts. Thus, the meaning of a term which designates observable events is viewed as the mental image of reality which is connected with it. *Weber was puzzled by the fact that certain empirical phenomena are grouped together and named by the same term*—subsumed under a concept of general form, e.g., "bureaucracy"—*which in the strict sense do not meet the necessary qualifications for subsumption under general or class concepts, as he understood them.* His trouble was that these phenomena do not constitute a *class* whose instances have certain absolute qualities (or elements) in common, but constitute a serial *order*. Thus, terms like "rational action" or "economic exchange" look as if they designate class concepts, but as soon as they are used in combinations like "not entirely rational" or "economic exchange which is partly governed by traditional considerations" it becomes apparent that they designate a scale on which phenomena are located according to the extent to which they exhibit particular features. Within the framework of his theory of meaning, it was impossible for Weber to conceive of a mental image—one single mental image, that is—depicting many phenomena which in the crucial aspects differ from each other by degrees.

This aspect of Weber's problem can be resolved once the idea is given up that knowledge and concepts consist of images in the mind and must be treated in a frame of reference which takes account of this. For methodological purposes the problem of what exactly goes on in the human mind when a person understands words and sentences is irrelevant.

Weber's conception that somehow a sign (the linguistic expression) is correlated with the mental picture of an object (or a number of objects) is incompatible with the fact that there are many terms which people understand without apparently having any mental images of objects at all. To be sure, something must be going on in the human mind when meanings are understood. But what this is, is a question of psychology.[6] Knowledge of the correct answer to this psychological question is not a prerequisite for communication and science. To the extent that Weber intended his definitions of ideal types as an attempt of providing a clear terminology, therefore, his theory of knowledge led him astray. For this problem is not solved by considerations about mental processes. For the purposes of science, it is solved simply by providing rules which insure that intersubjectively there is a (relatively) identical use of the scientific language. In this respect, however, Weber's definitions are incomplete, for although it is acknowledged by Weber that the objects to which his ideal types refer can be ranked in a serial order according to the degree in which they possess certain characteristics, the principle of ordering is not precisely defined.

Carl G. Hempel and Paul Oppenheim were the first to clarify the logical structure of ordering concepts.[7] In their book they argued that, just as the definition of a class concept must allow the differentiation between those objects which have a certain property (or number of properties) and those which do not, the definition of an ordering concept must make it possible to determine an order among the objects to which it refers. It must therefore contain the following specifications:[8] (a) it must spell out under what conditions two objects occupy the same place in an order, (b) it must be stipulated under what conditions an object precedes another in the order. The relation described in (a) must be transitive and symmetrical, the one described in (b) intransitive and symmetrical. Further, (c) the two relations must be connected with each other.[9]

The introduction of ordering concepts provides a solution to the problem of conceptualizing a continuous series of phenomena. All ideal types may be interpreted as representing the extreme poles of ordering, or comparative, concepts, no matter how complex the phenomena to which they refer.[10] It seems, however, that this approach does not really do justice to Weber's intent. Whereas it certainly provides a solution to his immediate difficulties, it misses what he ultimately wanted to convey. The crucial and problematic aspect of ideal types does not lie in their formal incompleteness, the fact that they are imperfect ordering concepts (although some of them undeniably can be usefully treated as such). Rather, their interesting feature is that they constitute an attempt at establishing generalizations about human social action.[11] This is what Weber wanted them to be. However, in order to express his intention, he had to make use of the notion of class concept, since this was the only logical form available to him.[12] Again it has to be remembered here that for Weber, general concepts are equivalent to (universal) statements about interrelationships between empirically existing elements of complex phenomena. The introduction of ordering concepts—incomplete and ambiguous as their definitions may be—is the only way, given the class-logic which Weber uses, in which generalizations, the formulation of laws, can be attempted in the cultural sciences. In this context it is imperative to realize, however, that Weber has a particular conception of "law." For him, "laws" are summary descriptions in terms of "cause"

and "effect" of a multitude of known, specific sequences of phenomena. They are not interpreted as hypotheses postulating certain
invariant *relationships* between particular variables. Rather, they are
meant to state that certain causes are known to exist frequently, and
in the ideal case always, (everywhere) in the empirical world, and
therefore certain effects, too. They state that identical constellations
of facts empirically exist in many instances (and ideally, everywhere)
and that therefore, due to the operation of causal laws, identical constellations of effects occur. In other words, *general concepts do not
postulate invariant relationships between instances of classes of phenomena, but describe recurrent occurrences of identical cause-effect
sequences.* They are conjunctions of singular statements, each describing such a sequence. Thus, in Weber's self-interpretation a general concept does not assert, for example, that people who feel that they belong
together act in ways expressing this feeling. Rather, it asserts that empirically there are many instances (whose location in time and space
is known) in which individuals actually have these feelings and therefore act in particular ways. These instances are grouped together and
given a name. By calling the general concepts occurring in the historical sciences "ideal types" Weber is indicating that empirically
the (complex) causes and effects whose existence is asserted in all those
instances to which the type is intended to refer (in the example, all
communal social relationships) do not quite occur as described by
the construct, but only approximately so. This is the state of affairs
which Weber has in mind when he describes the process of abstraction
by which an ideal type is constructed.

An ideal type is formed by the one-sided *exaggeration* (*Steigerung*) of
one or *several* points of view and by the synthesis of a great many diffusely and discretely existing component phenomena (*Einzelerscheinungen*)
which are sometimes more and sometimes less present and occasionally
absent, which are in accordance with those one-sidedly emphasized viewpoints, and which are arranged into an internally consistent (*in sich
einheitlich*) *thought-image*.[13]

All ideal types refer to constellations of ("component") phenomena,
i.e., elements of empirical reality, which exist as the result of the fact
that human individuals have consciously and exclusively enacted certain clearly defined[14] inner states (plans, emotions, reasons, etc.).
Thus, ideal types describe the phenomena, consisting of component
elements standing in specific relations to each other, which empirically
exist when certain conditions are fulfilled, *pretending for the purposes*

of concept formation that these conditions are given in all the instances which are intended to be covered by the type. To what extent they *actually are* fulfilled in each instance, is problematic. However—and this is important—in each instance they are assumed to be fulfilled to *some* degree.

2. THE PRINCIPLES OF IDEAL-TYPE CONSTRUCTION

In spite of the heavy and varied criticisms directed against Weber's methodological arguments, the constructs which he called "ideal types" continue to be used and produced. This is not really surprising once it is realized that Weber's analysis of ideal types is the attempt of a *rational reconstruction* of a *procedure in use*.[1] Since historians—or sociologists, for that matter—continue to produce accounts of the kind whose logical status Weber tried to clarify, it is understandable that the term "ideal type" is still employed. However, it becomes imperative now that sociologists free themselves of the presuppositions of Weber's theory and reanalyze those features of the actual scientific enterprise on which Weber was focusing.

The formulation of an ideal type, as it emerges from Weber's description, involves the following procedure:

(1) The social scientist chooses a universal statement which asserts that in a certain kind of social situation, humans decide to act in conformity with a particular maxim of conduct. According to Weber, this hypothesis is an inductively established generalization expressing that in all known instances of the kind of situation under consideration, individuals decided to act in conformity with the particular maxim.[2] Examples: (a) in politics, individuals try to optimize their control over others; (b) when undergoing changes in social status, people seek refuge in radical ideologies.

(2) The scientist constructs in his mind a situation of the kind referred to in the hypothesis. He specifies its features to some degree by giving it certain characteristics. In Weber's view, this situation is constructed through "idealizing" abstraction from the features of known situations of the requisite kind; accordingly, it resembles them in many respects. Examples: (a) a campaign for political office in a mass democracy; (b) the downward mobility of population groups in a Protestant society with a democratic political system.

(3) The scientist, with the help of the hypothesis about individuals' decisions listed under (1), then constructs in his mind what one actor, or a multiplicity of actors, when put in the situation described under (2), would do, i.e., what kinds of activities would ensue, and what phenomena would result from these activities (given certain facilities and obstacles). Examples: (a) attempts to get voter support by giving speeches, etc., the foundation of a political party, fund-raising efforts, etc.; (b) attempts to cope with the threat of status loss by creating suitable conservative religious and political ideologies.

(4) The scientist now formulates subclasses of the kind of situation referred to in (2) by giving its general characteristics various specific values. Examples: (a) the contenders for office are rich—the contenders for office are poor; (b) the downwardly mobile group are farmers—the downwardly mobile group are the petty bourgeoisie.

(5) With the help of the "nomological" hypothesis mentioned in (1), the scientist constructs in his mind the specific activities which would occur if actors were put in each of the situations referred to in (4), and what the results of these activities would be. Examples: (a) the contenders do not rely on the financial help of "fat cats" vying for political influence—the contenders rely on the financial help of "fat cats"; (b) downwardly mobile farmers are attracted by religious revivals—downwardly mobile petty bourgeoisie are attracted by right wing political parties. According to Weber, the operations listed under (3), (4), and (5) are performed while continually checking the available evidence.

(6) The configuration of activities and their results referred to in (3), (a hypothetical configuration of events), is what is described by an ideal type. (1) and (2) are frequently called the "assumptions" on which this type rests. A comparison of the varying activities and endproducts of actions referred to in (5), which result from the varying situational circumstances referred to in (4), allows the establishment of the covariations existing between various components of the scientists's imagined world, which is described by the ideal type. It is these interrelationships which are frequently presented as sociological or economic "laws." Examples: (a) the ideal type is that of a political power struggle in a democracy. The ideal-typical "law" is: "the wealthier the contenders in the struggle for political power in mass democracy, the smaller the political influence of fat cats." (b)

The ideal type is that of the reaction to downward social mobility in a Protestant society with a democratic political system. The "law" is: "the more rural a group threatened by status loss in a Protestant society with a democratic system, the higher the incidence of religious revival meetings; the more urban the group, the greater the strength of right wing political parties."

The examples given here are, of course, invented and not too precise. For the purpose of further illustration, it may be useful to present a short analysis of Weber's ideal type of bureaucracy:

(1) The hypothesis used in the construction of the ideal type of bureaucracy is: "In positions of political leadership, humans try to use the most efficient means available to them to exercise power (i.e., to have their way against resistance)."[3]

(2) The kind of social situation in which efforts of this type take place is characterized as an imperatively coordinated group, or "ruling organization" (*Herrschaftsverband*),[4] which is large enough for the ruler to require an administrative staff for the transmission of his orders and the supervision of their execution. It is posited that the ruler has sufficient facilities available to him to organize successfully an administrative staff which is best suited to his purposes, namely the exercise of (legitimate) power. The situation is also characterized by the existence, on the part of all relevant actors, of the following beliefs:

(a) Any given legal norm may be established by agreement or by imposition, on grounds of expediency or value-rationality or both, with a claim to obedience at least on the part of the members of the organization.

(b) Every body of law consists essentially in a consistent system of abstract rules which have normally been intentionally established. Administration of law is held to consist in the application of these rules to particular cases.

(c) The typical person in authority, the "superior," is himself subject to an impersonal order by orienting his actions to it in his own dispositions and commands.

(d) The person who obeys authority does so only in his capacity as a "member" of the organization, and what he obeys is only "the law."

(e) The members of the organization, insofar as they obey a person in authority, do not owe this obedience to him as an individual, but to the impersonal order.[5]

(3) On the part of the ruler, this leads to actions bringing about the following results:

(a) A continuous rule-bound conduct of official business.

(b) Specified spheres of competence.

(c) An organization of offices following the principle of hierarchy; that is, each lower office is under the control and supervision of a higher one.

(d) Technical rules or norms are regulating the conduct of an office; if their application is to be fully rational, specialized training is necessary. The administrative staff of a rational organization thus consists of "officials."

(e) The members of the administrative staff are completely separated from ownership of the means of administration.

(f) There is a complete absence of appropriation of his official position by the incumbent.

(g) Administrative acts, decisions, and rules are formulated and recorded in writing.

(h) The whole administrative staff under the supreme authority consists of individual officials.

(i) Officials are personally free and subject to authority only with respect to their impersonal office obligations.

(j) The office is filled by a free contractual relationship; thus, there is free selection.

(k) Officials are remunerated by fixed salaries in money.

(l) The office is treated as the sole occupation of the incumbent.

(m) It constitutes a career. There is a system of "promotion" according to seniority or to achievement, or both.

(n) The official is subject to strict and systematic discipline and control in the conduct of the office.[6]

(4) Two subclasses of this type are formed by assuming that:

(a) officials are tenured;

(b) officials are subject to discretionary dismissal or transfer.

(5) In the case of (4a), officials discharge their specific office duties in a strictly impersonal style, independent from any considerations of personal benefit. In the case of (4b), officials discharge their duties always with an eye on the implications of their actions with respect to their job security.

(6) The ideal type in question is that of bureaucracy. One "law" of bureaucracies is: "In the modern bureaucracy, the more materially secure the office holders, the less the role of personal considerations in the performance of their office duties, i.e., the more 'objective' their decisions."[7]

If the analysis of ideal-type construction as presented here is correct, then there can be no doubt that, strictly speaking, ideal types do not provide a description of any set of empirical phenomena; rather, they describe constellations or sequences of phenomena which would frequently exist if (1) people always decide to act in certain ways in certain kinds of situations (although actually they do not), and if (2) all empirical instances of these kinds of situations had the same features (which they actually have not). Thus, they describe hypothetical constellations of events, that is, mental constructs.

Weber arrived at the insight that the "abstract" theories of economics, sociology, and political science describe mental constructs, not classes of empirical phenomena, due to his interpretation of laws of nature as conjunctions of singular statements, i.e., as a result of his inductivist methodological approach. His view of laws as summarizations of statements describing individual empirical instances made him aware of the peculiar status of ideal-typical statements. This insight into their special character was a very keen one, and its astuteness is quite independent of the correctness of the peculiar premises from which it was derived. Weber realized (1) that the formulations he was analyzing do not inform about the real world, but about an ideal one, and (2) that this ideal world, or *model*,[8] which is a mental construct, is related to the real world in ways which—after analysis—can be specified for every relevant instance, though not in general (unless "idealizing" is accepted as such a specification). From this insight, two things immediately follow. (1) Statements about the model must not be treated as if they constituted a theory of a class of empirical phenomena.[9] (2) The construction or selection of a suitable model and its application to a particular case must not be confused with the testing of empirical hypotheses. Types are descriptions of constructed configurations, configurations which may not be found anywhere in empirical reality. In principle, they do not make any assertions about the actual empirical occurrence of these constellations of elements. However, they are constructed in such a fashion that the empirical occurrences of constellations of phenomena which are like the model configurations, are possible. This is accomplished by making sure (1) that the constructed configuration is related in a determinate fashion to another constructed configuration in such a way that the empirical occurrence of the latter configuration (a social situation of a particular kind, providing certain conditions and facilities) brings about (through the occurrence of a certain type of action) an empirical constellation of phenomena which is like the one described in the model, and (2) that the determining configuration (the social situation) is of a kind whose actual occurrence is empirically possible (i.e., would not violate any known laws of nature). Thus, models are built with the help of what appear to be nomological hypotheses about the decisions triggering human conduct, but the purpose of these constructions is *not* to be a *test* of these hypotheses. Nor is any of these constructions as a whole to be tested. Rather, for the purpose at hand the correctness of the implicitly or explicitly used nomological hypotheses is "assumed."[10]

Unfortunately, the hypothetical character of ideal types is all too easily obscured by the fashion in which they are presented. This presentation usually takes the form: "a bureaucracy is" (or, "by 'bureaucracy' is to be understood") "a social relationship characterized by the features x, y, and z," or it takes the form: "(all) bureaucracies have the features x, y, and z, (whereby x, y, and z may refer to phenomena or relationships between phenomena or both)." The former formulation may evoke the impression that what is given is a definition, the latter may evoke the idea that universal statements about empirical phenomena are intended. Both interpretations are erroneous, however. Ideal types are neither definitions nor empirical statements. They are descriptions of hypothetical constellations of phenomena, constellations which would exist if certain antecedent conditions were given empirically, since—by "assumption"—human behavior is "governed" by certain laws (i.e., since—by "assumption"—in situations of a certain kind humans invariably decide to act in certain ways). Thus, ideal types describe mental constructs. For identification purposes, these constructs are *named*, e.g., "bureaucracy," "handicraft economy," and so on. The names refer to sets of empirical constellations of phenomena, constellations which all have in common that they have resulted from antecedent constellations resembling (to a greater or lesser extent) the models' determining constellations.

Apart from their characterizing function in historical descriptions, the most general theoretical purpose of these models is to serve as substitutes for some sector of empirical reality, some recurrent relatively similar configurations of phenomena. Among other things, they are used for imaginary experiments in order to try out what would happen (or would have happened), if certain things were (had been) the case. Another use is as fixed points of reference in comparative studies. For these purposes, models seem to be indispensable, and from this it also follows that they cannot be completely unrelated to some actual phenomena.

As already indicated, the existing relation is twofold: first, the model world is constructed with the help of generalizations about the occurrence of decisions in favor of the kind of conduct which (presumably) characterizes its empirical counterpart. That is, the relationship asserted by the hypothesis employed in the construction of the model must be relevant to the empirical instances under consideration. Second, the antecedent conditions whose existence is postulated for the purpose of constructing the model world, must sufficiently resemble those which prevail in the relevant sector of empirical reality. Just exactly how this latter aspect of the construction of the model world is handled depends on what *kind* of model is desired to stand for a selected sector of empirical reality. The principle of construction is usually indicated by the declaration that the model's description constitutes a certain *kind* of type, e.g., an "ideal" type, or an "average" type. What this refers to is the feature of the model world that, as a "result" of the set of antecedent conditions postulated for the purpose of its construction, it represents what on the average exists in the relevant empiricial cases, or a somehow "ideal" configuration of phenomena, etc., whatever the case may be. This aspect of model construction has been treated at some length by McKinney and therefore needs no further elaboration in this context.[11]

It can now readily be seen why it is so easy to mistake the referent of types by assuming that they inform directly about empirical reality. One reason is that the label given to the model described by the type is also applied to the empirical phenomena for which the model is to stand. The rationale behind this labelling is, of course, to indicate by the label the sector of empiricial reality which the model is to represent. The other reason is that frequently empirical situations exist which exhibit exactly the same features as the model. As a matter of fact, it is precisely such cases which often suggest the construction of a certain model. In this event, the description of the model and the description of the empirical phenomenon are identical. It is easy to create confusion when this coincidence gives rise to the belief that ideal types (or any other kind of type) in general are intended as descriptively accurate accounts of aspects of empirically existing phenomena. The divergence of many relevant empirical instances from what is described by the type then may lead to all sorts of interpretations concerning the reality to which the type refers, e.g., the "essence" of phenomena, or some ontological "aspect" of reality which empirically supposedly is intermingled with other such aspects. The methodological debates in economics yield a number of examples of such strategies.[12]

A different sort of problem exists with regard to the ideal-typical "laws" which may be formulated about the relations holding between elements of the model world.[13] It centers around the fact that a specific relationship, e.g., that between the personal wealth of politicians and the political influence of fat cats, holds only in a particular kind of situation *and* as long as there are decisions to adopt a particular kind of action (that "assumed" by the model-builder) in this kind of situation. Now it might seem that a statement like "the wealthier the contenders in the political power struggle in mass democracy, the smaller the political influence of fat cats," can simply be interpreted as a nomological hypothesis which holds under specified conditions. However, there are some difficulties with such an interpretation. What these difficulties are is discussed in the next section.

3. SOCIOLOGICAL LAWS AND THE PROBLEM OF VOLUNTARISM

The idea of establishing a natural science of social phenomena, i.e., to find and formulate their laws, to a considerable extent has been constitutive for the development of sociology, and social science in general. Weber defended this idea by emphasizing that general concepts (laws) are indispensable for the purpose of scientific explanation. The ideal types which he constructed were intended to provide such concepts. However, it must be asked now whether they are able to fulfill the function which they are supposed to fulfill. A discussion of this question is the subject of the present section.

Notwithstanding his peculiar justification of the generalizing approach (natural science), Weber clearly appreciated the importance of nomological knowledge for explanatory purposes. He did not dwell on the differences between laws of a universal and those of a statistical character, and the concomitant distinctions between deductive and probabilistic inferences. For the issues here considered, however, this distinction between universal and statistical hypotheses is of secondary importance. To simplify the discussion, therefore, reference is limited to universal statements and deductive explanations.

The structure of deductive explanations is so well known that only a short sketch of its main features is required here. Such an explanation is essentially the drawing of a conclusion from premises. These premises must include two kinds of statements: first, statements asserting that universally certain variables are related in some specific ways; second, statements describing particular events, i.e., facts. Statements of the first kind are variously called "laws" or "universal statements"; those of the second kind are "singular statements," describing "initial conditions." Explaining an event, then, involves the logical derivation of the statement describing its occurrence from suitably chosen premises.[1]

A deductive nomological explanation "explains" by making explicit that the explanandum is a logical implication of the—in the simplest case, two—premises forming the explanans. Mere deducibility of the explanandum, however, is not sufficient for a set of premises to be regarded as explanatory. It "explains" only when the major premise states a genuinely universal relation between relevant variables. A nomological hypothesis is of this kind when it is considered capable of serving to support a counterfactual conditional,[2] i.e., when it can serve to support statements of the form, "If A were to occur, B would occur," when in fact A does not occur. This requirement seems to pose a problem when statements like, "The wealthier the contenders in a political power struggle in mass democracy, the smaller the political influence of fat cats," are considered. It could be argued that this hypothesis cannot with confidence be used to support the claim, "If this contender here (say, John Doe) had been wealthy, fat cats would not have political influence." Now, this lack of confidence may have two sources. On the one hand, it may derive from the vagueness of the formulation, especially from the failure to specify exactly under what conditions the postulated relationship is claimed to hold. This deficiency, of course, could in principle be repaired by providing a satisfactory list of such conditions. On the other hand, it may stem from the conviction that the statement asserts the universality of a relationship which really is not universal at all, but only seemingly so.

Since it is this latter position which is important to the discussion here, it is useful to state more clearly the distinction on which it rests. It is a distinction between two kinds of universal statements with regard to their capability in principle of supporting counterfactual conditionals, namely (1) statements asserting a "numerical," "accidental," or "de facto" universality, i.e., a universal contingent concomitance, and (2) statements asserting a "strict" or "nomic" universality, i.e., "laws of nature." Only strictly universal (nomic) statements can support counterfactual conditionals. They do so by "ruling out" the actual occurrence of certain events,[3] namely those incompatible with what is asserted by the laws in question, and by going beyond what is already known. De facto universals, in contrast, are mere restatements, conveniently summarized, of things already known; they are, as a matter of fact, equivalent to conjunctions of singular statements.[4] As such, when they are used as premises in deductive nomological explanations, they do not "explain" at all. They cannot explain because they do not postulate anything beyond what is already known; they are not explanatory hypotheses postulating universal relationships, but summary descriptions of "accidental" concomitances. Only nomic universals can "explain" if by "explanation" more is to be understood than a description of facts already known. It is these nomic universals, therefore, which scientists are trying to establish.

Nomic universal statements have a number of distinctive characteristics which distinguish them from de facto universals. The following is a list of such characteristics as compiled by Nagel.[5] Accordingly:

(1) Universal statements, in order to qualify as nomic universals, must have an unrestricted scope of predication. That is, the classes of objects, of which these statements affirm some predicates, must not be limited to things that fall into a specific spatio-temporal region. Whether or not this condition is fulfilled cannot be inferred from the syntactical structure of the statement in question, but requires familiarity with the relevant subject matter.

(2) Such statements must not be vacuously true, i.e., they must deal with classes of objects for which there are possible empirical instances. Or, at least, scientists must have "reason to believe" that there are such instances.

(3) Such statements must not be summary ways of asserting *finite conjunctions of singular statements*. That is, the classes of objects of which such statements affirm some predicates, must not be finite classes of which all the instances are known to possess the predicates in ques-

tion. Statements must not be accepted as laws when their formulation is based on the examination of some fixed number of objects which may be assumed to exhaust the statements' scopes of predication.

(4) Such statements must be so well-established through (direct and indirect) empirical evidence that rather overwhelming new evidence is needed for abandoning them. (This requirement must be interpreted as a rule of thumb.)

With the help of these criteria it is now possible to assess the status of statements like, "The wealthier the contestants in a political power struggle, the smaller the political influence of fat cats." However, the problem of empirical corroboration will not be raised. Instead, it is investigated whether these statements are such that they could not be interpreted as laws even if no contrary instances were known. In this context, a particular feature of such statements acquires importance. This is that the covariation or sequence of phenomena which they affirm is the result of human decisions to interfere with a course of events. Thus, the postulated relationships do not obtain "by themselves"; they are "made." They are due to the fact that humans decide to act in certain ways. Universal statements of the kind considered by Weber (e.g., Gresham's Law), therefore, implicitly always assert the universal occurrence of human decisions to adopt certain kinds of action in certain kinds of situations. In the case of the relationship between politicians' wealth and the influence of fat cats, this is the formers' decision to optimize their political control; in the case of Gresham's Law it is the decision made by participants in a market to pursue their material self-interest. In short, such statements imply the claim that in specified kinds of situations, a relevant number of humans decide to orient their conduct toward plans and considerations of a certain kind. Now, this implication must be seen in conjunction with the apparent fact that men stand in a very special relationship to some of the factors which influence their actions: ends, values, norms, cognitive knowledge, feelings, and assumptions concerning the relevant features of past, present and future situations (including the behavior of other actors). The problematic aspect is that (a) individuals seem to be able to transgress norms or disregard feelings and values, if only they want to, that (b) they seem to be "free" in the selection of the standard according to which they select means, that (c) they can decide what ends to pursue, and that (d) they often have several possible "definitions of the situation" which they can choose to impose on the "objective" facts. It is this prima facie capacity of humans to decide how to act, or to act "otherwise" if they want to, their capacity of letting themselves be influenced by some considerations rather than others (that is, to choose the determinants of their own behavior) which has given rise to, and is at the core of, a particular theoretical approach to the analysis of action phenomena, the so-called "voluntaristic theory of action."[6] This approach has been given the label "voluntaristic" because, according to Parsons's exposition, "as distinguished from both the positivistic and the idealistic alternatives it involves the element of effort as the mediating link between the normative and non-normative aspect of action systems."[7]

As mentioned, the generalizations produced in a voluntaristic action theory are always statements to the effect that certain things happen in a recurrent fashion. They claim that certain things are made to occur because human actors in certain kinds of situations (situations which they define as similar) recurrently *decide to adopt* certain kinds of action, i.e., behavior conforming to certain plans and norms. Actors do so because they "want" to, not because they cannot help it (in the sense of being compelled by something which is completely beyond their control); at the same time it is understood that actors, although they may have acted one way, could have decided to act differently had they wanted to do so.

When it is said that particular kinds of ends, values, norms, and definitions of the situation do not "automatically" serve as behavior guidelines (in the sense that individuals are unable to disregard them), this must not be understood to mean that individuals, when they act, can decide not to have any plans, etc., at all according to which they behave; this would not be considered to be "action" anymore. Rather it means that it is an individual's decision to adopt one set of such considerations rather than another. The implication of this tenet is that strict universality cannot be claimed for the generalizations which are formulated within the voluntaristic framework. Given the particularities of the approach, such statements must always involve the assertion that actors decide to adopt certain kinds of behavior in certain kinds of situations. However, on voluntaristic premises it always makes sense to ask why men should decide in favor of these alternatives of conduct rather than others. This question cannot be answered since it is acknowledged that there is nothing which "forces" a particular decision, that the decision in favor of particular alternatives does not "have" to take place. Voluntaristic generalizations, therefore, cannot be interpreted as laws. Rather, they are the equivalents of finite conjunctions of singular statements, each of which is to the effect that as the result of a decision in favor of a certain kind of behavior in a particular kind of situation, a specific type of phenomenon was brought about. Thus they are merely descriptions of things already known. As such, however, they must be interpreted as de facto universal statements, not as nomic ones.

A second consideration which has a bearing on the status of universal statements in a voluntaristic action theory is that of the origin of the cultural elements influencing human conduct. These elements are part of the cultural heritage of social groups. A group's culture, however, is not something which was given to it at the beginning of times, and which it has faithfully transmitted ever since (i.e., culture is not like a genetic code), but it is something which the group's members have produced, invented, or created, and which can be changed by them. The cultural products of different groups often differ significantly from each other (although it must not be overlooked that there are also similarities).[8] This means that frequently specific modes of conduct, since they are dependent on the adoption of certain cultural behavior determinants which are created by and available to the individuals, are limited in their occurrence to particular social groups. Furthermore, it seems that they are limited to certain time periods as well. What is significant here is that the cultural products in question are human creations, or inventions, whose production is the result of more or less deliberate considerations in the minds of individuals, and that these considerations are not completely subject to the influence of factors beyond the control of the individuals involved. Since universal statements within a voluntaristic theory of action are necessarily statements about the social consequences of the occurrence of culturally formed modes of conduct in certain situations, this means that their scope of predication is not spatio-temporally unrestricted, but limited to those areas and periods in which the cultural elements are present, to which they refer.

If the considerations put forward are valid, then it would indeed seem that the generalizations formulated within a voluntaristic theory of action must not be considered capable of nomic universality.[9] Accordingly, they cannot be used for deductive nomological explanation. If Parsons's interpretation is correct, according to which Weber espoused a voluntaristic approach, then it follows that it is not possible to turn ideal-typical generalizations (among which are the universal statements formulated in economics) into nomic universal statements by qualifying the conditions under which alone the affirmed relationships hold without exception. However, it most probably was not Weber's intention to deny that human decisions are "determined." At least this is the gist of his discussion of the significance of "free will" for explanations in history.[10] Nevertheless, his statements are by no means conclusive or even unambiguous. It is not possible here to deal with this problem in an exhaustive fashion. It must suffice to say that, regardless of what Weber's position in principle may have been, his theoretical language has voluntaristic connotations, that the question, "Couldn't individuals have decided differently, had they wanted to?" is a legitimate and meaningful question within his framework, and that nowhere does he attempt to show how, at least in principle, this question could be answered.

Under these circumstances it seems best to interpret Weber's ideal-typical laws not as incomplete nomological hypotheses (since, for a variety of reasons, no indication is given whether and how they could be completed), but to treat them as summary descriptions of a number of identical cause-effect sequences, i.e., not to interpret them as theoretical statements (laws), but as statements providing historical information. This is in line with Weber's view that universal statements are equivalent to conjunctions of a number of singular statements. At the same time, the distinction between de facto and nomic universal statements, which Weber's methodology tends to obliterate, clarifies the theoretical status of assertions like, "The wealthier the contenders in a political power struggle, the smaller the political influence of fat cats." They must not be understood to assert universal invariant relationships. They merely express that in all known instances particular kinds of phenomena were brought about or maintained as a result of decisions to adopt certain types of behavior in particular kinds of situations. They are summaries of a number of individual explanatory accounts.

This interpretation allows for the fact that the discovery of empirical instances which do not confirm such alleged generalizations, instead of leading to their rejection (as would be expected of disconfirmed laws), rather occasions their reformulation as weaker statements to the effect that in most, or many (rather than all) instances of some kind of social situation particular kinds of phenomena come about. Ideal types are such weaker formulations.

The adoption of a voluntaristic position is one way of resolving the dilemma created by the apparent impossibility to state the conditions under which people invariably decide to select certain behavior alternatives. However, there has been considerable reluctance to embrace this approach, since its implications are at odds with the regulative idea behind the development of sociology, namely that of a natural science of social phenomena. Not surprisingly, therefore, attempts have been made to avoid voluntaristic problems by formulating strictly "naturalistic" sociological theories, i.e., theories whose nomological statements do not refer to variables whose influence can be said to be under human control. These attempts have not convinced everyone, and thus there has been a third strategy through which authors have tried to secure the nomic character of universal statements in spite of the fact that they were formulated within a framework posing the voluntaristic problem. This procedure has been to present the statements in question (e.g., Gresham's Law) in conditional form. Thus it is often said that a given generalization must be understood to hold only when certain conditions are fulfilled, or *under certain assumptions*. The occurrence of a certain kind of conduct, or rather, the decision in favor of its occurrence, then is included among these assumptions. Gresham's Law, for instance, is claimed to hold only under the assumption that the relevant individuals have decided to rationally pursue their economic interests.

The conditional formulation of voluntaristic generalizations seems to have the great advantage of eliminating, at least in the immediate context, the necessity to deal with the problem, what makes individuals decide to select a particular action alternative. Unfortunately it is often not realized that as "laws" such statements are worthless since the described procedure renders them nonempirical. The cause of this was indicated earlier, when it was said that the kinds of relationships which are asserted to hold by the universal statements typically occurring in the voluntaristic action theory exist only due to human intervention. Therefore, it was argued that these generalizations implicitly assert the universal occurrence of decisions in favor of certain kinds of action in certain kinds of situations. Their nomological content, if they have one, can only lie in the relationship between the occurrence of a particular kind of conduct and a particular type of situation. To "assume" the occurrence of such a decision, however, empties the statement, which is made conditional on it, of all empirical content.

In spite of these undesirable implications, conditional formulations of voluntaristic generalizations are rather popular. For example, many of the statements formulated in Parsons's system theory about the dynamics of action systems appear to be of this kind. The appeal of the conditional form lies in the fact that it seems to provide a way around the voluntaristic problem. It appears to eliminate the necessity to claim the universal occurrence of particular kinds of conduct in specific kinds of situations. This impression is erroneous, however. The conditional formulation replaces by postulates what ought to be empirical hypotheses. Contrary to the hopes of those who think that this device makes the establishment of nomic universals possible, the "assumption" of behavior uniformities, as a matter of fact, amounts to the tacit admission that no relevant ones are known.[11] If they were known, it would not be necessary to assume them.

Weber did not resort to this strategy. As a matter of fact, it was his refusal to adopt such a solution (which Menger adopted) which led him to the conception of ideal type. However, the professed ideal-typical character of statements like, "The wealthier the contenders in a political power struggle, the smaller the political influence of fat cats," signifies nothing else than the admission that they are merely statements to the effect that sometimes, or frequently (even always) certain relationships have been found to obtain. The weak form of such statements is entirely necessitated by the incapacity to qualify the empirical conditions under which the asserted relationships would hold universally. It is not necessary to decide here whether in Weber's case this incapacity was more the result of voluntaristic convictions, ignorance, or an inductive procedure not carried through to its end. The fact remains that the generalizations under consideration are nothing but conjunctions of singular statements.

4. THE ROLE OF IDEAL-TYPE MODELS IN SOCIOLOGY

Ideal types, i.e., model constructs like "bureaucracy" or "charismatic authority," and ideal-typical "laws," i.e., summary statements about the recurrent occurrence of particular cause-effect sequences, are descriptive of empirically possible constellations and sequences of events. One value of such constructions which so far has not been mentioned lies in the fact that they show the *social-structural significance* of the interplay of many individual courses of conduct—for instance, what from a social-structural point of view is a bureaucracy is nothing but the cluster of on-going activities of individuals who are guided in their conduct by a variety of guidelines. What these considerations are in the minds of actors was described above. Thus, ideal types are informative by showing that what is, on the individual level, a series of efforts to implement a variety of plans, considerations and action maxims under a variety of circumstances, constitutes in its interplay an identifiable interaction network, such as a market, a household, a friendship, a state, or an army. Similarly, of course, ideal-typical laws describe sequences or covariations of social-structural attributes as successions of individual activities guided by particular considerations under successively changing circumstances. The statement, for instance, that bad money drives out good money (Gresham's Law) describes, with regard to its societal import, the occurrence of economically rational behavior taking place in certain situations (characterized by the presence of two kinds of currency which are in unequal demand).

The construction of ideal types is not trivial to the extent that the kinds of actions (i.e., the types of considerations guiding this construction) whose interplay constitutes some structural aspect of a social group are not immediately apparent. The more complicated the interplay, the less trivial is the ideal type. Ideal types are models in that they carry out the "translation" of structural properties of social groups into the interplay of diverse types of individual actions in a fashion which is exemplary for a whole set of empirical cases. From this it follows that the construction of ideal types in most cases makes sense only when there are empirical phenomena resembling them. Conversely, such models can be used for the purpose of reporting in a summary fashion that the occurrence of certain phenomena, which more or less resemble the model conception, characterizes a particular society or group in certain time periods or certain places. In this context, a model would be exemplary of a set of empirical phenomena in the sense that it represents a constellation of features whose presence—in a more or less similar form—is peculiar to a certain social group in comparison to some other group. An example would be the statement that in the latter half of the twentieth century, the government and the economy of the United States have been pervaded by ever larger bureaucracies. It is this use of ideal types which Weber, above all, had in mind when he developed his definition of rational bourgeois capitalism, for instance.

It seems that as long as sociologists are interested in characterizing in a summary fashion the peculiarities of group structures, they will have to rely on model constructions. Such constructs can be assembled in different ways. They may refer to those elements which on the average are displayed by the relevant phenomena, or they may be polar types.[1] Whatever is chosen depends on the purposes of the researcher when he assembles such constructs. These constructs describe the phenomena which would exist if certain conditions were fulfilled, i.e., phenomena whose occurrence is empirically possible. They are constructed when it is desirable or necessary to characterize in a summary fashion the kinds of social phenomena existing in certain time periods and in certain areas. This includes characteristic cause-effect sequences. Whenever sociologists want to describe how societies, or economies, developments, institutions, etc., *in general* are structured, they are required to build model-societies, model-economies, model-developments, etc. This is the only way in which they can present general descriptions of such phenomena. It seems, therefore, that as long as descriptions of general phenomena (in the sense of "repeatedly occurring relatively similar" phenomena), i.e., what may be called "generalized descriptions," are part of the sociological enterprise[2]— be it as an ultimate aim or a step thereto—models will be used and formulated.[3] *Such models are mental constructs, consisting of a number of elements standing in particular relationships to each other, which are designed to represent, for descriptive purposes, a specific segment of empirical reality and the interdependences existing in it.*

The elements of which a model is made up are simplified representations of empirical phenomena (i.e., phenomena which have been or can be observed), or phenomena that are empirically possible (i.e., whose occurrence is not ruled out by any known law of nature). The relationships in which these elements are thought to stand to each other may be those of temporal coexistence, temporal sequence, and / or of causal interdependence. The postulation of these relationships must not violate any known law of nature. The model is intended to represent a segment of empirical reality, i.e., a recurrent pattern of events. It does not correctly *describe* this segment, nor does it explain it; it *stands for it.* As a substitute for empirical reality, the constructed configuration of elements is arrived at by selecting a number of elements of the segment of empirical reality for representation by the mental construct. These elements may be common to all the empirical patterns for which the model is to stand, they may be possessed by most of them, or only by a few of them.

In sociology, models are usually presented in verbal form. The linguistic entities referring to models are commonly known as "types" —"ideal types," "average types," etc., depending on the kind of model. Formally, the presentation of type concepts resembles a definition.

However, properly interpreted, what seems to be a definition in truth is the description of a model. Unfortunately, not only have the descriptions of models frequently been taken for definitions, but moreover these supposed definitions have sometimes been held to constitute "real definitions" (i.e., empirical statements about the objects denoted by them). Thus, what was intended as the description of a model is turned into a set of general statements about empirical reality, which are correspondingly interpreted as the "laws" of the subject matter in question. This has happened, for instance, to Weber's ideal type of bureaucracy. Of course, the opposite has also happened. Authors have claimed the discovery of laws when all they did was to describe relationships between elements of a model. Michels's Iron Law of Oligarchy seems to be such an instance. All these misinterpretations are a result of the failure to realize that, for certain purposes (e.g., imaginary experiments) in sociology models are substituted for empirical reality, and that statements referring to such models must not be taken as statements about empirical reality. Relationships holding for the model often do not hold for specific empirical cases under consideration.

It is imperative that models be treated as such and only as such, that ideal-typical statements not be mistaken for empirical ones. It must not be taken for granted in an a priori fashion that the model is an exact replica (in the crucial aspects) of all the empirical instances to which it is intended to refer. As a matter of fact, the opposite is usually correct. The great danger lying in an unawareness of the ideal-typical character of many constructions, and thus of their relationships to the relevant part of empirical reality, is its conduciveness to the assumption that there is something like a distinct sphere in reality (a specific "nature" of a part of reality) of which these constructs give an adequate account, and that the generalizations which hold true on the level of the model are the empirical hypotheses required for the explanation of the phenomena belonging to this sphere (sui generis). Of course, the phenomena belonging to this sphere are empirically supposed to be intermingled with phenomena belonging to other spheres, but this is assumed not to affect the possibility of explaining them in a satisfactory manner with the help of these hypotheses. If one can believe its critics, it seems that this sort of thinking has characterized to a degree neoclassical economic theory,[4] where it has been frequently criticized and called a "platonism of models."[5] Since economic theory for many represents the state to which sociology is to aspire, it seems profitable to become aware of the implications. Thus, one has only to take a look at the several "analytic" systems which according to some sociologists constitute a concrete action system. They are said to be abstractions from reality and to have dynamics of their own, i.e., the elements constituting each system are claimed to be interrelated in ways specific to each system, subject to its own laws.[6]

The point of these comments is *not* to dispute the utility of model construction; on the contrary. The point is to emphasize that they *are* useful under certain conditions. The main condition is that such constructs are not mistaken—by their creators or their users—for something which they are not, namely accurate descriptive or explanatory accounts of empirical phenomena. When their empirical accuracy is at issue, it is not necessary to resort to all kinds of dubious strategies in order to "preserve" an empirical correctness to which they do not aspire. Weber managed to avoid the fallacies the commission of which the use of models makes seductive. This may have been a result of the fact that his theory of concept formation kept him acutely aware of the precarious methodological status of ideal-typical constructions. Another contributing factor may be found in his general lack of interest in a general theory of society. Thus he was much less subject to the temptation of confusing the construction of models with accounts of empirical reality, especially since he did not try to prove the existence of a social reality sui generis. Today this temptation may be rather strong due to the current emphasis on "deductive reasoning" and the construction of "systems of interrelated propositions." If it can be resisted, however, there seems to be no reason to doubt the utility of the typological procedure.

NOTES

INTRODUCTION.

1. Dennis Wrong (ed.), *Max Weber* (Englewood Cliffs: Prentice Hall, 1970), p. 8.

CHAPTER I.

I. 1

1. Max Weber, *Economy and Society*, 3 vols. (New York: Bedminster Press, 1968), pp. 3–22.
2. "Roscher und Knies und die logischen Probleme der historischen National-oekonomie" (Roscher and Knies and the Logical Problems of Historical Economics), published between 1903 and 1906, not available in English translation; hereafter referred to as "Roscher & Knies"; "The 'Objectivity' of Knowledge in Social Science and Social Policy," published in 1904, referred to as "Objectivity"; "Critical Studies in the Logic of the Cultural Sciences," published in 1906, referred to as "Critical Studies"; "R. Stammlers 'Ueberwindung' der materialistischen Geschichtsauffassung" (R. Stammler's "Overcoming" of the Materialistic Interpretation of History), published in 1907, not available in English translation; "The Meaning of the 'Ethical Neutrality' of the Sociological and Economic Sciences," published in 1917. This last essay together with "Objectivity" and "Critical Studies" was published as *The Methodology of the Social Sciences* (Glencoe: Free Press, 1949), hereafter referred to as *ET* (for "English translation").
3. "Die Grenznutzenlehre und das 'psychophysische Grundgesetz'" (The Doctrine of Marginal Utility and the "Basic Law of Psychophysics"); "'Energetische' Kulturtheorien" ("Energetic" Theories of Culture); "Ueber einige Kategorien der verstehenden Soziologie" (On Some Categories of Interpretive Sociology); and—the only one existing in an English translation—"Science as a Vocation" (In Hans Gerth & C. Wright Mills, eds., *From Max Weber* [New York: Oxford University Press, 1946]).
4. Tuebingen: Mohr, 1921. Hereafter referred to as *GAzWL*.
5. *GAzWL*, pp. 1–145.
6. *Op. cit.*, pp. 146–214; *ET*, pp. 50–112.
7. *Op. cit.*, pp. 215–290; *ET*, pp. 112–188.
8. *Op. cit.*, p. 146 n. 2; *ET*, p. 51 n. 1.
9. *Op. cit.*, p. 451 n. 1; *ET*, p. 1 n. missing.
10. "Die Genesis der Methodologie Max Webers," *Koelner Zeitschrift fuer Soziologie und Sozialpsychologie* 11 (1959): 573–630; pp. 574–575.
11. This, for instance, is Alexander von Schelting's assumption. Cf. Alexander von Schelting, "Die logische Theorie der historischen Kulturwissenschaft von Max Weber und im besonderen sein Begriff des Idealtypus," *Archiv fuer Sozialwissenschaft und Sozialpolitik* 49 (1922): 623–752; p. 630. Hereafter referred to as "Logische Theorie."
12. Dieter Henrich, *Die Einheit der Wissenschaftslehre Max Webers* (Tuebingen: Mohr, 1952), p. 2.
13. *Op. cit.*, p. 5. (Original emphasis in all quotations unless otherwise noted.)
14. Tenbruck, *op. cit.*, p. 580.

15. *Op. cit.*, p. 581.
16. *Op. cit.*, p. 583.
17. *Op. cit.*, p. 576.
18. *Op. cit.*, p. 582.
19. Especially von Schelting.
20. This is, e.g., Bennion's impression. Cf., Lowell L. Bennion, *Max Weber's Methodology* (Paris: Les Presses Modernes, 1932), p. 7.
21. Marianne Weber, *Max Weber. Ein Lebensbild* (Tuebingen: Mohr, 1926), pp. 272–273, 278, 319–321, 340.
22. *GAzWL*, pp. 217–218; *ET*, pp. 115–116.
23. Cf. Werner Bienfait, "Max Webers Lehre vom geschichtlichen Erkennen. Ein Beitrag zur Frage der Bedeutung des 'Idealtypus' fuer die Geschichtswissenschaft," *Historische Studien* 194 (1930): 5–93; p. 13.
24. Alexander von Schelting, *Max Webers Wissenschaftslehre* (Tuebingen: Mohr, 1934), p. 6 n. 2. Hereafter referred to as *Wissenschaftslehre*.
25. *Op. cit.*, p. 6.
26. Interestingly, Tenbruck (*op. cit.*, p. 582) found that in the second edition of Marianne Weber's biography, which appeared after the publication of von Schelting's *Wissenschaftslehre*, the references to Max Weber's methodological concerns had been altered to convey the impression of a more active interest of Weber's in these matters.
27. Tenbruck, *op. cit.*, pp. 579–580.
28. Von Schelting, *Wissenschaftslehre*, p. 7 n.
29. *Op. cit.*, pp. 9, 9–10 n. 2, 54 n. 1, 55.
30. *Op. cit.*, pp. 207–208. Cf. Wolfgang Schluchter, *Wertfreiheit und Verantwortungsethik* (Gesellschaft und Wissenschaft 3; Tuebingen: Mohr, 1971).
31. *GAzWL*, p. 7 n. 1.
32. Heinrich Rickert, *Die Grenzen der naturwissenschaftlichen Bergriffsbildung* (Tuebingen: Mohr, 1902). Hereafter referred to as *Grenzen*.
33. *GAzWL*, pp. 3, 3–4 n. 2.
34. *Op. cit.*, pp. 230 n. 1, 277 n. 1; *ET*, pp. 128 n. 13, 175 n. missing.
35. *Op. cit.*, pp. 251–252; *ET*, pp. 149–150.
36. This identity in almost all respects is also acknowledged by von Schelting, *Wissenschaftslehre*, pp. 232–233 n. 2, and Henrich, *op. cit.*, pp. 4–5. However, both authors also claim that there are a few important differences. Henrich thinks that Weber, "although in the field of methodology he is in closest agreement with Rickert, in his justification of this methodology leaves Rickert and the philosophical position of Neo-Kantianism completely behind" (*op. cit.*, pp. 4–5). See also von Schelting, "Logische Theorie," p. 629. It will be shown that Henrich's statement is erroneous.
37. An opinion also held by Judith Janoska-Bendl in her book *Methodologische Aspekte des Idealtypus. Max Weber und die Soziologie der Geschichte* (Berlin: Duncker & Humblot, 1965), p. 9. Runciman, in contrast, though acknowledging inconsistencies in Weber's position, does not think that Weber changed his mind. See W. G. Runciman, *A Critique of Max Weber's Philosophy of Social Science* (Cambridge University Press, 1972). Hereafter referred to as *Critique*.
38. For instance, Bernhard Pfister, *Die Entwicklung zum Idealtypus. Eine methodologische Untersuchung ueber das Verhaeltnis von Theorie und Geschichte bei Menger, Schmoller und Max Weber* (Tuebingen: Mohr, 1928). Johannes Winckelmann in his book *Legitimitaet und Legalitaet in*

Max Webers Herrschaftssoziologie (Tuebingen: Mohr, 1952), pp. 12–19, holds that there has been an a priori overestimation of Rickert's influence and an underestimation of Dilthey's and Husserl's. His support of this contention, however, is rather poor, and to the present author seems mistaken.

39. Don Martindale, "Sociological Theory and the Ideal Type," in Llewellyn Gross (ed.), *Symposium on Sociological Theory* (Evanston, White Plains: Row, Peterson, 1959) pp. 57–89; p. 57. Hereafter referred to as "Theory & Type."

40. For an overview, cf. Werner J. Cahnman, "Max Weber and the Methodological Controversy in the Social Sciences," in Werner J. Cahnman & Alvin Boskoff, *Sociology and History* (New York: Free Press, 1964) pp. 103–127.

41. Christoph Sigwart, *Logic*, 2 vols. (New York: Macmillan, 1895).

42. Wilhelm Windelband, "Geschichte und Naturwissenschaft," in Wilhelm Windelband, *Praeludien* (Tuebingen: Mohr, 3rd ed., 1907) pp. 355–379.

43. Georg Simmel, *Die Probleme der Geschichtsphilosophie* (Leipzig: Duncker und Humblot, 3rd ed., 1907).

44. Carl Menger, *Problems of Economics and Sociology* (Urbana: University of Illinois Press, 1963).

45. John Stuart Mill, *A System of Logic* (London and New York: Longmans, Green, 1947). Walther Wegener's book, whose title—*Die Quellen der Wissenschaftsauffassung Max Webers und die Problematik der Werturteilsfreiheit der Nationaloekonomie* (The Sources of Max Weber's Conception of Science, and the Problem of Ethical Neutrality in Economics) (Berlin: Duncker und Humblot, 1962)—would lead one to believe that it deals with a special aspect of the intellectual tradition behind Weber, in fact does not hold this promise. In a book claiming to show the sources of Max Weber's conception of science one should expect an analysis and presentation of these sources together with a documentation of Weber's indebtedness. This, however, is not Wegener's procedure. He does not present an analysis of either the original sources from which Weber drew, or of Weber's own writings, but bases his claims on what other interpreters have said the influences on Weber were. The first part of the book (ca. 115 pages), supposedly dealing with the sources of Weber's conception of science, is nothing but a confusing collation of quotations from secondary sources. The bibliography appended to the book lists 357 titles, not counting Weber's works. Thirty-eight of these might have been known by Weber since they were published while he was still alive. Twenty-two of them are nowhere referred to in the text. The remaining 16 are referred to in (in footnotes) 33 times, plus twice a reference to Kant who is not included in the bibliography. Of the 33 references, 18 are to Rickert. Gottl's *Die Herrschaft des Wortes* is not mentioned, Jellinek is not mentioned, Menger's work is never referred to, nor are J. S. Mill's *System of Logic*, Sigwart's *Logic*, or Simmel's *Probleme der Geschichtsphilosophie*. Chapter II of the first part of the book, entitled "The Reception of Neo-Kantianism by Max Weber," contains exactly one reference to Weber. The following chapter—"The Reception of Positivism and Historicism by Max Weber"—contains 6 such references. This shows that Wegener practically never uses original sources to demonstrate and document his claims. In any case, he is in no position to show anything in this respect since the books most important for an understanding of Weber's background do not even appear in the bibliography.

Wegener's book must easily be the worst production within the secondary literature on Weber, where there is certainly no lack of bad studies.

46. *GAzWL*, p. 92.

47. *Op. cit.*, p. 146 n. 1; *ET*, pp. 49–50.

48. *Op. cit.*, p. 288 n. 1; *ET*, p. 186 n. 42.

49. In this whole essay, the terms "science," "scientific" are used to refer to both the natural sciences and the social sciences including history.

50. At the time when Weber wrote his essays.

51. *GAzWL*, p. 91.

52. See below, pp. 135–151.

53. Henrich, *op. cit.*, p. 6.

54. Marianne Weber, *op. cit.*, p. 273.

55. Tenbruck's opinion that Rickert's only influence on Weber consisted in the latter's adoption of the principle of value-relevance is completely wrong. Cf. Tenbruck, *op. cit.*, p. 629 n. 25.

56. This is the title of Henrich's book; cf. Henrich, *op. cit.* Henrich's contention that the foundation of Max Weber's methodological theory is entirely different from that of Rickert's, in spite of all terminological identity (*op. cit.*, p. 5), will be discussed below, chapter 3, sections 2 and 3.

57. In agreement with this, Henrich, *op. cit.*, p. 5.

58. Tenbruck, *op. cit.*, p. 626.

I. 2

1. Rickert, *op. cit.* All quotations are taken from the 1902 edition.

2. Henry Thomas Buckle, *History of Civilization in England* 2 vols. (New York: Appleton, 1870), vol. I, p. 3.

3. *Op. cit.*, p. 4.

4. See below, section 5.

5. Heinrich Rickert, *Zur Lehre von der Definition* (On Definition) (Tuebingen: Mohr, 3rd impr. ed., 1929), p. 64. Hereafter referred to as *Definition*.

6. Rickert, *Grenzen*, p. 7.

7. Henrich Rickert, *Der Gegenstand der Erkenntnis* (Tuebingen: Mohr, 6th impr. ed., 1928). Hereafter referred to as *Gegenstand*.

8. Cf. Sigwart, *op. cit.*, vol. I, p. 26. "For us, then, the investigation of the nature of the judgment consists in a consideration of the mental act which takes place when we are actively engaged in judging, and to which we proceed to give expression in words." See also Windelband, *op. cit.*, J. S. Mill, *op. cit.*, Simmel, *op. cit.*

9. Rickert, *Gegenstand*, pp. 15–22, 30.

10. *Op. cit.*, pp. 127–131.

11. *Op. cit.*, pp. 178–187.

12. *Op. cit.*, p. 354

13. *Op. cit.*, pp. 140–150.

14. It has to be emphasized that Rickert, when he speaks of "assertions," "judgments," "forms," etc., always refers to mental states and activities. Verbal statements are their rendition on a linguistic level. Cf. Sigwart, *op. cit.*, vol. I, p. 25. "The Proposition, in which something is stated about something, is the verbal expression of the Judgment. This originates as an active movement of Thought (*lebendiger Denkakt*), and always presupposes that there are present to the person forming and uttering the judgment, two ideas (*Vorstellungen*)—the Subject and Predicate ideas. . . ."

15. Rickert, *Gegenstand*, p. 188.
16. See above, this section.
17. Rickert, *Gegenstand*, pp. 199–200.
18. *Op. cit.*, p. 216.
19. *Op. cit.* pp. 366–368.
20. *Op. cit.*, pp. 371–378.
21. Rickert, *Grenzen*, p. 32.
22. Rickert, *Gegenstand*, pp. 401–404.
23. For Rickert, laws of nature are summarized presentations of recurrent series of events, i.e., constellations of facts which repeatedly occur. For a more detailed exposition, see below, section 3, and chapter 3, section 7.
24. Rickert, *Grenzen*, p. 34.
25. Rickert, *Gegenstand*, pp. 425–426.
26. Rickert, *Grenzen*, p. 34.
27. Rickert, *Gegenstand*, p. 140. An idea was described as a reproduction on another mental level of some immediate sensations. See above, this section.
28. This is also the meaning in which Max Weber uses the term "objectivity."
29. See section 6, this chapter.
30. Rickert, *Grenzen*, p. 15.
31. Not every scientist makes use of all valid methods of abstraction. Due to specialization, each scientist is concerned only with the standards relevant to his special tasks.
32. Rickert, *Grenzen*.
33. *Op. cit.*, p. 10.
34. *Op. cit.*, p. 583 n. Max Weber uses "logic" and "logical" in the same sense as Rickert.
35. *Op. cit.*, p. vii.
36. *Op. cit.*, p. 13.
37. See above, this section.
38. *Op. cit.*, p. 23.
39. "Irrational," since it is not conceivable by reason.
40. Rickert, *Gegenstand*, pp. 427, 449–450.
41. *Op. cit.*, p. 404.
42. *Op. cit.*, pp. 425–426.
43. See above, this section.
44. *Op. cit.*, pp. 392–393.
45. *Op. cit.*, pp. 405–421.

I. 3

1. Rickert, *Grenzen*, p. 33.
2. Rickert, *Gegenstand*, p. 136.
3. Rickert, *Grenzen*, p. 34.
4. *Op. cit.*, p. 36.
5. *Op. cit.*, p. 43.
6. Rickert, *Definition*, p. 40.
7. Rickert, *Grenzen*, pp. 42–43.
8. "The logical particularity of an empirical science must be understood on the basis of the relationship between the content of its concepts and empirical reality." *Op. cit.*, pp. 527–528. In modern philosophy of science, the problem of abstraction is treated as a problem of psychology. Cf. Heinrich

Scholz & Hermann Schweitzer, *Die sogenannten Definitionen durch Abstraktion* (Leipzig: Meiner, 1935), p. 14.
9. Rickert, *Grenzen*, p. 50.
10. *Op. cit.*, p. 86.
11. *Op. cit.*, p. 40.
12. *Op. cit.*, p. 53.
13. Rickert, *Definition*, p. 46.
14. Rickert, *Grenzen*, pp. 54–55.
15. Rickert, *Definition*, p. 50.
16. *Ibid.*
17. "Of course, this is not to say that each time we hear the concept used in scientific discourse we explicitly have to make the judgments which establish the meaningful content of the term. Psychologically speaking, there may again occur an abbreviated process whose nature does not concern us here." *Grenzen*, p. 55. The result of this "abbreviated process" seems to be the vague particular content which usually passes for a general image.
18. *Grenzen*, p. 55.
19. *Op. cit.*, p. 77.
20. *Op. cit.*, p. 79.
21. *Op. cit.*, p. 80.
22. *Op. cit.*, p. 88.
23. *Op. cit.*, p. 90.
24. *Op. cit.*, p 92.
25. See above, section 2.
26. For a critique of this view, cf. Ernest Nagel, *The Structure of Science* (New York, Burlingame: Harcourt, Brace and World, 1961), pp. 117–129.
27. Rickert, *Definition*, pp. 20–21.
28. *Op. cit.*, p. 49.
29. Rickert, *Grenzen*, p. 41.
30. See below, chapter 3, section 4.
31. Sigwart devoted a few pages in his two-volume work to this question. Sigwart, *op. cit.*, vol. II, pp. 165–166.
32. Rickert, *Grenzen*, p. 68.
33. Thus, Rickert says that in the case of concepts defined according to the principle of genus proximum and differentia specifica "the generic concept is, to us, the expression for the timelessly valid law which time and again we uncover in the changing phenomena." *Definition*, p. 66.
34. Rickert, *Definition*, p. 67.
35. Rickert, *Grenzen*, p. 63. Concerning the special significance of this assumption, cf. below, section 6.

I. 4

1. Cf. above, section 3.
2. Rickert, *Grenzen*, p. 236.
3. *Op. cit.*, p. 230.
4. *Op. cit.*, pp. 252, 501–504.
5. *Op. cit.*, pp. 249–250.
6. *Op. cit.*, p. 339.
7. *Op. cit.*, pp. 328–329.
8. *Op. cit.*, p. 351.
9. *Op. cit.*, pp. 353–354.

10. *Op. cit.*, p. 371.
11. *Op. cit.*, p. 363. This argument also represents the systematic foundation for Weber's advocacy of "ethical neutrality" in science.
12. Heinrich Rickert, *Science and History* (Princeton: Van Nostrand, 1962), pp. 18–19. *Grenzen*, p. 577.
13. Rickert, *Science and History*, p. 22. See also *Grenzen*, p. 578.
14. Rickert, *Grenzen*, pp. 364–365.
15. *Op. cit.*, p. 632. The empirical correctness of this may seem debatable.
16. *Op. cit.*, p. 371. This is patently false. An historical description of, e.g., Lincoln has to mention, or imply, e.g., that he is a human being, which is a generic feature.
17. This is what Weber calls the "transcendental presupposition of all cultural sciences." See below, chapter 2, section 5.
18. Rickert, *Grenzen*, p. 365.
19. *Op. cit.*, pp. 342–343.
20. On the justifiability of this assumption, see below, section 6.
21. Rickert, *Grenzen*, p. 390.
22. *Op. cit.*, p. 703.
23. *Op. cit.*, pp. 382–386.
24. *Op. cit.*, p. 327.
25. Concept formation on the basis of value-relevance Rickert also calls "teleological" concept formation. Cf. *Grenzen*, p. 307.
26. Rickert, *Grenzen*, pp. 382–383.
27. *Op. cit.*, p. 382.
28. *Op. cit.*, p. 385.

I. 5

1. Again, this reference to the idea of a science of concrete reality is made to justify the inclusion of elements other than those which are value-relevant.
2. Rickert, *Grenzen*, p. 392.
3. *Op. cit.*, p. 395.
4. *Op. cit.*, p. 409.
5. *Op. cit.*, p. 437.
6. *Op. cit.*, pp. 471–472.
7. *Op. cit.*, p. 438.
8. *Op. cit.*, p. 474.
9. *Op. cit.*, p. 477.
10. *Op. cit.*, p. 478.
11. *Op. cit.*, pp. 412–413.
12. *Op. cit.*, pp. 413–414.
13. *Op. cit.*, p. 414.
14. *Op. cit.*, pp. 419–420.
15. *Op. cit.*, p. 422.
16. *Op. cit.*, pp. 337–340.
17. *Op. cit.*, p. 430.
18. *Op. cit.*, p. 431

I. 6

1. Rickert, *Grenzen*, p. 492.
2. *Op. cit.*, p. 665. Cf. above, section 2.

3. *Op. cit.*, p. 673.
4. Above, section 2.
5. *Op. cit.*, p. 675.
6. I.e., knowledge of the extensive infinity of the world.
7. *Op. cit.*, p. 680.
8. *Op. cit.*, p. 686.
9. *Op. cit.*, p. 692.
10. Cf. Maurice Mandelbaum, *The Problem of Historical Knowledge* (New York, Evanston, London: Harper Torchbooks, 1967), p. 135.
11. "Historical Explanation in the Social Sciences," *British Journal for the Philosophy of Science* 8 (1957): 104–117; p. 104.
12. Rickert, *Grenzen*, p. 255.
13. *Op. cit.*, pp. 560–561.
14. *Op. cit.*, p. 561.
15. *Op. cit.*, p. 567.
16. *Op. cit.*, p. 574.
17. *Op. cit.*, p. 589.
18. *Op. cit.*, p. 298.
19. *Op. cit.*, p. 270.
20. *Op. cit.*, p. 481.
21. Cf. Erich Becher, *Geisteswissenschaften und Naturwissenschaften* (Muenchen, Leipzig: Duncker & Humblot, 1921), pp. 186–197. Ernst Cassirer, *Substance and Function* (New York: Dover, 1953), pp. 221–233. Raymond Aron, *La philosophie critique de l'histoire* (Paris: Vrin, 2nd ed, 1950), pp. 113–157. Oskar Kraus, *Die Wertheorien. Geschichte und Kritik* (Bruenn, Wien, Leipzig: Rohrer, 1937), pp. 286–293. Max Frischeisen-Koehler, *Wissenschaft und Wirklichkeit* (Leipzig, Berlin: Teubner, 1912), pp. 99–187. Mandelbaum, *op. cit.*, pp. 119–147. Ernst Troeltsch, "Ueber den Begriff einer historischen Dialektik. Windelband-Rickert und Hegel," *Historische Zeitschrift* 119 (1919): 373–426.
22. Cf. Bienfait, *op. cit.*, p. 49.
23. *Op. cit.*, pp. 57–58.
24. *Op. cit.*, p. 54.
25. Cf. F. A. Hayek in the preface to Rickert's *Science and History*, p. vi. Also Frischeisen-Koehler, *op. cit.*, pp. 157–159.

CHAPTER II.

II. 1

1. Eugène Fleischmann, "De Weber à Nietzsche," *Archives Européennes de Sociologie* 5 (1964): 190–238; p. 199 n. 36. Fleischmann is echoed by Runciman, *Critique*, pp. 9, 11, 12.
2. *Op. cit.*, p. 199.
3. Friedrich H. Tenbruck, "Formal Sociology," in Lewis A. Coser (ed.), *Georg Simmel* (Englewood Cliffs: Prentice-Hall, 1965), pp. 77–96; p. 88. Cf. also Winckelmann, *op. cit.*, p. 22.
4. Von Schelting, "Logische Theorie," p. 629. Henrich, *op. cit.*, pp. 4–5; see also Pfister, *op. cit.*
5. See below, section 6.

II. 2

1. Albert Salomon, "Max Weber's Methodology," *Social Research* 1 (1934): 147–168.
2. *GAzWL*, p. 265 n. 1, also p. 11; *ET*, p. 163 n. 30.
3. *GAzWL*, pp. 71, 80, 103.
4. *Op. cit.*, pp. 12 n. 1, 125–126.
5. This can either be an interest in the generic features of everything which exists, or an interest in the unique features of particular, individual segments of concrete reality.
6. *GAzWL*, p. 178; *ET*, p. 79.
7. *GAzWL*, p. 6.
8. *GAzWL*, p. 176; *ET*, p. 77.
9. *GAzWL*, p. 212; *ET*, p. 110.
10. *GAzWL*, p. 60.
11. *Ibid.*
12. *GAzWL*, p. 187; *ET*, p. 87.
13. *GAzWL*, p. 180; *ET*, p. 80.
14. Julien Freund, *The Sociology of Max Weber* (New York: Vintage Books, 1969), pp. 38–39.
15. *Op. cit.*, p. 40.
16. Cf. above, chapter 1, section 1.
17. *GAzWL*, p. 150. *ET*, p. 54, renders it as "analytical ordering" which does not have the mentalistic connotations of the original expression whose significance will become clear through the analysis here presented. See also *GAzWL*, pp. 155, 156, 160, 213; *ET*, pp. 58, 59, 63, 111.
18. *GAzWL*, p. 208; *ET*, p. 106.
19. Actually it is stated in several instances where the ideal type is called a "thought-picture" (*Gedankenbild*), e.g., pp. 190, 193 in *GAzWL*; *ET*, p. 90 ("conceptual pattern"), 93. It seems desirable, though, at this point not to rely on statements concerning the ideal type, since so much controversy centers around their interpretation. Weber also uses the expression "conceptual pictures," *GAzWL*, p. 195; *ET*, p. 94 ("theoretical constructs"). What is not easily recognizable is that these terms are not metaphorical. To the knowledge of this author, no interpreter has ever paid any attention to the fact that Weber's theory is mentalistic. Also, nobody ever seems to have been puzzled by many statements of Weber's which make sense only in reference to such a conception, e.g., those concerning the limits of the human mind. The mind is conceived by Weber in analogy to a bucket that can hold only so much water. See below, section 3.
20. *GAzWL*, p. 110. Concerning the meaning of "experience," see below, this section and section 3.
21. *GAZWL*, p. 280; see also pp. 5, 92 n. 1, 113, 171, 177, 192–193; *ET*, pp. 178, 72, 78, 92.
22. *GAzWL*, p. 170, also p. 14; *ET*, p. 72.
23. *GAzWL*, p. 4.
24. Cf. von Schelting, *Wissenschaftslehre*, p. 322 n. 1.
25. Cf. above, chapter 1, sections 2 and 3.
26. *GAzWL*, p. 96 n. 1.
27. *Op. cit.*, pp. 89, 96, 104, 107–108, 119, 121–122, 209; *ET*, p. 107.
28. This is Julius Jakob Schaaf's opinion, who apparently has understood neither Rickert nor Weber, since he declares that in this respect Weber fully agrees

with Rickert. See Julius Jakob Schaaf, *Geschichte und Begriff. Eine kritische Studie zur Geschichtsmethodologie von Ernst Troeltsch und Max Weber* (Tuebingen: Mohr, 1946), p. 42. As Henrich, *op. cit.*, p. 2 correctly states, this basic mistake completely invalidates Schaaf's analysis.

29. Von Schelting, "Logische Theorie," pp. 632–633, and Henrich correctly state that Weber makes the distinction between methodological and constitutive forms. Constitutive forms, for Weber as well as for Rickert, belong to the realm of epistemology, not to methodology. It is, therefore, not entirely correct when Henrich says that there are no epistemological implications in Weber's methodology, and claims: "Rather, it will be shown that the key to its understanding can be found only when it is realized how undisturbed its construction is by epistemological implications." Henrich, *op. cit.*, p. 2.

30. I.e., everything that goes on in the minds of humans.

31. *GAzWL*, pp. 102–103.

32. *Op. cit.*, p. 73.

33. *Op. cit.*, p. 104.

34. *Op. cit.*, p. 279; *ET*, p. 177.

35. *Op. cit.*, p. 290; *ET*, p. 188.

36. *Op. cit.*, p. 89.

37. *Op. cit.*, p. 110.

38. *Op. cit.*, pp. 72–73.

39. *Op. cit.*, p. 157; *ET*, p. 60 ("analysis of facts").

40. *Op. cit.*, p. 156; *ET*, p. 59, Cf. above, chapter 1, section 2.

41. *Op. cit.*, p. 119.

42. *Op. cit.*, p. 104.

43. *Op. cit.*, p. 184; *ET*, p. 84.

44. *Op. cit.*, p. 104. Weber here uses the term "category" loosely in the general sense of "mode of thought." Here it obviously does not refer to the form given to a sensation. Also, the two quotations taken from *GAzWL*, p. 104 stand in a context in which "experience" has a meaning other than "sensation." Here it refers to an actor's feelings, emotions, thoughts, etc. In this sense of the word, experiences can be either immediate sensations, or categorically formed facts. In the context of p. 104, the experiences have the logical status of "direct experience," i.e., immediate sensations, not "facts." Cf. below, section 3.

45. *GAzWL*, p. 134.

46. *Op. cit.*, pp. 134–135.

47. *Op. cit.*, p. 135.

48. *Ibid.*

49. *Op. cit.*, pp. 85, 144, 178, 186; *ET*, pp. 78–79, 86.

50. Cf. above, chapter 1, sections 2 and 4.

51. Freund, *op. cit.*, pp. 49–50. Freund's account is full of such inaccuracies.

52. *GAzWL*, p. 89.

53. Cf. above, chapter 1, section 2.

54. *GAzWL*, p. 89.

II. 3

1. *GAzWL*, p. 237; *ET*, p. 135.

2. To take a particular scientific account as *the* account of reality is to mistake an aspect for the concrete totality. Cf. *GAzWL*, p. 75 n. 2.

3. *GAzWL*, pp. 4, 14, 75 n. 2, 92 n. 1, 171, 177; *ET*, pp. 72, 78.

4. *Op. cit.*, p. 171; *ET*, p. 72.

5. This plainly is not the Kantian argument against the possibility of knowledge of the thing-in-itself, as Schaaf declares, *op. cit.*, p. 45.

6. *GAzWL*, p. 92, n. 1. This has nothing whatsoever to do with the hypothetical character of all knowledge, as Freund holds, *op. cit.*, pp. 60–61. Nor is the idea of knowledge as a complete picture of reality rejected by Weber because this presupposes the presence of objective structures in reality (Tenbruck, *op. cit.*, p. 601). Weber's efforts do not, as Tenbruck declares, "result fom the lack of structure of the naturalistic conception of reality" (*op. cit.*, p. 600). Weber's conception of reality is an implication of his Neo-Kantian epistemology. In this sense it is wrong, therefore, when Tenbruck interprets Weber's methodology as an "attack upon naturalism" (*op. cit.*, p. 598).

7. *GAzWL*, pp. 5, 113.

8. For all this, cf. above, chapter 1, sections 2 and 3.

9. Cf. below, this section and section 6.

10. *GAzWL*, p. 5. This is not knowledge of a value, as Bienfait, *op. cit.*, p. 30, declares, but knowledge of the embodiment of a value; it is knowledge of reality from the point of view of a value. Cf. above, chapter 1, section 3.

11. *GAzWL*, p. 217; *ET*, p. 115. Thus, what Weber claims he is doing is the rational reconstruction of procedures in use.

12. *Op. cit.*, pp. 5, 86, 171; *ET*, p. 72. It hardly needs emphasis that "essential," as Weber uses it, has nothing to do with the "nature" of things.

13. *Op. cit.*, pp. 176, 180; *ET*, pp. 77, 80.

14. *Op. cit.*, pp. 5, 15, 176, 180; *ET*, pp. 77, 80.

15. *Op. cit.*, p. 5.

16. *Ibid.*

17. *Op. cit.*, p. 11.

18. *Op. cit.*, pp. 11, 174; *ET*, p. 75.

19. Cf. above, chapter 1, sections 3 and 4. Runciman's claim (*Critique*, p. 12) that Weber's position is not the same as Rickert's, is mistaken.

20. Talcott Parsons, *The Structure of Social Action* (New York: Free Press, 1949), p. 591.

21. *Op. cit.*, pp. 592–593.

22. *Op. cit.*, pp. 595–596.

23. *GAzWL*, p. 207; *ET*, p. 105 ("analytical rearrangement").

24. *Op. cit.*, p. 208; *ET*, p. 106.

25. *Op. cit.*, p. 6 n. 6.

26. *Op. cit.*, p. 93.

27. *Op. cit.*, p. 6.

28. *I.e.*, the thinking of a multiplicity of facts in one concept.

29. Cf. *op. cit.*, pp. 100–101 n. 2.

30. This is what Weber means when he says that "concepts are primarily means of thought for the intellectual mastery of empirical data..." (*op. cit.*, p. 208; *ET*, p. 106).

31. *Op. cit.*, pp. 109–110.

32. *Op. cit.*, p. 5. An analogous statement regarding history can be found *op. cit.*, p. 6. See also pp. 195, 237; *ET*, pp. 94, 135, for "concept" as end-product.

33. *Op. cit.*, pp. 177, 178, 179, 180, 193, 208; *ET*, pp. 78, 79, 80, 90, 92, 106. It

is not entirely clear how Runciman can state that Weber is "wrong to conclude [from the impossibility of laws of history] that there are no laws
of any kind to which historical explanation implicitly, if not explicitly, ap-
peals" (*Critique*, p. 68).

34. See below, section 5.

35. Should be "conceptual forms."

36. *ET*: "analytical instruments."

37. And, combined with contents, cannot be exact copies of empirical reality
in the human mind.

38. I.e., general concept.

39. I.e., general concepts.

40. In history.

41. Of explanation.

42. *GAzWL*, pp. 208–209; *ET*, p. 106.

43. *Op. cit.*, p. 4.

44. See chapter 1, sections 3 and 4.

45. See chapter 1, section 6.

46. *GAzWL*, p. 254; *ET*, p. 152.

47. *Op. cit.*, pp. 212–213; *ET*, pp. 110–111.

48. Cf. below, section 6.

49. *GAzWL*, pp. 75 n. 2, I; 92 n. 1.

50. *Op. cit.*, p. 92. n. 1.

51. *Ibid.*

52. *Op. cit.*, pp. 125–126; also p. 53 n. 1.

53. *Op. cit.*, p. 71.

54. *Op. cit.*, pp. 12–13 n. 1.

55. It may seem that Weber's own procedure is not in accord with this insight.
For, as will be seen in the next section, the formation of individual concepts
requires meaningful objects (*op. cit.*, p. 101). However, it must be realized
that the meaningful character of certain facts merely makes history possible;
it in no way requires an historical treatment. What makes history necessary
is the human goal to have knowledge of phenomena in their uniqueness.
The fact that this interest focuses on the meaningful parts of reality logically
is a consequence of the standard of selection in use (*GAzWL*, p. 99). Of
course, without these special features of parts of reality there would be no
sense in applying the standard. But these parts can also be treated in a
generalizing fashion (cf. *op. cit.*, pp. 12 n. 1, 79 n. 1, 173; *ET*, p. 75).

56. *Op. cit.*, p. 5.

57. *Op. cit.*, p. 6, also p. 179; *ET*, p. 80. See above, chapter 1, section 3.

58. Cf. Walter Dubislav, *Die Definition* (Leipzig: Meiner, 3rd ed., 1931), esp.
pp. 7–17, 118–122. Schaaf has criticized Weber's doctrine and his theory of
abstraction in general (Schaaf, *op. cit.*, pp. 46, 49), without being able to
profit from this insight, though. He did not realize that the problematic
aspects of the ideal type are closely related to the theory of abstraction used
by Weber. Cf. below, chapter 3, section 4.

II. 4

1. *GAzWL*, p. 5.

2. *Op. cit.*, p. 4; also p. 177; *ET*, p. 78. This multiplicity—which Weber calls
a "chaos"—is not the same as Kant's "chaos of sensations," but refers to facts.

Cf. Henrich, *op. cit.*, p. 11. "Reality" always refers to the *infinity* of facts, their *totality*. Knowledge of this *limitless totality* is the problem with which Weber is concerned in his methodological reflections, not knowledge of *single* facts.

3. *GAzWL*, pp. 5, 110, 177, 272; *ET*, pp. 78, 169.
4. *Op. cit.*, p. 171; *ET*, p. 72.
5. *Op. cit.*, p. 15.
6. *Op. cit.*, p. 6.
7. *Op. cit.*, p. 13.
8. *Op. cit.*, p. 14.
9. *Op. cit.*, p. 11.
10. *Op. cit.*, pp. 4, 13, 13 n. 1.
11. *Op. cit.*, pp. 4, 13 n. 1, 80.
12. *Op. cit.*, p. 91.
13. *Op. cit.*, p. 15.
14. *Ibid.*
15. *Op. cit.*, p. 176; *ET*, p. 77.
16. *Ibid.*
17. In Rickert's work, the complementary name, equally misunderstandable, for the natural sciences is "sciences of the concept" (*Wissenschaften vom Begriff*). An influential author who makes use of the notion of "science of reality" (*Wirklichkeitswissenschaft*) is Hans Freyer. It is important to realize, however, that Rickert/Weber and Freyer do not understand the same thing by it. Whereas the former employ it in order to characterize the logical character of historical sciences, the latter denotes by it a systematic, i.e., theoretical, science (in his book *Soziologie als Wirklichkeitswissenschaft* [Leipzig-Berlin: Teubner, 1930]). Furthermore, whereas Rickert/Weber justify the sciences of (concrete) reality on the basis of their contribution to the humanly attainable type of knowledge, Freyer claims that they are required since the object with which they deal demands a particular logical treatment (*op. cit.*, p. 199). Sciences of reality, in Freyer's scheme of things, constitute one of three types of sciences, the other two being natural sciences and sciences of meaning structures (*Logoswissenschaften*). The procedures of the natural sciences are declared to be appropriate to a realm of objects which can be thought ordered according to timelessly valid laws. The sciences of meaning structures deal with systems of meaning, with self-contained meaningful wholes (*op. cit.*, p. 201). Sciences of reality are called for whenever the object which is to be grasped cognitively is neither "nature" nor "objective spirit," but an ongoing meaningful process of which the knowing subject himself is an active part (*op. cit.*, p. 204). The dependence of this process on the active will of the humans who are existentially involved in it (including the scientist) precludes its treatment as an accomplished fact. Rather, its scientific analysis is to be regarded as the articulation of the self-consciousness of subjects who are existentially involved in, and responsible for, something which is in the process of emerging through their activity. The concepts of sociology as a science of reality therefore must refer to the present phenomena as phenomena which contain within them the forces and directions of their transcendence, the emergence of the future (*op. cit.*, p. 206). Freyer's position owes much to Weber, yet the differences are considerable. The main source of the divergences lies in the fact that for Weber the postulate of a science of reality is derived from a certain conception of

knowledge. Freyer, in contrast, bases it on the circumstance that certain segments of empirical reality are subject to human interference.

18. *GAzWL*, p. 4.

19. *Op. cit.*, pp. 23, 96.

20. *Op. cit.*, p. 8.

21. Toward ever more abstract concepts; therefore, the name "sciences of the concept."

22. I.e., nonconcrete.

23. *GAzWL*, pp. 4–5.

24. As a matter of fact, Weber intended it to be a short outline of Rickert's theory of concept formation in the natural sciences. Cf. *op. cit.*, p. 7 n. 1.

25. Cf. above, chapter 1, section 3.

26. *Ibid.*

27. *Ibid.* Compare Rickert's treatment of "definition" as the making explicit of the judgments constituting the content of the concept, and the mentalistic conception of "judgment" with the statement of Weber's "that we comprehend reality only through a chain of changing mental images (*Vorstellungsveraenderungen*). . . ." *GAzWL*, p. 195; *ET*, p. 94.

28. See above, chapter 1, section 3.

29. *Ibid.*

30. *Ibid.*

31. *GAzWL*, p. 180; *ET*, p. 80.

32. *Op. cit.*, p. 91.

33. *Op. cit.*, p. 180; *ET*, p. 80. Joseph Lopreato & Letitia Alston in their article "Ideal Types and the Idealization Strategy," *American Sociological Review* 35 (1970): 88–96, criticize this statement (p. 89), but since they are not familiar with Weber's terminology they miss the point.

34. *GAzWL*, pp. 75 n. 2, II; 134.

35. *Op. cit.*, pp. 13, 18, 28, 174; *ET*, p 75.

36. *Op. cit.*, p. 13 n. 1.

37. *Op. cit.*, p. 172; *ET*, p. 73. Tenbruck's interpretation of this statement is as follows: "Only this opinion is refuted [by Weber], that reality can be deduced from laws, that is, that events can be predicted" ("Die Genesis der Methodologie Max Webers," p. 591). Tenbruck here is obviously way off the mark.

II. 5

1. *GAzWL*, p. 4.

2. *Op. cit.*, pp. 83, 112, 176; *ET*, pp. 76–77.

3. *Op. cit.*, p. 6, also p. 186; *ET*, p. 86.

4. *Op. cit.*, pp. 172–173; *ET*, p. 74.

5. Cf. above, chapter 1, section 3.

6. I.e., concrete, not abstract.

7. *Op. cit.*, p. 113.

8. *Op. cit.*, p. 173; *ET*, p. 74.

9. *Op. cit.*, p. 175; *ET*, pp. 75–76.

10. *Op. cit.*, pp. 86, 96.

11. *Op. cit.*, p. 116, see also pp. 252–253; *ET*, pp. 150–151. This quotation substantiates Henrich's point (*op. cit.*, pp. 75–76) that Weber also has a substantive conception of culture, not only a logical one.

12. *Op. cit.*, p. 245; *ET*, p. 143. This does not imply, as Weber points out,

NOTES TO CHAPTER II.5

that always only the uniqueness of things is valued. Cf. *op. cit.*, p. 92 n. 1.
13. *Op. cit.*, p. 156; *ET*, p. 59. How Carlo Antoni can say *(From History to Sociology* [Detroit: Wayne State Press, 1959], p. 142) that Weber's distinction between value judgment and science arose from practical necessity and not out of an intellectual need for clarity is not entirely obvious, unless he should subscribe to a psychoanalytic explanation like Arthur Mitzman's in *The Iron Cage* (New York: Knopf, 1970), pp. 51, 61, 169–170.
14. *GAzWL*, p. 91. According to Tenbruck, this is Rickert's only true contribution to Weber's methodology (Tenbruck, *op. cit.*, p. 629 n. 25).
15. *GAzWL*, pp. 174, 175; *ET*, pp. 75, 76.
16. *Op. cit.*, pp. 252–253; *ET*, p. 150.
17. *Op. cit.*, pp. 83, 100–101 n. 2, 126, 163, 173; *ET*, pp. 65, 74.
18. See chapter 1, section 4.
19. *Op. cit.*, p. 177; *ET*, p. 78. "Chaos" here merely means the "infinite unordered multiplicity of empirical phenomena," and has nothing to do with Kant's "chaos of sensations."
20. *Op. cit.*, p. 178; *ET*, p. 78. Also *op. cit.*, p. 177; *ET*, p. 78.
21. Cf. above, chapter 1, section 4.
22. *Op. cit.*, p. 181; *ET*, p. 81.
23. I.e., particular concrete phenomena as the embodiments of particular values.
24. I.e., by making value judgments about this culture, since he is concerned with it.
25. *Op. cit.*, pp. 180–181; *ET*, p. 81. See also *op. cit.*, pp. 54, 100–101 n. 2. Completely erroneous is Tenbruck, *op. cit.*, p. 596. "Weber's 'transcendental presupposition' of the cultural sciences is the reinstatement of an historical heritage by means of the methodology." It is, of course, true that Rickert's and Weber's thought was a product of its time and was successful at the time because it appealed to a current world view. But it is also a reasoned argument.
26. *GAzWL*, p. 192; *ET*, p. 91.
27. *Op. cit.*, p. 83.
28. *Op. cit.*, p. 86.
29. *Op. cit.*, p. 181; *ET*, p. 81. The logical structure of the principle of value-relevance has gone almost completely unanalyzed in the secondary literature, although it is one of the least clear parts of Rickert's and Weber's thought. Take, for example, Raymond Aron's statement: "The term *value-reference* [or value-relevance] . . . simply means that the sociologist . . . can explore . . . reality by placing it in relation to the specific value [chosen as a point of reference]. . . ." Raymond Aron, *Main Currents in Sociological Thought* (Garden City: Anchor Books, 1965, 1967), vol. II. p. 230; hereafter referred to as *Main Currents*. Unfortunately, the explanation is not as simple as that. Failure to understand the function and exact nature of the principle of value-relevance is a flaw in Runciman's otherwise excellent *Critique*. Runciman does not seem to be aware that Weber's main problem was the justification of writing history; this is the frame of reference within which many of Weber's statements must be interpreted, not that provided by the problem of *explanation*. From the fact that history "is not a producer but only a consumer of laws" (*Critique*, pp. 69–70) Weber does not draw any conclusions whatsoever (it is one of his conclusions), especially not the one that there is "something other than 'reference to laws' by which historical explanation has to be justified" (*op. cit.*, p. 70). The principle of value-relevance

is designed to show that it is justifiable to attempt historical explanations at all. It is not a "further justification" (*ibid.*) for the historian's *explanation*, in *addition* to his application of whatever laws he has available. It is a justification of the historian's existence. Today, this may be a trivial issue; in Weber's time it was not.

30. *GAzWL*, p. 213; *ET*, p. 111.

31. I.e., inessential from the logical point of view.

32. *Op. cit.*, p. 124 n. 1.

33. *Op. cit.*, p. 183; *ET*, p. 83.

34. "Interest" here means "arouse the curiosity of." It does not imply that some people deem these phenomena worth knowing, essential, and others do not. Everybody thinks they are essential, but not everybody wants to make the description of any particular one his scientific preoccupation.

35. *Op. cit.*, pp. 183–184; *ET*, pp. 83–84.

36. *Op. cit.*, p. 181, also pp. 164, 168, 170, 192; *ET*, pp. 81, 66, 69, 71, 91. It is imperative not to confuse the referent of "viewpoint" in these contexts, i.e., the decision to focus one's scientific interest in *historical* knowledge on *particular* value-embodiments, from another use, where the term refers to the decision to adopt either the procedure of the natural sciences or that of the historical ones. Cf. *op. cit.*, p. 6.

37. Henrich completely misunderstands this (Henrich, *op. cit.*, pp. 23–24, 26–27). Especially he is confused about what a viewpoint is. Georg Weippert also is mistaken when he accusingly says that "an earthquake perhaps, or a battlefield may become historical concepts in the same way as an individual person or a collective phenomenon." Georg Weippert, "Die ideal-typische Sinn-und Wesenserfassung und die Denkgebilde der formalen Theorie. Zur Logik des 'Idealtypus' und der rationalen Schemata,'" *Zeitschrift fuer die gesamte Staatswissenschaft* 100 (1940): 257–308; p. 266. An earthquake, e.g., does not embody any values.

38. *GAzWL*, p. 181; *ET*, pp. 81–82.

39. *Op. cit.*, p. 97.

40. *Op. cit.*, p. 181; *ET*, p. 81.

41. Henrich, *op. cit.*, pp. 27, 32.

42. *GAzWL*, p. 97 n. 3.

43. *Op. cit.*, p. 170; *ET*, p. 71.

44. *Op. cit.*, p. 116 n. 2. Cf. von Schelting's critique in *Wissenschaftslehre*, pp. 406 f.

45. Because of this inclusion of the environment in historical accounts Weber rejects the claim that history is part of psychology—apart from the fact that psychology for him is a natural science. Cf. *GAzWL*, pp. 78, 83.

46. *GAzWL*, p. 261; *ET*, p. 159.

47. *Ibid.*

48. *Op. cit.*, p. 121. Cf. above, chapter 1, section 5.

49. *Op. cit.*, p. 166; *ET*, p. 68.

50. *Op. cit.*, pp. 163–164; *ET*, pp. 65–66.

51. *Op. cit.*, p. 162; *ET*, p. 64.

52. *Ibid.*

53. *Op. cit.*, p. 162; *ET*, p. 65.

54. *Op. cit.*, p. 167; also p. 164; *ET*, pp. 68, 66.

55. *Op. cit.*, p. 168; *ET*, p. 70.

56. *Op. cit.*, p. 164; *ET*, p. 66.

57. I.e., intellectually not conceivable in its totality by human reason.
58. *Op. cit.*, p. 213; *ET*, p. 111.
59. Cf. Henrich, *op. cit.*, p. 34. Parsons's claims to the contrary are simply wrong. Cf. Parsons, *op. cit.*, p. 601. Runciman's impression that "Weber goes on to suggest that because cultural evolution is subjective and open-ended the social scientist not only need not but cannot rest his explanations on general laws, and cannot frame his explanations without implicit dependence upon pre-suppositions of a 'value-relevant' kind" (*Critique*, p. 35), is mistaken. It is based on his failure to distinguish the justification of an explanation in history from the justification of history as such.
60. *GAzWL*, p. 184, also p. 206; *ET*, pp. 84, 104. Freund declares that no one scientist "can exhaust what we know of reality; on the contrary, reality becomes increasingly intelligible in its complexity as more and more historians, sociologists, economists, and students of politics examine it in the light of yet other values. For that very reason, a contemporary historian will find Thucydides' account of the Peloponnesian War fully as interesting as that of a more modern author . . ." (Freund, *op. cit.*, p. 54). This is not at all correct, for it ascribes to Weber a cumulative view of historical investigation, whereas Weber's real problem was to explain that history is *not* and *cannot* be cumulative.
61. *GAzWL*, p. 181; *ET*, p. 82.
62. *Op. cit.*, p. 182; *ET*, p. 82.
63. *Ibid.*
64. *Op. cit.*, pp. 5, 6 n. 2, 164, 172; *ET*, pp. 67, 74.
65. *Op. cit.*, p. 183; *ET*, p. 83.
66. *Op. cit.*, p. 186; *ET*, p 86.
67. *Op. cit.*, p. 182; *ET*, p. 82. This position is criticized by Antoni, *op. cit.*, p. 160.
68. *GAzWL*, pp. 95, 134. All historical events are causally determined. Cf. *op. cit.*, p. 54.
69. The fact that historical accounts contain understandable elements has nothing to do with this, for it is possible to establish understandable regularities. *Op. cit.*, p. 173; *ET*, p. 74.
70. *Op. cit.*, pp. 48 n. 1, 50, 63.
71. *Op. cit.*, p. 80
72. Troeltsch's statement in *Der Historismus und seine Probleme* (*Gesammelte Schriften*, vol. III) (Tuebingen: Mohr, 1922), p. 566, that Weber replaced Rickert's doctrine of "individual causality" by the methods of "objective possibility" and "adequate causation" is patently false. Those methods, in any case, have relevance only in relation to the problem of establishing individual causal chains.
73. *GAzWL*, p. 172, also p. 177; *ET*, p. 73, also p. 78.
74. *Op. cit.*, p. 179; *ET*, p. 79.
75. *Ibid.* Thus, Runciman's suggestion that Weber denies "the applicability of general laws in the social sciences . . ." (*Critique*, p. 61), cannot be justified.
76. *ET*: "heuristic means," p. 76.
77. *GAzWL*, p. 175, also pp. 178–179; *ET*, p. 76, also p. 80. Because of this function of general concepts in the establishment of historical knowledge Weber insists that the formation of individual concepts is only the specific means of history, but not the exclusive one. *Op. cit.*, p. 6 n. 1.

II. 6

1. See above, chapter 1, section 6.
2. Henrich, *op. cit.*, p. 45.
3. *GAzWL*, p. 183; *ET*, p. 83. Cf. Raymond Aron, *German Sociology* (Glencoe: Free Press, 1957), p. 96. Don Martindale, *The Nature and Types of Sociological Theory* (Boston: Houghton Mifflin, 1960), p. 379, hereafter referred to as *Nature & Types*. Bennion, *op. cit.*, p. 42; Bienfait, *op. cit.*, p. 39; Aron, *Main Currents*, vol. II, pp. 233–234; Schaaf, *op. cit.*, pp. 58–59; Hans Oppenheimer, *Die Logik der soziologischen Begriffsbildung, mit besonderer Beruecksichtigung von Max Weber* (Tuebingen: Mohr, 1925), p. 51. Troeltsch, *op. cit.*, p. 566; Janoska-Bendl, *op. cit.*, pp. 22–23. Marcel Weinreich, *Max Weber. L'homme et le savant. Etudes sur ses idées directrices* (Paris: Vrin, 1938), pp. 68–69. Freyer, *op. cit.*, p. 155, also p. 147.
4. Andreas Walther, "Max Weber als Soziologe," *Jahrbuch fuer Soziologie* 2 (1926): 1–65; p. 5.
5. Von Schelting, *Wissenschaftslehre*, p. 228. In his earlier discussion, von Schelting left the issue undecided, stating that Weber did not discuss the problem. Cf. von Schelting, "Logische Theorie," pp. 669–670.
6. Fleischmann, *op. cit.*, p. 198.
7. I.e., the natural sciences.
8. *GAzWL*, p. 4.
9. *Ibid.*
10. Rickert, *Grenzen*, pp. 635–640.
11. *GAzWL*, p. 160; *ET*, p. 63.
12. *Op. cit.*, p. 170; *ET*, p. 72.
13. Cf. section 5 above.
14. *Op. cit.*, pp. 183–184; *ET*, pp. 83–84.
15. This interpretation is confirmed by similar thoughts elsewhere. "The intellectual apparatus [i.e., concepts] developed by the past through intellectual treatment—that is, in reality: transformation in thought—of the concretely given reality and its ordering into those concepts which were in accordance with the state of knowledge and the direction of interest of this past, is continually challenged by the new knowledge which we can and *want* to derive from reality . . . but this is due to *that* circumstance that in the sciences which deal with human culture concept formation depends on the way in which the problems are posed, and that this changes with the content of culture itself. . . . The most far-reaching steps forward in the social sciences are *substantively* tied to a shift in the practical cultural problems." *Op. cit.*, pp. 207–208; *ET*, pp. 105–106.
16. *GAzWL*, pp. 261–262; *ET*, pp. 159–160.
17. "This imputation of causes is, as a matter of principle, made with the goal of being 'objectively' valid as an empirical truth with the same absoluteness as any other empirical knowldege." *Op. cit.*, p. 261; *ET*, p. 159.
18. *Op. cit.*, p. 213; *ET*, p. 111.
19. I.e., the theory of historical knowledge.
20. *GAzWL*, p. 47 n. 1.
21. Cf. Bennion, *op. cit.*, pp. 42, 167; Bienfait, *op. cit.*, p. 39; Aron, *German Sociology*, p. 97; Oppenheimer, *op. cit.*, p. 55; Max Horkheimer, *The Eclipse of Reason* (New York: Oxford University Press, 1947), p. 75.
22. Tenbruck, *op. cit.*, p. 602. Tenbruck has obviously failed to understand Weber's postulate of the "immanence" of reality, the role of categories, the

role of concepts, and the conception of objectivity.

23. Von Schelting, *Wissenschaftslehre*, p. 233; Troeltsch, *op. cit.*, p. 566; Bien-fait, *op. cit.*, p. 39; Pfister, *op. cit.*, pp. 154–156.
24. Aron, *Main Currents*, vol. II, pp. 233–234.
25. *Op. cit.*, pp. 234–235.
26. *Op. cit.*, p. 239.
27. Von Schelting, *Wissenschaftslehre*, p. 234.
28. Bienfait, *op. cit.*, p. 39.
29. Tenbruck, *op. cit.*, p. 600.

CHAPTER III.

III. 1

1. See above, chapter 2, section 5.
2. *Ibid.*
3. *GAzWL*, p. 184; *ET*, p. 84.
4. *Op. cit.*, p. 124. "Understanding" designates the phenomenologically distinct mode in which humans have knowledge of meaningful phenomena, (i.e., phenomena in which values are embodied). Cf. below, section 3.
5. *Op. cit.*, p. 123. "Feeling" here means "having sensations."
6. *Op. cit.*, pp. 123–124.
7. *Op. cit.*, p. 123.
8. *Op. cit.*, p. 245; *ET*, p. 143.
9. *Op. cit.*, p. 248; *ET*, p. 146.
10. *Op. cit.*, pp. 245–246; *ET*, p. 143.
11. Weber also calls it "value-relating interpretation" (*op. cit.*, p. 122). This is not the same as "value-relevance." Rather, it designates the process of re-viewing all the possible value-relevances of a concrete object.
12. *Op. cit.*, p. 123.
13. *Op. cit.*, p. 248; *ET*, p. 146.
14. *Op. cit.*, p. 246; *ET*, p. 144.
15. *Op. cit.*, p. 247; *ET*, pp. 144–145.
16. *Op. cit.*, p. 251; *ET*, p. 149.
17. The historical individuals holding these values are the "historical centers" of the historical account in question. Cf. *op. cit.*, p. 116 n. 2.
18. *Op. cit.*, p. 149; *ET*, p. 52.

III. 2

1. *GAzWL*, p. 172; *ET*, p. 73.
2. See above, chapter 1, section 6.
3. *Op. cit.*, p. 254; *ET*, p. 152. Cf. above, chapter 1, section 6.
4. Bienfait (*op. cit.*, p. 24) is one of the few authors who takes notice of Weber's equivocation.
5. *GAzWL*, pp. 170–171, also 14; *ET*, p. 72.
6. *Op. cit.*, p. 168; *ET*, p. 70. This argument is directed against primitive "vulgar" Marxism. Other occurrences of "significant[L]" are on pp. 175, lines 9, 6, and 3 from the bottom of the page; 176, lines 2 and 11 from the top; 177, lines 21–22 from top; 181, line 12 from bottom; 231, lines 6 and 1–2 from the bottom. *ET*, pp. 76, lines 13, 10, and 10 from the bottom; 76, line 3 from

the bottom (translated as "meaning"); 77, lines 5–6 from top; 78, line 10 from top; 82, line 2 from top; 129, lines 4 and 1 from the bottom.

7. *Op. cit.*, p. 161; *ET*, p. 64.

8. *Op. cit.*, p. 180; *ET*, pp. 80–81. Other occurrences, cf. *GAzWL*, pp. 162, lines 3 and 14 from the top; especially 172, lines 18–19 from the top; 176, line 5 from top; 181, line 3 from top; 183, lines 14–15 and 6 from bottom; 253, lines 9 and 27 from top. *ET*, pp. 64, lines 17 and 9 from bottom; 73, line 11 from bottom; 76, line 1 from bottom (translated as "meaning"); 77, line 4 from top; 81, line 17 from top (translated as "meaningful"); 83, lines 7–8, 1 from bottom; 151, lines 6 (translated as "meaning") and 22 from top.

9. Here: "causally important."

10. *Op. cit.*, p. 155; *ET*, p. 58.

11. In the logical sense, not in the substantive one.

12. *Op. cit.*, pp. 175–176; *ET*, p. 76.

13. *Op. cit.*, pp. 54 line 19 from top; 163, line 27 from bottom; 170, line 4 from top; 174, lines 10–11 from bottom; 176, line 8 from top; 177, line 19 from top; 183, line 16 from bottom; 184; 192, lines 16, 20, and 23 from top; 240, bottom line. *ET*, pp. 65, line 15 from bottom; 71, line 17 from bottom; 75, line 10 from bottom; 78, lines 7–8 from top, lines 13 and 9–10 from bottom; 79, line 8 from top; 81, lines 20, 15, and 8 from bottom; 83, line 8 from bottom; 84; 91, lines 12 (translated as "meaningful"), 9 (left out in translation,) and 7 from bottom; 138, line 17 from bottom.

14. *Op. cit.*, pp. 158, 183–184; *ET*, pp. 61, 83–84.

15. Henrich, *op. cit.*, p. 8.

16. See chapter 1, section 4. See also below, section 3.

17. *GAzWL*, p. 69.

18. *Op. cit.*, p. 177, line 15 from top; *ET*, p. 78, line 5 from top.

19. *Op. cit.*, pp. 176–177; *ET*, p. 77. Other instances occur *GAzWL*, pp. 153, line 13 from bottom; 163, line 5 from top; 164, lines 1–2 and 25 from top, 165, lines 9 and 21–22 from top; 166, line 14 from bottom; 167, line 20 from bottom; 169, line 4 from top; 170, line 2 from bottom; 174, line 4 from top, 175, lines, 1, 3, 6–7, 22, 23, and 24 from top; 176, lines 22–23, 17–18, 11, 9–10, and 3 from bottom; 177, lines 4 and 8–9 from top; 178, line 6 from bottom; 183, lines 3–4, 15, and 18 from top; 189, lines 24, 21, and 12–13 from bottom; 195; 224 n. 1; 231, line 17 from top. *ET*, pp. 56, line 9 from bottom; 65, line 16 from top; 66, lines 9 and 26 from top; 67, lines 10 and 19–20 from top; 68, line 16 from top; 69, line 8 from top; 70, line 15 from bottom (translated as "meaning"); 72, line 14 from top; 75, lines 30 and 2 from bottom; 76, lines 1, 6, 17, and 18 from top, 77, lines 11, 15, 20, 22–23, and 28 from top; 78, lines 6 and 1 (translated as "meaningful") from bottom; 79, line 13 from top; 83, lines 9, 21, and 24 from top; 89, lines 1, 3–4, and 11 (left out in the translation) from top; 94; 122–123 n. 6; 129, line 18 from top.

20. *Op.cit.*, pp. 170, line 1 from top; 236 n. 1; 253, line 10 from top; 260; 266; *ET*, pp. 71, line 18 from top; 133–134 n. 16; 151, line 7 from top; 158, line 13 from top; 164, line 8 from bottom.

21. *Op. cit.*, p. 289; *ET*, p. 187. There is, finally, one instance where "cultural significance" means "cultural value" (*op. cit.*, p. 232; *ET*, p. 130). It is not entirely clear to this interpreter why Weber uses here "significance," which he puts between quotation marks, but the meaning is certainly unambiguous.

III.3

1. *GAzWL*, pp. 100–101.
2. *Op. cit.*, p. 164; *ET*, p. 66.
3. Cf. Felix Kaufmann, *Methodenlehre der Sozialwissenschaften* (Wien: Springer, 1936), pp. 157, 159.
4. *GAzWL*, p. 93.
5. *Op. cit.*, p. 96 n. 1, 103.
6. Not the exclusive one, for in historical accounts occur not only things and processes going on "within" humans but also those "outside" them. *Op. cit.*, p. 171; *ET*, p. 72.
7. *Op. cit.*, p. 89.
8. Cf. von Schelting, *Wissenschaftslehre*, p. 325.
9. *GAzWL*, p. 105.
10. *Ibid.*
11. *Op. cit.*, p. 107.
12. *Op. cit.*, p. 104.
13. *Op. cit.*, p. 93.
14. Weippert, *op. cit.*, pp. 259–260.
15. *Op. cit.*, p. 260.
16. *Op. cit.*, p. 261.
17. For a comparison of Weber's and Rickert's conceptions of *Verstehen*, cf. von Schelting, *Wissenschaftslehre*, pp. 364–373.
18. Von Schelting, "Logische Theorie," p. 691; Walther, *op. cit.*, p. 31.
19. Von Schelting, *op. cit.*, pp. 695–696, 699.
20. Theodore Abel, *Systematic Sociology in Germany* (New York: Octagon Books, 1965), p. 133.
21. Dennis Wrong (ed.), *Max Weber*, p. 19.
22. "Methodological" means "concerning the methods of concept formation," or "concerning the methods of abstracting concepts from empirical reality." Weber's rejection of "intuitionism" is clearly recognized by Runciman, *Critique*, pp. 24 ff.
23. Tenbruck, *op. cit.*, p. 607; Freund, *op. cit.*, p. 98; Theodore Abel's article, "The Operation Called 'Verstehen,'" *American Journal of Sociology* 54 (1948): 211–218—which, incidentally, does not essentially go beyond what Weber (in *Economy and Society*, vol. I, pp. 4–22) or Georg Simmel, *op. cit.*, said on the subject—does not specify whether he argues against *Verstehen* as a *method*.
24. Henrich, *op. cit.*, p. 42.
25. *Op. cit.*, p. 101.
26. *Op. cit.*, pp. 44–45.
27. *Op. cit.*, p. 37.
28. *Op. cit.*, pp. 36–37.
29. *Op. cit.*, pp. 82–83.
30. *Op. cit.*, pp. 2, 35.
31. Above, chapter 1, section 4.
32. Building on Weber, its construction has been attempted by Alfred Schuetz in his book *The Phenomenology of the Social World* (Evanston: Northwestern University Press, 1967).
33. Cf. Aron, *German Sociology*, p. 105; von Schelting, *Wissenschaftslehre*, p. 362.

34. *GAzWL*, p. 89.
35. *Op. cit.*, p. 70 n. 2.
36. *Op. cit.*, pp. 89, 91, also 94.
37. *Op. cit.*, p. 104.
38. *Op. cit.*, p. 83.
39. *Op. cit.*, pp. 12–13 n. 1, 93, 100, 101–102 n. 1.
40. *Economy and Society*, vol. I, pp. 5–6.
41. *GAzWL*, p. 100.
42. *Op. cit.*, p. 89.
43. *Op. cit.*, p. 70.
44. Cf. also *op. cit.*, pp. 91, 100.
45. *Op. cit.*, p. 101 n. Von Schelting, *Wissenschaftslehre*, p. 116 does not get to the core of the problem when he remarks that *Verstehen* makes reference to those things which can be objectively possible contents of the observer's psyche.
46. Aron, *German Sociology*, p. 105, correctly notes this problem.
47. *GAzWL*, p. 89. Weber distinguishes two other kinds of interpretation which are of no concern here: (1) the attempt to elicit a certain valuing attitude; e.g., the aesthetic interpretation of a work of art; (2) value-analysis, i.e., the listing of several possible value-relevances of a phenomenon as a preparatory step to the final adoption of a particular value-viewpoint. Cf. *op. cit.*, p. 89 and n.
48. *Op. cit.*, p. 89.
49. *Op. cit.*, p. 94, also pp. 89, 95 n. 1.
50. *Economy and Society*, vol. I, p. 9.
51. *GAzWL*, p. 94.
52. Cf. the statement: "Psychologically, 'understanding' sets in as an undifferentiated unit of valuation and causal interpretation, but when 'historical individuals' are formed, the logical treatment replaces valuation by a merely theoretical 'relating' to values." *Op. cit.*, p. 124 n. 1.
53. *Op. cit.*, p. 186; *ET*, p. 86.
54. *Op. cit.*, pp. 89, 134.
55. Von Schelting, *Wissenschaftslehre*, p. 328.
56. *Op. cit.*, p. 376.
57. *Op. cit.*, p. 381.
58. *GAzWL*, p. 173; *ET*, p. 74.
59. *Op. cit.*, p. 136.
60. I.e., in history.
61. *Op. cit.*, p. 173; *ET*, p. 74.
62. *Op. cit.*, p. 115.
63. *Economy and Society*, vol. I, p. 5. cf. also p. 58 n. 6.
64. Cf. Kaufmann, *op. cit.*, pp. 7–13.
65. *GAzWL*, pp. 116, 126.
66. *Op. cit.*, p. 115.
67. *Economy and Society*, vol. I, p. 5.
68. Cf. Henrich, *op. cit.*, p. 37.
69. *GAzWL*, p. 127. The function which Weber ascribes to the "certainty" of understanding has repercussions on his formation of ideal types. Given the necessity to work with ideal types, it seems best to construct types of rational behavior. They can be unambiguously constructed and can be understood with a maximum of "certainty" (*Economy and Society*, vol. I, p. 6).

70. *GAzWL*, p. 116.
71. *Ibid.*
72. *Op. cit.*, p. 68, also p. 111.
73. Cf. Schuetz, *op. cit.*; also Kaufmann, *op. cit.*, pp. 154–169; Siegfried Landshut, *Kritik der Soziologie und andere Schriften zur Politik* (Neuwied: Luchterhand, 1969), pp. 41–42.

III. 4

1. See above, chapter 1, section 5.
2. See above, chapter 2, section 5.
3. It is, therefore, not correct to see, as e.g., Weinreich, *op. cit.*, p. 110 does, in these concepts "relatively historical concepts" in Rickert's sense (cf. above, chapter 1, section 6). For the latter result when the process of forming general concepts for some reason is not carried through to the very end, whereas the present problem concerns the logical impossibility of forming general concepts of certain aspects of cultural phenomena. "For the purpose of ideal-typical concept formation is everywhere to make clearly explicit *not* the generic features of cultural phenomena but rather their particularity." *GAzWL*, p. 202, see also pp. 194–195, 201; *ET*, p. 101, also pp. 93–94, 100.
4. *GAzWL*, p. 116.
5. *Op. cit.*, p. 87.
6. Aron, *Main Currents*, vol. II, p. 244.
7. Ludwig M. Lachmann, *The Legacy of Max Weber* (Berkeley: Glendessary Press, 1971), p. 3.
8. Von Schelting, "Logische Theorie," p. 677.
9. I.e., general concepts.
10. *GAzWL*, p. 187, also p. 185; *ET*, p. 87, also p. 85.
11. *Op. cit.*, p. 187; *ET*, p. 87.
12. Tenbruck seems right in declaring that this concrete situation compelled Weber to deal with methodological problems, but not, as he thinks, because for Weber this conflict "endangers the objectivity of social science" (Tenbruck, *op. cit.*, p. 589). On the contrary, it is Weber's opinion that both approaches are necessary and justified. His problem is to show in what sense this is the case.
13. *GAzWL*, p. 187; *ET*, p. 87.
14. *Op. cit.*, p. 188; *ET*, p. 88.
15. *Op. cit.*, p. 9.
16. *Op. cit.*, p. 42.
17. *Op. cit.*, pp. 189–190; *ET*, p. 89.
18. The statement that ideal types are peculiar to the cultural sciences is criticized by Carl Hempel, "Problems of Concept and Theory Formation in the Social Sciences," in *Science, Language, and Human Rights*, American Philosophical Association, Eastern Division, vol. 1 (Philadelphia: University of Pennsylvania Press, 1952), pp. 65–86; and W. G. Runciman, *Critique*, pp. 33ff. This criticism is entirely justified. Nevertheless, within Weber's framework, his assertion is a necessary consequence of the premises of his theory. Contrary to Aron's statement (*German Sociology*, p. 99), "ideal type" is not the generic term for all general concepts used in the cultural sciences. Weber mentions others, e.g., average types and genuinely general concepts.
19. Freund, *op. cit.*, p. 70.
20. Alexander Ruestow, "Der Idealtypus, oder die Gestalt als Norm," *Studium*

Generale 6 (1953): 54–59; p. 55 n. 5. Paul Lazarsfeld, "Philosophy of Science and Empirical Social Research," in Ernest Nagel, Patrick Suppes, & Alfred Tarski (eds.), *Logic, Methodology and Philosophy of Science* (Stanford: Stanford University Press, 1962), pp. 463–473; p. 466. R. Stephen Warner, "The Role of Religious Ideas and the Use of Models in Max Weber's Comparative Studies of Non-Capitalist Societies," *Journal of Economic History* 30 (1970): 74–99; p. 88 n. 45. Juergen von Kempski, "Zur Logik der Ordnungsbegriffe, besonders in den Sozialwissenschaften," in Hans Albert (ed.), *Theorie und Realitaet* (Tuebingen: Mohr, 1964), 209–232; p. 214.

21. Von Schelting, *Wissenschaftslehre*, p. 329.
22. E.g., J. W. N. Watkins, "Ideal Types and Historical Explanation," in Herbert Feigl & May Brodbeck (eds.), *Readings in the Philosophy of Science* (New York: Appleton-Century-Crofts, 1953), 723–743; pp. 723–724, 727.
23. Ruestow, *op. cit.*, p. 55 n. 5.
24. *GAzWL*, p. 202; *ET*, p. 100.
25. Below, section 5.
26. *GAzWL*, p. 201; *ET*, p. 100.
27. Strangely enough, in the whole secondary literature only Rudner has paid any attention to this. Cf. Richard S. Rudner, *Philosophy of Social Science* (Englewood Cliffs: Prentice-Hall, 1966), p. 56.
28. Above, chapter 1, section 3; chapter 2, section 3.
29. *GAzWL*, pp. 140, 179, 189–190; *ET*, pp. 80, 89–90. Zittel's opinion ("Der Typus in der Geschichtswissenschaft," *Studium Generale* 5 [1952]: 378–384) that logically the ideal type stands between the individual and the generic concept (p. 378) is too vague to be correct. His statement that to the nature of history the average type corresponds better than anything else (p. 380) is not backed up by any argument. Completely wrong is Erich Voegelin in his article "Ueber Max Weber," *Deutsche Vierteljahresschrift fuer Literaturwissenschaft und Geistesgeschichte* 3 (1925): 177–193, where he says (p. 190): "Max Weber calls the guiding value-ideas . . . ideal types. . . ."
30. *GAzWL*, p. 190; *ET*, p. 90 ("can be indispensable . . .").
31. This statement is an exaggeration and in this form untenable. It should be seen in conjunction with the following more modest and correct version: "Those interpretive schemas [i.e., ideal types] . . . are not *only* 'hypotheses' in analogy to the hypothetical 'laws' of natural science. When concrete processes are heuristically interpreted, they can *function* as hypotheses. But in contrast to the hypotheses of the natural sciences the insight that in a concrete instance they do *not* contain a valid interpretation does not affect their usefulness for the establishment of knowledge. . . ." *Op. cit.*, p. 131.
32. *Op. cit.*, p. 190; *ET*, p. 90.
33. *Op. cit.*, p. 193, also p. 194; *ET*, p. 92, also p. 93.
34. *Op. cit.*, p. 202, also p. 198; *ET*, pp. 100–101, also p. 97.
35. *Op. cit.*, p. 201; *ET*, p. 100.
36. Von Schelting, "Logische Theorie," p. 711, also p. 713.
37. *GAzWL*, p. 193; *ET*, p. 92.
38. *Op. cit.*, p. 202; *ET*, p. 101.
39. *Op. cit.*, p. 191; *ET*, p. 90.
40. Cf. Janoska-Bendl, *op. cit.*, p. 26. Since such a situation by definition—within Rickert's and Weber's theory—cannot occur in the natural sciences, Weber can state that ideal types are concepts "peculiar" to the historical sciences. *GAzWL*, p. 190; *ET*, p. 89.

41. Concerning the meaning of "genetic," see below, this section.
42. *GAzWL*, p. 202; *ET*, p. 100. According to Weippert, the difference between a class concept and an ideal type—which is also a general concept—lies in the fact that the conceptual content of the latter is "understood," whereas that of the former is not (Weippert, *op. cit.*, pp. 266–267). This is a half-truth at best. The main difference between the two is the relationship in each case of the conceptual content to empirical reality. Weippert is correct insofar as in the case of the ideal type this specific relationship is a consequence of the fact that the reality in question is meaningful and, therefore, understood. However, the formation of truly general concepts whose content is meaningful reality is definitely possible.
43. Correctly seen by Walther, *op. cit.*, p. 11. Cf. Carl Hempel & Paul Oppenheim, *Der Typusbegriff im Lichte der neuen Logik* (Leiden: A. W. Sijthoff's Uitgeversmaatschappij N. V., 1936). Ludwig von Mises denies the foundation of the whole argument by declaring that the concepts of economics are obtained "through reflection having in view the comprehension of what is contained in *each* of the individual phenomena taken into consideration," *Epistemological Problems of Economics* (Princeton: Van Nostrand, 1960), pp. 78–79. Thus the laws of sociology and economics are not ideal types (pp. 90–91). Von Mises fails to give any supporting arguments for his claim. It helps him to conclude, however, that Weber "has implicitly answered the question that had once constituted the substance of the *Methodenstreit* entirely in the sense of those who denied the legitimacy of a theoretical science of social phenomena" (p. 77).
44. This is correctly perceived by Aron, *Main Currents*, vol. II, p. 254; *German Sociology*, p. 99.
45. Cf. below, this section.
46. *GAzWL*, pp. 194–195; *ET*, pp. 93–94.
47. *Op. cit.*, pp. 195, 202; *ET*, pp. 94, 101.
48. *Op. cit.*, pp. 190, 191; *ET*, p. 90.
49. Parsons, *op. cit.*, p. 602.
50. *Op. cit.*, p. 593.
51. *Ibid.*
52. Von Schelting, "Logische Theorie," pp. 711–712 n. 364.
53. August Seiffert, *Die kategoriale Stellung des Typus. Beiheft zur Zeitschrift fuer philosophische Forschung*, Heft 7 (1953), p. 61.
54. Cf. Bennion, *op. cit.*, p. 142; Antoni, *op. cit.*, p. 174; Henrich, *op. cit.*, p. 92.
55. *GAzWL*, p. 183; *ET*, p. 83. Note the contrasting of "observe" and "understand" which supports the claim that "understanding" denotes a phenomenological characteristic, not a logical one.
56. *Op. cit.*, pp. 140, 190; *ET*, pp. 89–90. Cf. also Talcott Parsons, "Introduction" to Weber's *The Theory of Social and Economic Organization* (New York: Free Press, 1964), p. 12.
57. *GAzWL*, p. 190; *ET*, p. 90.
58. Weippert, *op. cit.*, pp. 270–272.
59. Oppenheimer, *op. cit.*, p. 14.
60. *Op. cit.*, p. 59.
61. *Op. cit.*, p. 47.
62. *GAzWL*, p. 191; *ET*, pp. 90–91.
63. *Op. cit.*, pp. 194, 208; *ET*, pp. 93, 106.
64. *Op. cit.*, p. 194; *ET*, p. 93. Cf. Abel, *Systematic Theory*, p. 150.

65. Henrich, *op. cit.*, pp. 86–87.
66. *Op. cit.*, p. 88.
67. *Ibid.*
68. Concerning the anthropological considerations involved in Weber's reasoning, cf. Henrich, *op. cit.*, pp. 94, 101–103.
69. I.e., one or several of the considerations motivating the actor(s).
70. *GAzWL*, p. 191; *ET*, p. 90.
71. *Op. cit.*, pp. 206–207; *ET*, p. 105.
72. Walter Eucken, *The Foundations of Economics* (Chicago: University of Chicago Press, 1951), p. 69.
73. *Op. cit.*, p. 326.
74. *Ibid.*
75. *Op. cit.*, p. 300.
76. *Op. cit.*, p. 348.
77. *Op. cit.*, p. 349.
78. *Op. cit.*, p. 173.
79. *GAzWL*, p. 192; *ET*, p. 91.
80. I.e., concepts.
81. I.e., which are significant from an adopted viewpoint.
82. Because they influence the adoption of certain viewpoints.
83. *Op. cit.*, pp. 207–208; *ET*, p. 105–106.
84. *Op. cit.*, p. 198; *ET*, p. 97. Runciman's interpretation of Weber's position here is not quite correct. According to Runciman, Weber holds "that the social scientist's formulation of his hypotheses about his chosen topic cannot but have relevance to his 'values' in a way that the natural scientist's does not have to be" (*Critique*, p. 38). This he interprets to mean that "social scientists do not, and cannot, have a theory of culture in the sense that chemists have theories of chemistry or physicists of physics; they must, however, have presuppositions which dictate the terms of their proposed hypotheses; since these cannot be drawn from a theory which doesn't exist, they must be drawn from somewhere else; accordingly their source can only lie in the criteria of 'cultural significance' (*Kulturbedeutung*), and therefore the 'cultural value-ideas' (*Kulturwertideen*) which every social scientist brings to the subject matter he has chosen to study" (pp. 38–39). In response to this, the following comments are in order: (1) "Social scientist," to Weber, above all, means "historian." The "hypotheses" advanced by social scientists are about individual developments, e.g., the emergence of capitalism. "Hypothesis," for Weber, does not mean (nomological) "sociological hypothesis," but refers to a suggested explanation of an historical individual, e.g., the emergence of capitalism. (2) Hypotheses, in Weber's sense, of course, must vary with the different conceptualizations of the same concrete events that are to be explained; e.g., the acceptance of Marx's conception of capitalism leads to a different hypothesis about the emergence of capitalism than the acceptance of Weber's conception. The reason is obvious: the hypotheses differ because they are designed to explain different aspects of the same concrete phenomenon. (3) Runciman is correct when he says: "If explicability in principle has once been accepted, it doesn't matter where the social scientist's concepts and, therefore, his hypotheses come from but only whether the hypotheses are so framed that in principle, at least, they are capable of empirical disconfirmation" (p. 39). However, the principle of value-relevance does not concern the problem of explanation,

but that of the selection of the phenomena that are to be explained. (4) Runciman has not properly understood the function of the principle of value-relevance. This function is that of a standard of selection. It allows one to determine what phenomena are worth knowing, and thus explaining. Once the interest in explaining a particular phenomenon is recognized as legitimate, this entails the legitimacy of those concepts which are necessary for the explanation. Thus, the legitimacy of investigating those (cultural) phenomena which are the result of the economic considerations which humans entertain entails the legitimacy of using "class," for instance, as long as it seems to have any explanatory value. In this sense, the acceptance of "class" as a theoretical term is indeed a matter of its relevance to values (cf. *Critique*, pp. 40–41). (5) It seems that Runciman is not entirely clear about the distinction between "value-relevance" and "evaluation." Otherwise he could not accuse Weber of a "confusion of theoretical presuppositions with value judgment" (p. 41). (6) Runciman uses "validity" in a different sense than Weber. Valid knowledge to the latter, is knowledge of phenomena which are worth knowing. To Runciman, it is empirically valid knowledge, i.e., falsifiable statements.

III. 5

1. Von Schelting is right when he says: "The 'ideal type' is a logical discovery, not an 'invention'" ("Logische Theorie," p. 714).
2. *GAzWL*, p. 201; *ET*, p. 100.
3. *Ibid.*
4. This is the question asked by von Schelting, *Wissenschaftslehre*, p. 335, and Watkins, "Ideal Types and Historical Explanation," p. 726.
5. Cf. von Schelting, "Logische Theorie," pp. 730–731, *Wissenschaftslehre*, pp. 330 n. 1, 333, 334–335; Walther, *op. cit.*, pp. 12, 13; Bienfait, *op. cit.*, p. 83; Weippert, *op. cit.*, p. 275.
6. *GAzWL*, p. 191; *ET*, p. 90.
7. *Op. cit.*, p. 193, *ET*, p. 92.
8. See above, section 4.
9. *Op. cit.*, p. 203; *ET*, p. 101.
10. *Op. cit.*, p. 201; *ET*, p. 100.
11. *Ibid.* This is a very unfortunate formulation indeed, for it seems to state that individual ideal types are concepts describing single phenomena. Nevertheless, Weber also clearly states that they are abstracted from, and therefore, refer to, a multitude of recurrent and similar phenomena (*op. cit.*, p. 191; *ET*, p. 90); thus, they must be general. Only as general concepts do they make sense.
12. *Op. cit.*, p. 201; *ET*, p. 100.
13. *Op. cit.*, p. 202; *ET*, p. 100.
14. *Op. cit.*, p. 197; *ET*, p. 96
15. This is correctly perceived by Aron, *German Sociology*, p. 108.
16. Weippert, *op. cit.*, p. 278.
17. *GAzWL*, p. 197; *ET*, p. 96.
18. *Op. cit.*, p. 195; *ET*, p. 94.
19. *Op. cit.*, p. 203; *ET*, p. 101.
20. *Ibid.*
21. Weber, *Economy and Society*, vol. I, p. 25.
22. Von Schelting, *Wissenschaftslehre*, p. 73, to alleviate his difficulties proposes

to distinguish generic ideal types and concepts of historical totalities. Following him, the same distinction has been made by Parsons, *Structure of Social Action*, p. 604, and "Introduction" (to *The Theory of Social and Economic Organization*), p. 13; Pfister, *op. cit.*, p. 170; Freyer, *op. cit.*, p. 149; Bennion, *op. cit.*, p. 142; Walther, *op. cit.*, p. 16; Bienfait, *op. cit.*, pp. 83, 87; Janoska-Bendl, *op. cit.*, p. 49; Rolf E. Rogers, *Max Weber's Ideal Type Theory* (New York: Philosophical Library, 1969), pp. 87–88. Aron differentiates three kinds of ideal type: historical types, general types, and types of rational behavior (*German Sociology*, p. 104; *Main Currents*, vol. 11, pp. 246–247).

23. E.g., Oppenheimer, *op. cit.*, p. 70.
24. Weippert, *op. cit.*, pp. 292–293.
25. *Op. cit.*, p. 290.
26. *Op. cit.*, p. 306.
27. *Op. cit.*, p. 308.
28. *Op. cit.*, pp. 292–293.

III. 6

1. *GAzWL*, p. 195; *ET*, p. 94.
2. *Op. cit.*, p. 193; *ET*, p. 92.
3. *Op. cit.*, p. 193; *ET*, pp. 92–93.
4. *Op. cit.*, p. 209; *ET*, p. 107.
5. *Op. cit.*, p. 194; *ET*, p. 93.
6. *Economy and Society*, vol. I, p. 19.
7. *GAzWL*, p. 193; *ET*, p. 92.
8. *Op. cit.*, p. 130. Schaaf, *op. cit.*, p. 150, thinks—and Weinreich, *op. cit.*, p. 108, agrees with him—that circular reasoning is involved in this argument since reality, to be known, must be in conceptual form. Thus it can be compared with the ideal type only when it is known. It is the ideal type, however, which is supposed to provide the conceptual form to begin with. Schaaf would be right only on the assumption that ideal types form immediate sensations. This is not true, though. They give a form to concrete facts. Facts, however, can be known without being conceptualized (in Weber's sense).
9. *GAzWL*, p. 190, *ET*, p. 90.
10. *Op. cit.*, p. 205; *ET*, p. 103.
11. *Economy and Society*, vol. I, p. 19.
12. Antoni, *op. cit.*, p. 177. See also von Schelting's statement: "Thus the aim of economics finds its fulfillment in economic history" ("Logische Theorie," p. 703). Also Weippert, *op. cit.*, p. 276.
13. Weippert, *op. cit.*, p. 275. Also Bienfait, *op. cit.*, p. 23 n. 15.
14. Von Mises, *op. cit.*, p. 74.
15. Parsons, *Structure of Social Action*, p. 607 and n.
16. *Op. cit.*, p. 601.
17. *Ibid.*
18. *GAzWL*, p. 130.
19. *Op. cit.*, p. 203; *ET*, p. 102.
20. Cf. *op. cit.*, p. 194, also p. 179; *ET*, p. 93, also p. 80.
21. *Op. cit.*, p. 191; *ET*, p. 90. To Martindale, this is a "startling" suggestion. "This is nothing but a form of intellectual acrobatics, for actual individuals ought to deviate from the ideal type just as much as one made them deviate

in the first place" (*Nature & Types*, p. 382). He continues: "We compare different empirical configurations and types" (*op. cit.*, p. 383).

22. *Economy and Society*, vol. I, p. 21.
23. I.e., a concept.
24. *GAzWL*, p. 194, also pp. 198–199; *ET*, p. 93, also p. 97.
25. *Op. cit.*, p. 131.
26. *Op. cit.*, p. 214; *ET*, p. 112.

III. 7

1. Above, chapter 1, section 1.
2. Weber justified his involvement in methodological studies in almost the same terms as Menger. Cf. above, chapter 1, section 1, and Carl Menger, *Untersuchungen ueber die Methode der Socialwissenschaften und der Politischen Oekonomie insbesondere* (Leipzig: Duncker und Humblot, 1883), translated as *Problems of Economics and Sociology* (Urbana: University of Illinois Press, 1963). Hereafter referred to as *Untersuchungen*, with page indications first to the German edition, then to the English translation (*ET*); pp. XII–XIII; *ET*, p. 37.
3. *GAzWL*, pp. 187, 189 ff.; *ET*, pp. 87, 89 ff.
4. Since the concern here is with the problems of concept formation, only those arguments are presented which are relevant to these problems. For further information, see Gerhard Ritzel, *Schmoller versus Menger. Eine Analyse des Methodenstreites* (Frankfurt, 1950); Werner Hasbach, "Zur Geschichte des Methodenstreites in der politischen Oekonomie," *Schmollers Jahrbuch* 19 (1895): 465–490, 751–808.
5. Schmoller, although admitting Menger's intelligence, accuses him of a lack of philosophical and historical education as well as of narrow-mindedness (Gustav Schmoller, "Zur Methodologie der Staats-und Sozial-Wissenschaften," *Schmollers Jahrbuch* 7 [1883]: 975–994; p. 987. Hereafter referred to as "Methodologie.") To the truly monumental conceit displayed by Schmoller here and elsewhere, Menger replied in kind. He called Schmoller a man "who without the slightest orientation in the questions of scientific methodology acts like a fully qualified judge of the value, or lack thereof, of the results of methodological inquiries" (Carl Menger, *Die Irrthuemer des Historismus in der deutschen Nationaloekonomie* [Wien: Hoelder, 1884], p. 71, hereafter referred to as *Irrthuemer*), and a scientist "the totality of whose halfways original knowledge consists in the primordial slime of historical-statistical material" (*op. cit.*, p. 72).
6. Menger, *Untersuchungen*, p. 14; *ET*, p. 43. Gustav Schmoller, "Volkswirtschaft, Volkswirtschaftslehre und -methode," in J. Conrad, L. Elster, W. Lexis, E. Loening (eds.), *Handwoerterbuch der Staatswissenschaften* (Jena: Fischer, 1st ed., 1894), vol. 6, pp. 532, 546–547, hereafter referred to as "Volkswirtschaft, etc."
7. Menger, *Untersuchungen*, pp. VI, IX; *ET*, pp. 23–24, 25. Schmoller, "Volkswirtschaft, etc.," p. 532.
8. Menger, *op. cit.*, pp. 68, 126, Anhang II; *ET*, pp. 79, 119, appendix II. Cf. the interesting articles concerning Menger's Aristotelian background by Emil Kauder, "Intellectual and Political Roots of the Older Austrian School," *Zeitschrift fuer Nationaloekonomie* 17 (1957/58): 411–425; and Oskar Kraus, "Die Aristotelische Werttheorie in ihren Beziehungen zu den Lehren der

modernen Psychologenschule," *Zeitschrift fuer die gesamte Staatswissenschaft* 61 (1905): 573–592. In contrast, see Josef Dobretsberger's "Zur Methodenlehre C. Mengers und der oesterreichischen Schule," *Zeitschrift fuer Nationaloekonomie* 12 (1948/49): 88–89; Schmoller, *op. cit.*, pp. 530–531.

9. Walter Eucken, "Wissenschaft in Stile Schmollers," *Weltwirtschaftliches Archiv* 59 (1940): 468–506; pp. 484–485.
10. Weber, *GAzWL*, pp. 185–187; *ET*, pp. 85–87.
11. Cf. Gustav Schmoller, "Wechselnde Theorien und feststehende Wahrheiten im Gebiete der Staats-und Social-Wissenschaften und die heutige deutsche Volkswirtschaftslehre," *Schmollers Jahrbuch* 21 (1897): 1387–1408; pp. 1393, 1395, 1399, 1402. Schmoller, "Volkswirtschaft, etc.," p. 546.
12. Schmoller, "Volkswirtschaft, etc.," pp. 537, 546.
13. *Op. cit.*, pp. 545, 550, 551.
14. *Op. cit.*, pp. 529–530. It is clear, then, that not all adherents of the Historical School rejected the formulation of laws. What they rejected were the laws of classical economics. Cf. *op. cit.*, p. 532.
15. *Op. cit.*, pp. 529–530, 539, 546, 550–551, 559.
16. Menger, *Untersuchungen*, pp. 54, 78–79; *ET*, pp. 69, 87.
17. Schmoller, *op. cit.*, pp. 550–552.
18. Menger, *op. cit.*, pp. 79–80, 264, 265; *ET*, pp. 88, 217, 218.
19. Schmoller, *op. cit.*, pp. 553–555; Menger, *op. cit.*, pp. 54, 288–289; *ET*, pp. 69, 235–236.
20. Menger, *op. cit.*, pp. 18–19, 44, 56–57, 63, 65, 67–69, 127 n. 43; *ET*, pp. 45–46, 62–63, 70–71, 76, 77–78, 79–80, 120 n. 43.
21. Rickert borrowed this distinction from Menger.
22. Menger *op. cit.*, p. 4; *ET*, p. 36.
23. *Op. cit.*, pp. 3, 7; *ET*, pp. 35, 38.
24. *Op. cit.*, p. 14; *ET*, p. 43.
25. *Op. cit.*, p. 17; *ET*, p. 45.
26. Cf. *op. cit.*, pp. 46–47; *ET*, pp. 64–65.
27. *Op. cit.*, pp. 18–19; *ET*, pp. 45–46.
28. *Op. cit.*, p. 23; *ET*, p. 49.
29. *Op. cit.*, pp. 44, 64; *ET*, pp. 62–63, 77.
30. *Op. cit.*, p. 67; *ET*, p. 79.
31. *Op. cit.*, p. 36; *ET*, p. 57.
32. Cf. *op. cit.*, pp. 59, 65–68, 265; *ET*, pp. 72–73 ,77–80, 218.
33. *Op. cit.*, p. 35; *ET*, pp. 56–57.
34. *Op. cit.*, pp. 40–41; *ET*, pp. 60–61.
35. *Op. cit.*, pp. 64–65; *ET*, p. 77.
36. *Op. cit.*, p. 77; *ET*, p. 86.
37. *Op. cit.*, pp. 54, 78; *ET*, pp. 69–70, 86.
38. Schmoller, "Methodologie," pp. 977–978, 978–979.
39. *Op. cit.*, pp. 981, 985; also Schmoller, "Volkswirtschaft, etc.," pp. 550–551.
40. Schmoller, "Methodologie," p. 980.
41. *Op. cit.*, p. 979. Menger replied to this that, of course, he would never dream of abstracting from anything but the accidental elements. (Menger, *Irrthuemer*, p. 7 n.). He misses the issue, though; the question precisely is: What is essential?
42. Schmoller, "Volkswirtschaft, etc.," pp. 551, 559–560.
43. Othmar Spann, *The History of Economics* (New York: W. W. Norton, 1930) (title of the British edition: *Types of Economic Theory*), pp. 244–245.

44. Schmoller, *op. cit.*, pp. 545–546.
45. Menger, *Untersuchungen*, p. 48; *ET*, p. 65.
46. Weber, *GAzWL*, p. 187; *ET*, p. 87.
47. Weber even accuses the Historical School that partly as a *result* of its activities (although intended as a countermovement) the viewpoints of what he called "naturalism" had not been overcome, i.e., the notions that the adequate scientific treatment of social phenomena is to be found in the formulation of laws (*GAzWL*, p. 187; *ET*, pp. 86–87). What he refers to is the idea held by many representatives of the Historical School that the laws of social phenomena (possibly in all their concreteness) must be found through induction (cf. *op. cit.*, p. 11). This still amounts to the idea that it is the *laws* of history that must be grasped; however, if the *historical* character of social phenomena is to be grasped, then there is no room for the formulation of any law whatsoever, be they derived inductively or otherwise.
48. *Irrthuemer*, pp. 21–22.
49. Schmoller, "Methodologie," p. 977.
50. Cf. above, chapter 2, section 5.
51. *GAzWL*, pp. 187–188; *ET*, pp. 87–88.
52. *Op. cit.*, p. 188; *ET*, p. 88.
53. *Ibid.*
54. *Op. cit.*, pp. 189–190; *ET*, p. 89.
55. Chapter 3, section 4.
56. See above, section 6. This is an opinion shared by Menger. Cf. *Untersuchungen*, p. 18; *ET*, p. 46.

CHAPTER IV.

IV. 1

1. To confine the answer to only one aspect is a mistake, e.g., to view ideal types essentially as measuring devices. Cf. Lachmann, *op. cit.*, pp. 26–27; Howard Becker, "Historical Sociology," in Harry Elmer Barnes, Howard Becker & Frances Becker (eds.), *Contemporary Social Theory* (New York, London: Appleton-Century, 1940), pp. 527–528. John C. McKinney, *Constructive Typology and Social Theory* (New York: Appleton-Century-Crofts, 1966), pp. 3, 23. Martindale, "Theory & Type," p. 59.
2. Cf. Rogers, *op. cit.*, p. 87.
3. Hempel & Oppenheim, *op. cit.*, Henrich, *op. cit.*, Runciman, *Critique.*
4. Janoska-Bendl, *op. cit.*, pp. 77, 84.
5. The ultimate source of this impossibility is easily discovered: the basic feature of Rickert's and Weber's methodology is the determination and derivation of what humans *want* to know from what they *can* know, i.e., from the fact that knowledge must be in conceptual form and that there are two specific methodological forms available to the human mind. The occurrence of general concepts in history creates problems because here the situation is reversed. In history it has already been determined (through value-relevance) what scientists *want* to know, and an appropriate methodological form for the general concepts occurring in historical writings is required. This situation is incompatible with the conception of the primacy of the two conceptual forms—or principles of abstraction—i.e., the idea that only those parts of reality are worth knowing which can be fitted into the

forms available to the mind. It puts Weber into the awkward position of having to allow for a third form without contradicting the premises of his methodology, which postulates only two. Appropriately enough, he alters the reality which these concepts describe rather than the principles of his theory.

6. Cf. Viktor Kraft, *Erkenntnislehre* (Wien: Springer, 1960, pp. 52–58, 87–103.
7. Hempel & Oppenheim, *op. cit.*
8. In the case of a one-dimensional ordering concept; in the case of multidimensional orders, appropriate requirements have to be added.
9. *Op. cit.*, pp. 21–35. The same argument in shorter form can be found in Carl G. Hempel, *Fundamentals of Concept Formation in Empirical Science*. International Encyclopedia of Unified Science, vol. III, no. 7 (Chicago: University of Chicago Press, 1952); Rudolf Carnap, *Philosophical Foundations of Physics* (New York, London: Basic Books, 1966,) pp. 51–61.
10. These phenomena may be Gestalt phenomena or systems of interrelationships (*Wirkungssysteme*). Cf. Kurt Grelling & Paul Oppenheim, "Der Gestaltbegriff in Lichte der neuen Logik," *Erkenntnis* 7 (1938): 211–225. See also von Kempski, *op. cit.*, pp. 214–215.
11. Although generalizations of a peculiar kind. Cf. also Hempel, *op. cit.*, p. 71.
12. Cf. von Kempski, *op. cit.*, p. 215.
13. *GAzWL*, p. 191; *ET*, p. 90.
14. This is the "exaggeration" mentioned by Weber.

IV. 2

1. Kaufmann, *op. cit.*, p. 227.
2. As the examples show, interpreted as nomological hypotheses these statements are usually false; nevertheless, they are not discarded. The reasons for this seemingly strange procedure are discussed below, section 3.
3. Weber never states this hypothesis. It can be easily derived, however, from his statements about politics and his definition of power. Cf. *Economy & Society*, I, p. 285.
4. *Economy & Society*, I, p. 53, "The existence of legal parties, because of the fact that in principle they are based on *voluntary* adherence (as a result of free competition for adherents), in practice *always* means that the business of politics is one of *interests* (whereby at this point the idea, that these are 'economic' interests, must not be brought in at all; these interests are *political*, i.e., interests which are ideologically oriented or oriented toward the possessions of power as such)." For Weber's definition of "power," see *Economy & Society*, I, p. 53.
5. *Op. cit.*, I, pp. 217–218.
6. *Op. cit.*, I, pp. 218–221.
7. This is pieced together from statements made in *Economy & Society*, III, p. 962.
8. It is perhaps not wise to make use of the term "model" in this context, since it has so many meanings. On the other hand, ideal types have been called "models" before. Cf. Edward Baumgarten, *Max Weber. Werk und Person* (Tuebingen: Mohr, 1964), pp. 595–596; Janoska-Bendl, *op. cit.*, p. 57; Warner, *op. cit.*, p. 92. See also Everett E. Hagen, "Analytical Models in the Study of Social Systems," *American Journal of Sociology* 67 (1961): 144–154, pp. 144–145; von Kempski, *op. cit.*, pp. 217, 219; James Beshers, "Models and Theory Construction," in Milton L. Barron (ed.), *Contemporary So-*

ciology (New York, Toronto: Dodd, Mead & Company, 1968), p. 591; John C. McKinney, "Methodology, Procedures and Techniques in Sociology," in Howard Becker & Alvin Boskoff (eds.), *Modern Sociological Theory* (New York: Dryden, 1957), p. 227. Cahnman, *op. cit.*, p. 116. Social scientists have been using the term in the sense here indicated in order to distinguish the constructs in question from deductive theories, and there is good sense in this. It may perhaps be better to settle for a rather uncompromised term, though, like "constructed type."

9. As von Kempski argues, *op. cit.*, p. 215; also Hempel, *op. cit.*, pp. 73–82.
10. It may be asked here what sense it makes to "assume" the correctness of nomological hypotheses although one knows better. An attempt at giving an answer will be made below, section 3.
11. McKinney, *Constructive Typology and Social Theory* (New York: Appleton-Century-Crofts, 1966).
12. Cf. Hans Albert, *Marktsoziologie und Entscheidungslogik* (Neuwied-Berlin: Luchterhand, 1967); Terence Wilmot Hutchison, *The Significance and Basic Postulates of Economic Theory* (New York: Kelley, 1965).
13. Cf. above, this section.

IV. 3

1. Richard S. Rudner, *Philosophy of Social Science* (Englewood Cliffs: Prentice-Hall, 1966), p. 60.
2. Carl G. Hempel, *Philosophy of Natural Science* (Englewood Cliffs: Prentice-Hall, 1966), pp. 55–58.
3. Karl Raimund Popper, *The Logic of Scientific Discovery* (New York: Harper Torchbooks, 1965), p. 428.
4. *Op. cit.*, p. 62.
5. Ernest Nagel, *The Structure of Science* (New York, Burlingame: Harcourt, Brace & World, 1961), pp. 56–67.
6. Parsons, *Structure*, pp. 76, 250–254, 439–440, 709, 719.
7. *Op. cit.*, p. 253, n. 1.
8. It would seem that the existence of such similar patterns, like the incest taboo, constitutes a problem which is difficult to solve on a voluntaristic basis. It does not affect the quesions with which this section deals, though. It is not the adequacy of the voluntaristic theory of action which is discussed, but its methodological status.
9. This holds also with regard to statistical laws. It is fallacious to assume that the problem of voluntarism can be circumnavigated with the help of statistical generalizations. What is at issue is the peculiar kind of relationship asserted by certain sociological statements, i.e., its nomic or accidental character. This distinction is also applicable to statistical statements. Probabilistic formulations are not a solution to "free" choice and decision.
10. *GAzWL*, pp. 44–49, 64.
11. Milton Friedman, "The Methodology of Positive Economics," in *Essays in Positive Economics* (Chicago: University of Chicago Press, 1959). Ernest Nagel, "Assumptions in Economic Theory," *American Economic Review* 53 (1963, Supplement): 211–219.

IV. 4

1. For a variety of types, cf. McKinney, *op. cit.*
2. Cf. Martindale, "Theory & Type," p. 62.

3. *Op. cit.*, p. 88.
4. Cf. Terence Wilmot Hutchison, *The Significance and Basic Postulates of Economics* (New York: Kelley, 1965); Hans Albert, *Marktsoziologie und Entcheidungslogik* (Neuwied, Berlin: Luchterhand, 1967); Gerhard Kade, *Die Grundannahmen der Preistheorie* (Berlin, Frankfurt: Vahlen, 1962).
5. Albert, *op. cit.*, p. 331.
6. For an instructive illustration of the nonsense to which this can lead, see Jane Richardson & Alfred L. Kroeber, "Three Centuries of Women's Dress Fashion," *Anthropological Records* 5, no. 2 (1940).

BIBLIOGRAPHY

Abel, Theodore. *Systematic Sociology in Germany*. New York: Octagon Books, 1965. (Reprint of the 1929 edition.)
———. "The Operation Called 'Verstehen.'" *American Journal of Sociology*, 54 (1948): 212–218. Reprinted in Herbert Feigl & May Brodbeck (eds.). *Readings in the Philosophy of Science*. New York: Appleton-Century-Crofts, 1953: 677–687.
Abramowski, Guenter. *Das Geschichtsbild Max Webers*. Stuttgart: Klett, 1966. (Kieler Historische Studien, Band 1).
Adler, Max *et al.* (eds.). *Festschrift fuer Carl Gruenberg*. Leipzig: Hirschfeld, 1932.
Albert, Hans, (ed.). *Theorie und Realitaet*. Tuebingen: Mohr, 1964.
———. *Marktsoziologie und Entscheidungslogik*. Neuwied, Berlin: Luchterhand, 1967.
Antoni, Carlo. *From History to Sociology*. Detroit: Wayne State Press, 1959.
Archibald, G. C. "The State of Economic Science." *British Journal for the Philosophy of Science*, 10 (1959/60): 58–69.
Aron, Raymond. *Essai sur la théorie de l'histoire dans l'Allemagne contemporaine*. Paris, 1938.
———. *La philosophie critique de l'histoire. Essai sur une théorie allemande de l'histoire*. 2nd ed. Paris: Vrin, 1950.
———. *German Sociology*. Glencoe: Free Press, 1957.
———. *Main Currents in Sociological Thought*. 2 Vols. Garden City: Anchor Books, 1970.
Barnes, Harry Elmer & Howard Becker. *Social Thought From Lore to Science*. 3 vols. 3rd ed. New York: Dover, 1961.
Barton, Allen. "The Concept of Property-Space in Social Research." In Paul F. Lazarsfeld & Morris Rosenberg (eds.). *The Language of Social Research*. New York: Free Press, 1955: 40–53.
Baumgarten, Eduard. *Max Weber. Werk und Person*. Tuebingen: Mohr, 1964.
Becher, Erich. *Geisteswissenschaften und Naturwissenschaften*. Muenchen, Leipzig: Duncker und Humblot, 1921.
Becker, Howard. "Culture Case Study and Ideal-Typical Method, with Special Reference to Max Weber." *Social Forces*, 12 (1934): 399–405.
———. "Constructive Typology in the Social Sciences." In Harry Elmer Barnes, Howard Becker & Frances Becker (eds.). *Contemporary Social Theory*. New York, London: Appleton-Century, 1940: 17–42.
———. "Historical Sociology." In Harry Elmer Barnes, Howard Becker & Frances Becker (eds.). *Contemporary Social Theory*. New York, London: Appleton-Century, 1940: 491–541.
———. "Interpretive Sociology and Constructive Typology." In Georges Gurvitch & Wilbert E. Moore (eds.). *Twentieth Century Sociology*. New York: Philosophical Library, 1945: 70–95.
———. *Through Values to Social Interpretation*. Durham: Duke University Press, 1950.
Bendix, Reinhard. "Max Weber's Interpretation of Conduct and History." *American Journal of Sociology*, 51 (1946): 518–526.
———. *Max Weber. An Intellectual Portrait*. Garden City: Doubleday, 1962.
Bendix, Reinhard & Guenther Roth. *Scholarship and Partisanship. Essays on Max Weber*. Berkeley: University of California Press, 1971.

Bennion, Lowell L. *Max Weber's Methodology*. Paris: Les Presses Modernes, 1932.

Beshers, James M. "Models and Theory Construction." *American Sociological Review*, 22 (1959): 32–38. Reprinted in Milton L. Barron (ed.), *Contemporary Sociology*. New York, Toronto: Dodd, Mead, and Company, 1968: 590–597.

Bienfait, Werner. "Max Webers Lehre vom geschichtlichen Erkennen. Ein Beitrag zur Frage der Bedeutung des 'Idealtypus' fuer die Geschichtswissenschaft." *Historische Studien*, 194 (1930): 5–93.

Blalock, Hubert M. *Toward a Theory of Minority Group Relations*. New York: Capricorn Books. 1967.

——. *Theory Construction*. Englewood Cliffs: Prentice-Hall. 1969.

Blau, Peter M. & W. Richard Scott. *Formal Organizations*. San Francisco: Chandler, 1962.

Bloombaum, Milton. "A Contribution to the Theory of Typology Construction." *Sociological Quarterly*, 5 (1964): 157–162.

Blum, Fred A. "Max Weber's Postulate of 'Freedom' from Value Judgments." *American Journal of Sociology*, 50 (1944): 46–52.

Boumann, P. J. "Kausalitaet und Funktionszusammenhang in der Soziologie Max Webers." *Zeitschrift fuer die gesamte Staatswissenschaft*, 105 (1949): 463–474.

Brodbeck, May. "Models, Meaning and Theories." In Llewellyn Gross (ed.). *Symposium on Sociological Theory*. Evanston, White Plains: Row, Peterson, 1959: 373–403.

——. *Readings in the Philosophy of the Social Sciences*. London: Collier-Macmillan, 1968.

Buckle, Henry Thomas. *History of Civilization in England*. 2 Vols. New York: Appleton, 1870.

Cahnman, Werner J. "Max Weber and the Methodological Controversy in the Social Sciences." In Werner J. Cahnman & Alvin Boskoff (eds.). *Sociology and History*. New York: Free Press, 1964: 103–127.

——. "Ideal Type Theory: Max Weber's Concept and Some of its Derivations." *Sociological Quarterly*, 6 (1965): 268–280.

Carnap, Rudolf. *Philosophical Foundations of Physics*. New York, London: Basic Books, 1966.

Cassirer, Ernst. *Substance and Function*. New York: Dover, 1953.

Dobretsberger, Josef. "Zur Methodenlehre C. Mengers und der oesterreichischen Schule." *Zeitschrift fuer Nationaloekonomie*, 12 (1948/49): 78–89.

Dubin, Robert. *Theory Building*. New York: Free Press, 1969.

Dubislav, Walter. *Die Definition*. 3rd ed. Leipzig: Meiner, 1931.

Engisch, Karl, Bernhard Pfister & Johannes Winckelmann. *Max Weber. Gedaechtnisschrift der Ludwig-Maximilian-Universitaet Muenchen*. Berlin: Duncker und Humblot, 1960.

Eucken, Walter. *The Foundations of Economics*. Chicago: University of Chicago Press, 1951.

——. "Wissenschaft im Stile Schmollers." *Weltwirtschaftliches Archiv*, 59 (1940): 468–506.

Feigl, Herbert & May Brodbeck (eds.). *Readings in the Philosophy of Science*. New York: Appleton-Century-Crofts, 1953.

Ferber, Christian von. "Der Werturteilsstreit 1909–1959." *Koelner Zeitschrift fuer Soziologie und Sozialpsychologie*, 11 (1959): 21–37.

Fleischmann, Eugène. "De Weber à Nietzsche." *Archives Européennes de Sociologie*, 5 (1964): 190–238.

Freund, Julien. *The Sociology of Max Weber*. New York: Vintage Books, 1969.

Freyer, Hans. *Soziologie als Wirklichkeitswissenschaft*. Leipzig, Berlin: Teubner, 1930.

Friedman, Milton. "The Methodology of Positive Economics." In *Essays in Positive Economics*. Chicago: University of Chicago Press, 1959.

Frischeisen-Koehler, Max. "Ueber die Grenzen der naturwissenschaftlichen Begriffsbildung." *Archiv fuer systematische Philosophie*, N. F. 12 (1906): 225–266, 450–483; 13 (1907): 1–21.

———. *Wissenschaft und Wirklichkeit*. Leipzig, Berlin: Teubner, 1912.

Gardiner, Patrick. *Theories of History*. New York: Free Press, 1959.

Gerth, Hans & C. Wright Mills (eds.). *From Max Weber*. New York: Oxford University Press, 1946.

Gide, Charles & Charles Rist. *A History of Economic Doctrines*. Boston, New York, Chicago: Heath, 1913.

Goldenweiser, Alexander. "The Relation of the Natural Sciences to the Social Sciences." In Harry Elmer Barnes, Howard Becker & Frances Becker (eds.). *Contemporary Social Theory*. New York, London: Appleton-Century, 1940: 93–109.

Goode, William J. "A Note on the Ideal Type." *American Sociological Review*, 12 (1947): 473–475.

Gottl-Ottlilienfeld, Friedrich von. "Die Herrschaft des Wortes." In Friedrich von Gottl-Ottlilienfeld. *Wirtschaft als Leben*. Jena: Fischer, 1925: 83–335.

Grab, Hermann J. *Der Begriff des Rationalen in der Soziologie Max Webers. Ein Beitrag zu dem Problem der philosophischen Grundlegung der Sozialwissenschaft*. Karlsruhe: Braun, 1927. (Sozialwissenschaftliche Abhandlungen, vol. 3.)

Grelling, Kurt & Paul Oppenheim. "Der Gestaltbegriff im Lichte der neuen Logik." *Erkenntnis*, 7 (1938): 211–225.

Gross, Llewellyn (ed.). *Symposium on Sociological Theory*. Evanston, White Plains: Row, Peterson, 1959.

Hagen, Everett E. "Analytical Model in the Study of Social Systems." *American Journal of Sociology*, 67 (1961): 144–151.

Hasbach, Werner. "Zur Geschichte des Methodenstreits in der politischen Oekonomie." *Schmollers Jahrbuch*, 19 (1895): 465–490, 751–808.

Heimann, Eduard. *History of Economic Doctrines*. New York: Oxford University Press, 1964.

Hempel, Carl G. "The Function of General Laws in History." *Journal of Philosophy*, 39 (1942): 35–48. Reprinted in Herbert Feigl & Wilfrid Sellars (eds.). *Readings in Philosophical Analysis*. New York: Appleton-Century-Crofts, 1949: 459–471.

———. "Problems of Concept and Theory Formation in the Social Sciences." In *Science, Language, and Human Rights*. American Philosophical Association, Eastern Division, vol. I. Philadelphia: University of Pennsylvania Press, 1952: 65–86.

———. *Fundamentals of Concept Formation in Empirical Science*. International Encyclopedia of Unified Science, Vol. I, no. 7. Chicago: University of Chicago Press, 1952.

———. *Philosophy of Natural Science*. Englewood Cliffs: Prentice-Hall, 1966.

Hempel, Carl G. & Paul Oppenheim. *Der Typusbegriff im Lichte der neuen Logik.* Leiden: A. W. Sijthoff's Uitgeversmaatschappij N.V., 1936.

Henrich, Dieter. *Die Einheit der Wissenschaftslehre Max Webers.* Tuebingen: Mohr, 1952.

Honigsheim, Paul, *On Max Weber.* New York: Free Press, 1968.

Horkheimer, Max. *The Eclipse of Reason.* New York: Oxford University Press, 1947.

Horowitz, Irving Louis. "Max Weber and the Spirit of American Sociology." *Sociological Quarterly,* 5 (1964): 344–354.

Hughes, H. Stuart. *Consciousness and Society.* New York: Vintage Books, 1958.

Hutchison, Terence Wilmot. *The Significance and Basic Postulates of Economic Theory.* New York: Kelley, 1965. (Reprint of the 1938 edition.)

Janoska-Bendl, Judith. *Methodologische Aspekte des Idealtypus. Max Weber und die Soziologie der Geschichte.* Berlin: Duncker und Humblot, 1965.

Jaspers, Karl. *Allgemeine Psychopathologie.* 4th ed. Berlin, Heidelberg: Springer, 1946.

————. *Aneignung und Polemik. Gesammelte Reden und Aufsaetze zur Geschichte der Philosophie.* Muenchen: Piper, 1968.

————. *Leonardo, Descartes, Max Weber.* London: Routledge & Kegan Paul, 1965.

Jordan, Heinrich P. "Some Philosophical Implications of Max Weber's Methodology." *Ethics,* 48 (1938): 221–231.

Kade, Gerhard. "Die Verdaechtigung der exakten Wirtschaftstheorie." *Jahrbuecher fuer Nationaloekonomie und Statistik,* 169 (1957): 1–42.

————. *Die Grundannahmen der Preistheorie.* Berlin, Frankfurt: Vahlen, 1962.

Kaplan, Abraham. *The Conduct of Inquiry.* San Francisco: Chandler, 1964.

Kauder, Emil. "Intellectual and Political Roots of the Older Austrian School." *Zeitschrift fuer Nationaloekonomie,* 17 (1957/58): 411–425.

Kaufmann, Felix. *Methodenlehre der Sozialwissenschaften.* Wien: Springer, 1936. (Kaufmann's book, *Methodology of the Social Sciences* [New York, 1944], is *not* a translation of this book.)

Kempski, Juergen von. "Zur Logik der Ordnungsbegriffe, besonders in den Sozialwissenschaften." *Studium Generale,* 5 (1952): 205–218. Reprinted in Hans Albert (ed.). *Theorie und Realitaet.* Tuebingen: Mohr, 1964: 209–232.

Kluever, Heinrich. "Max Weber's 'Ideal Type' in Psychology." *Journal of Philosophy,* 23 (1926): 29–35.

Kocka, Juergen. "Karl Marx und Max Weber." *Zeitschrift fuer die gesamte Staatswissenschaft,* 122 (1966): 328–357.

Koenig, René. "Einige Ueberlegungen zur Frage der Werturteilsfreiheit bei Max Weber." *Koelner Zeitschrift fuer Soziologie und Sozialpsychologie,* 16 (1964): 1–29.

Koenig, René & Johannes Winckelmann. *Max Weber zum Gedaechtnis. Koelner Zeitschrift fuer Soziologie und Sozialpsychologie.* Sonderheft 7, (1963).

Kraft, Viktor. *Die Grundlagen einer wissenschaftlichen Wertlehre.* Wien: Springer, 1952.

————. *Erkenntnislehre.* Wien: Springer, 1960.

Kraus, Oskar. *Die Werttheorien. Geschichte und Kritik.* Bruenn, Wien, Leipzig: Rohrer, 1937.

————. "Die Aristotelische Werttheorie in ihren Beziehungen zu den Lehren der modernen Psychologenschule." *Zeitschrift fuer die gesamte Staatswissenschaft,* 61 (1905): 573–592.

Lachmann, Ludwig M. *The Legacy of Max Weber.* Berkeley: Glendessary Press, 1971.

Landshut, Siegfried. *Kritik der Soziologie und andere Schriften zur Politik.* Neuwied: Luchterhand, 1969.

Lazarsfeld, Paul F. "Some Remarks on the Typological Procedures in Social Research." *Zeitschrift fuer Sozialforschung,* 6 (1937): 119–139.

————. "Philosophy of Science and Empirical Social Research." In Ernest Nagel, Patrick Suppes, & Alfred Tarski (eds.). *Logic, Methodology, and Philosophy of Science.* Stanford: Stanford University Press, 1962: 463–473.

Lazarsfeld, Paul F. "Some Remarks on the Typological Procedures in Social Sciences. Classifications, Typologies, and Indices." in Daniel Lerner & Harold D. Lasswell (eds.). *The Policy Sciences.* Stanford: Stanford Univerity Press, 1951: 155–192.

Loewith, Karl. "Max Weber und Karl Marx." In Karl Loewith. *Gesammelte Abhandlungen.* Stuttgart, Berlin, Koeln, Mainz: Kohlhammer 1960: 1–67. A partial translation can be found in Dennis Wrong (ed.). *Max Weber.* Englewood Cliffs: Prentice-Hall, 1970: 101–122.

Lopreato, Joseph & Letitia Alston. "Ideal Types and the Idealization Strategy." *American Sociological Review,* 35 (1970): 88–96.

Machlup, Fritz. "Idealtypus, Wirklichkeit und Konstruktion." *Ordo,* 12 (1960/61): 21–57.

MacIver, Robert M. "The Imputation of Motives." *American Journal of Sociology,* 46 (1941): 1–12.

McKinney, John C. "Methodology, Procedures and Techniques in Sociology." In Howard Becker & Alvin Boskoff (eds.). *Modern Sociological Theory.* New York: Dryden, 1957: 186–235.

————. *Constructive Typology and Social Theory.* New York: Appleton-Century-Crofts, 1966.

————. "Constructive Typology: Structure and Function." In J. R. Doby (ed.). *An Introduction to Social Research.* New York: Appleton-Century-Crofts, 1967: 230–243.

Mandelbaum, Maurice. *The Problem of Historical Knowledge.* New York, Evanston, London: Harper Torchbooks, 1967.

Marcuse, Herbert. *Negations. Essays in Critical Theory.* Boston: Beacon, 1968.

Martindale, Don. "Sociological Theory and the Ideal Type." In Llewellyn Gross (ed.). *Symposium on Sociological Theory.* Evanston, White Plains: Row, Peterson, 1959: 57–91.

————. *The Nature and Types of Sociological Theory.* Boston: Houghton Mifflin, 1960.

Meadows, Paul. "Models, Systems, and Sciences." *American Sociological Review,* 22 (1957): 3–9.

Menger, Carl. *Problems of Economics and Sociology.* Urbana: University of Illinois Press, 1963.

————. *Untersuchungen ueber die Methode der Socialwissenschaften und der Politischen Oekonomie insbesondere.* Leipzig: Duncker und Humblot, 1883.

————. *Die Irrthuemer des Historismus in der deutschen Nationaloekonomie.* Wien: Hoelder, 1884.

————. *Zur Kritik der politischen Oekonomie.* Wien, Hoelder, 1887.

————. *Grundzuege einer Klassifikation der Wirtschaftswissenschaften.* Jena: Fischer, 1889.

Mill, John Stuart. *A System of Logic.* London, New York: Longmans, Green, 1947.

Mises, Ludwig von. *Epistemological Problems of Economics,* Princeton: Van Nostrand, 1960.

Mitzman. Arthur. *The Iron Cage.* New York: Knopf, 1970.

Nagel, Ernest. "Problems of Concept and Theory Formation in the Social Sciences." In *Science, Language, and Human Rights.* American Philosophical Association, Eastern Division, vol. I. Philadelphia: University of Pennsylvania Press, 1952: 43–64.

————. *The Structure of Science.* New York, Burlingame: Harcourt, Brace & World, 1961.

————. "Assumptions in Economic Theory." *American Economic Review,* 53 (1963, Supplement): 211–219.

Nefzger, Ben. "The Ideal Type: Some Conceptions and Misconceptions." *Sociological Quarterly,* 6 (1965): 166–174.

Oppenheimer, Hans. *Die Logik der soziologischen Begriffsbildung, mit besonderer Beruecksichtigung von Max Weber.* Tuebingen: Mohr, 1925.

Palyi, Melchior, *et al.* (eds.). *Hauptprobleme der Soziologie. Erinnerungsgabe fuer Max Weber.* Muenchen, Leipzig: Duncker und Humblot, 1923.

Parsons, Talcott, Review of Alexander von Schelting's *Max Webers Wissenschaftslehre. American Sociological Review,* 1 (1936): 675–681.

————. *The Structure of Social Action.* New York: Free Press, 1949.

————. *Essays in Sociological Theory.* Rev. ed. Glencoe: Free Press, 1954.

————. "Introduction." In Max Weber. *The Theory of Social and Economic Organization.* New York: Oxford University Press, 1947.

————. "Evaluation and Objectivity in Social Science: An Interpretation of Max Weber's Contribution." *International Social Science Journal,* 17 (1965): 46–63.

————. "Max Weber 1864–1964." *American Sociological Review,* 30 (1965): 171–175.

Pepper, George B. "A Re-examination of the Ideal Type Concept." *The American Catholic Sociological Review,* 24 (1963): 185–201.

Pfister, Bernhard. *Die Entwicklung zum Idealtypus. Eine methodologische Untersuchung ueber das Verhaeltnis von Theorie und Geschichte bei Menger, Schmoller und Max Weber.* Tuebingen: Mohr, 1928.

Pierce, Albert. "Empiricism and the Social Sciences." *American Sociological Review,* 21 (1956): 135–137.

Popper, Karl Raimund. *The Logic of Scientific Discovery.* New York: Harper Torchbooks, 1965.

Richardson, Jane & Alfred L. Kroeber. "Three Centuries of Women's Dress Fashion." *Anthropological Record,* 5, no. 2 (1940).

Rickert, Heinrich. *Zur Lehre von der Definition.* 3rd. ed. Tuebingen: Mohr, 1929.

————. *Der Gegenstand der Erkenntnis.* 6th ed. Tuebingen: Mohr, 1928.

————. "Les quatres modes de 'l'universel' dans l'histoire." *Revue de Synthèse Historique,* 2 (1901): 121–140.

————. *Die Grenzen der naturwissenschaftlichen Begriffsbildung.* Tuebingen: Mohr, 1902; 5th enlarged ed., 1929.

———. "Max Weber und seine Stellung zur Wissenschaft." *Logos*, 15(1926): 222–237.

———. *Science and History*. Princeton: Van Nostrand, 1962.

Ritzel, Gerhard. *Schmoller versus Menger. Eine Analyse des Methodenstreits.* Frankfurt, 1950.

Robinson, Richard. *Definition*. Oxford: Clarendon Press, 1950.

Rogers, Rolf E. *Max Weber's Ideal Type Theory*. New York: Philosophical Library, 1969.

Rose, Arnold. "A Deductive Ideal-Type Method." *American Journal of Sociology*, 56 (1950): 35–42.

Rossi, Pietro. "Scientific Objectivity and Value Hypotheses." *International Social Science Journal*, 17 (1965): 64–70.

Roth, Guether. "Das historische Verhaeltnis der Weberschen Soziologie zum Marxismus." *Koelner Zeitschrift fuer Soziologie und Sozialpsychologie*, 20 (1968): 429–447.

Rudner, Richard S. *Philosophy of Social Science*. Englewood Cliffs: Prentice-Hall, 1966.

Ruestow, Alexander. "Der Idealtypus, oder die Gestalt als Norm." *Studium Generale*, 6 (1953): 54–59.

Rumpf, Max. "Von rein formaler zu typologisch-empirischer Soziologie." *Schmollers Jahrbuch*, 48 (1924): 917–962.

Runciman, W. G. *A Critique of Max Weber's Philosophy of Social Science*. Cambridge University Press, 1972.

Salomon, Albert. "Max Weber's Methodology." *Social Research*, 1 (1934): 147–168.

———. "Max Weber's Sociology." *Social Research*, 2 (1935): 60–73.

———. "Max Weber's Political Ideas." *Social Research*, 2 (1935): 368–384.

Schaaf, Julius Jakob. *Geschichte und Begriff. Eine kritische Studie zur Geschichtsmethodologie von Ernst Troeltsch und Max Weber*. Tuebingen: Mohr, 1946.

Schelting, Alexander von. "Die logische Theorie der historischen Kulturwissenschaft von Max Weber und im besonderen sein Begriff des Idealtypus." *Archiv fuer Sozialwissenschaft und Sozialpolitik*, 49 (1922): 623–752.

———. *Max Webers Wissenschaftslehre. Das logische Problem der historischen Kulturerkenntnis. Die Grenzen der Soziologie des Wissens*. Tuebingen: Mohr, 1934.

Schmoller, Gustav. "Zur Methodologie der Staats- und Sozial-Wissenschaften." *Schmollers Jahrbuch*, 2 (1883): 975–994.

———. Letter to Menger (instead of a review of Menger's *Die Irrthuemer des Historismus in der deutschen Nationaloekonomie*). *Schmollers Jahrbuch*, 8 (1884): 677.

———. "Volkswirtschaft, Volkswirtschaftslehre und -methode." In J. Conrad, L. Elster, W. Lexis, & E. Loening (eds.). *Handwoerterbuch der Staatswissenschaften*. Jena: Fischer. 1st ed., 1894: vol. 6, pp. 527–563; 3rd ed., 1911: vol. 8, pp. 426–501.

———. "Wechselnde Theorien und feststehende Wahrheiten im Gebiete der Staats- und Sozialwissenschaften und die heutige deutsche Volkswirtschaftslehre." *Schmollers Jahrbuch*, 21 (1897): 1387–1408.

Scholz, Heinrich & Hermann Schweitzer. *Die sogenannten Definitionen durch Abstraktion*. Leipzig: Meiner, 1935.

Schluchter, Wolfgang. *Wertfreiheit und Verantwortungsethik.* Tuebingen: Mohr, 1971. (Gesellschaft und Wissenschaft 3.)

Schuetz, Alfred. *The Phenomenology of the Social World.* Evanston: Northwestern University Press, 1967.

———. *Collected Papers.* The Hague: Martinus Nijhoff, 1962.

Schumpeter, Joseph. *Economic Doctrine and Method.* London: Allen & Unwin, 1954.

———. *History of Economic Analysis.* New York: Oxford University Press, 1964.

Schweitzer, Arthur. "Vom Idealtypus zum Prototyp." *Zeitschrift fuer die gesamte Staatswissenschaft,* 120 (1964): 13–55.

Seiffert, August. *Die kategoriale Stellung des Typus. Beihefte zur Zeitschrift fuer philosophische Forschung.* Heft 7 (1953).

Sigwart, Christoph. *Logic.* 2 vols. New York: Macmillan, 1895.

Simey, T. S. "Weber's Sociological Theory of Value. An Appraisal in Midcentury." *Sociological Review,* N.S. 13 (1965): 45–64.

Simmel, Georg. *Die Probleme der Geschichtsphilosophie.* 3rd ed. Leipzig: Duncker und Humblot, 1907.

Smelser, Neil J. *Essays in Sociological Explanation.* Englewood Cliffs: Prentice-Hall, 1968.

Spann, Othmar. *The History of Economics.* New York: W. W. Norton, 1930. (Reprinted by Arno Press, 1972).

Spiethoff, Arthur. "Die allgemeine Volkswirtschaftslehre als geschichtliche Theorie. Die Wirtschaftsstile." *Schmollers Jahrbuch,* 56 (1932): 891–924.

Stammer, Otto *et al.* (eds.). *Max Weber und die Soziologie heute. Verhandlungen des 15. Deutschen Soziologentages.* Tuebingen: Mohr, 1965.

Stinchcombe, Arthur L. *Constructing Social Theories.* New York: Harcourt, Brace, and World, 1968.

Tatarkiewicz, Wladyslaw. "Nomological and Typological Sciences." *Journal of Philosophy,* 57 (1960): 234–240.

Tenbruck, Friedrich H. "Formal Sociology." In Lewis A. Coser (ed.). *Georg Simmel.* Englewood Cliffs: Prentice-Hall, 1965: 77–96.

———. "Die Genesis der Methodologie Max Webers." *Koelner Zeitschrift fuer Soziologie und Sozialpsychologie,* 11 (1959): 573–630.

Tiryakian, Edward. "Typologies." Article in the *International Encyclopedia of the Social Sciences.* New York: Macmillan, 1968.

Topitsch, Ernst. "Der Historismus." *Studium Generale,* 7 (1954): 430–439.

Troeltsch, Ernst, "Ueber den Begriff einer historischen Dialektik. Windelband-Rickert und Hegel." *Historische Zeitschrift,* 119 (1919): 373–426.

———. *Der Historismus und seine Probleme. (Gesammelte Schriften,* vol. 3.) Tuebingen: Mohr, 1922.

Voegelin, Erich. "Ueber Max Weber." *Deutsche Vierteljahresschrift fuer Literaturwissenschaft und Geistesgeschichte,* 3 (1925): 177–193.

Walther, Andreas. "Max Weber als Soziologe." *Jahrbuch fuer Soziologie,* 2 (1926): 1–65.

Warner, R. Stephen. "The Role of Religious Ideas and the Use of Models in Max Weber's Comparative Studies of Non-Capitalist Societies." *Journal of Economic History,* 30 (1970): 74–99.

Watkins, J. W. N. "Ideal Types and Historical Explanation." *British Journal for the Philosophy of Science,* 3 (1952): 22–42. Reprinted in Herbert Feigl

& May Brodbeck (eds.). *Readings in the Philosophy of Science.* New York: Appleton-Century-Crofts, 1953: 723–743.

Watkins, J. W. N. "Historical Explanation in the Social Sciences." *British Journal for the Philosophy of Science,* 8 (1957): 104–117. Reprinted in Patrick Gardiner (ed.). *Theories of History.* New York: Free Press, 1959: 503–515.

Weber, Marianne. *Max Weber. Ein Lebensbild.* Tuebingen: Mohr, 1926.

Weber, Max. *Gesammelte Aufsaetze zur Wissenschaftslehre.* 3rd ed. Tuebingen: Mohr, 1968.

———. *The Methodology of the Social Sciences.* Glencoe: Free Press, 1949.

———. *The Theory of Social and Economic Organization.* New York: Free Press, 1968.

———. *Economy and Society.* 3 vols. New York: Bedminster Press, 1968.

Wegener, Walter. *Die Quellen der Wissenschaftsauffassung Max Webers.* Berlin: Duncker und Humblot, 1962.

Weinreich, Marcel. *Max Weber, l'homme et le savant. Etudes sur ses idées directrices.* Paris: Vrin, 1938.

Weippert, Georg. "Die idealtypische Sinn- und Wesenserfassung und die Denkgebilde der formalen Theorie. Zur Logik des 'Idealtypus' und der 'rationalen Schemata.'" *Zeitschrift fuer die gesamte Staatswissenschaft,* 100 (1940): 257–308.

Winch, Peter. *The Idea of a Social Science.* London: Routledge & Kegan Paul, 1958.

Winch, Robert F. "Heuristic and Empirical Typologies." *American Sociological Review,* 12 (1947): 68–75.

Winckelmann, Johannes. *Legitimitaet und Legalitaet in Max Webers Herrschaftssoziologie.* Tuebingen: Mohr, 1952.

———. "Max Weber–Das soziologische Werk. Zu dem Buch gleichen Themas von Reinhard Bendix." *Koelner Zeitschrift fuer Soziologie und Sozialpsychologie,* 17 (1965): 743–790.

Windelband, Wilhelm. "Geschichte und Naturwissenschaft," in Wilhelm Windelband, *Praeludien.* 3rd ed. Tuebingen: Mohr, 1907: 355–379.

Wright, Georg Henrik von. *Explanation and Understanding.* London: Routledge & Kegan Paul, 1971.

Wrong, Dennis (ed.). *Max Weber.* Englewood Cliffs: Prentice-Hall, 1970.

Zeitlin, Irving M. *Ideology and the Development of Sociological Theory.* Englewood Cliffs: Prentice-Hall, 1968.

Zittel, B. "Der Typus in der Geschichtswissenschaft." *Studium Generale,* 5 (1952): 378–384.

INDEX OF NAMES

References to Heinrich Rickert and Max Weber can be found on practically every page. They are therefore omitted from this index.

INDEX OF SUBJECTS

2975